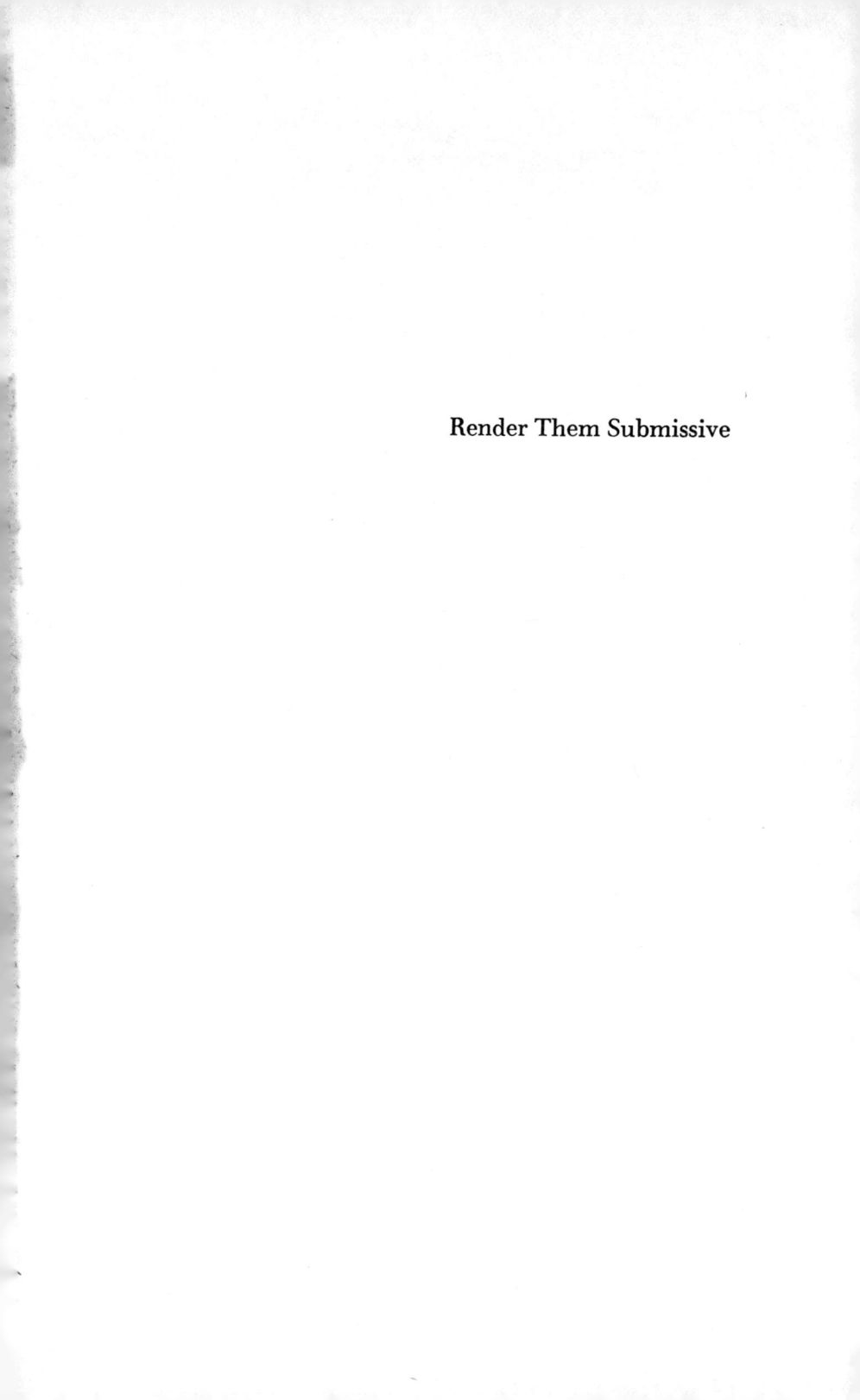

Render Them Submissive

Render Them Submissive

Responses to Poverty in Philadelphia, 1760–1800

John K. Alexander

The University of Massachusetts Press

Amherst, 1980

Copyright © 1980 by
The University of Massachusetts Press
All rights reserved
Library of Congress Catalog Card Number 79-22638
Printed in the United States of America
Library of Congress Cataloging in Publication Data
Alexander, John K
Render them submissive.
Bibliography: p. 223
Includes index.
  1. Philadelphia—Poor—History—18th century.
  2. Philadelphia—Social conditions. 3. Poverty.
I. Title.
HV4046.P5A4   362.5′09748′11   79-22638
ISBN 0-87023-289-4

For my favorite historian
June Granatir Alexander

Contents

Preface *ix*
Introduction *1*
1. "The Punishment of Dependence": Living Poor in Philadelphia, 1760–1800 *11*
2. The Context: Change, Anxiety, and the Desire for Control in the City *26*
3. Perceptions of "The Other Half": The Increasing Quest for Control *48*
4. Social Disorder, Crime, and Punishment: Reform and the Quest for Control *61*
5. Public Poor Relief, 1760–1776: Turbulent Innovation before the Revolution *86*
6. Public Poor Relief, 1776–1800: Change and Continuity *103*
7. Private Poor Relief: Increasing Emphasis on "A Judicious Choice of Objects" *122*
8. Educating the Poor: The Postwar Quest for Teaching Industrious Poverty *142*
Conclusion *160*
Appendix A: Methodology of Biographical Tracing *175*
Appendix B: Criminals in Philadelphia, 1794–1800 *179*

Abbreviations   *183*
Notes   *186*
Bibliographic Note   *223*
Index   *229*

Preface

This study of poverty and the response to proverty in the Philadelphia of 1760–1800 grows out of a desire to understand what impact the American Revolution had on society. The work focuses almost exclusively on Philadelphia, in part because we as yet have few detailed studies of poverty in this era and especially of poverty in the postindependence years. But the focus is limited to Philadelphia for another, equally important reason. I am convinced that we need to investigate poverty and the response to poverty by examining far more than poor laws and charity records. It is necessary to attempt to see how the poor lived and what it meant to be poor. We must seek to learn how the wider community perceived and responded to the poor in their midst and to understand the general social, political, and attitudinal context of the community as it confronted the issue of poverty and the poor. To do this, the historian needs to study the wide range of sources that may reveal how a community perceived and dealt with poverty and the poor. Hence, in most instances, it is necessary to analyze one city or one community. This is especially the case when dealing with a large and complex urban area such as Philadelphia. For these reasons, this work does not provide a comparative analysis, but the study is designed to offer the kind of detailed community investigation that can make such meaningful comparative analysis possible.

Although this work focuses on one major city in the years 1760–1800, the results raise questions about historical interpretations of the nature and meaning of the American Revolution, as well as of Philadelphia. The Philadelphia that emerges from this study was not a unified community that provided real economic benefits and opportunity for virtually all of its inhabitants. Rather, the city had far more social distance between classes and far more class conflict than is often supposed. The story of poverty in the Philadelphia of 1760–1800 thus questions the claim that the late colonial and revolutionary periods were marked by a high degree of social unity, harmony, and simple humanitarianism.

In the course of preparing this work, I have amassed innumerable debts that cannot be canceled by mere words. But some words are in order. The staffs of the libraries, archives, and churches that I visited were not only helpful but, invariably, kind in aiding my research efforts. John Daly, who has since left the Philadelphia City Archives, deserves special mention in this regard. Hannah B. Roach has, over the years, always been most generous in sharing her extensive knowledge of the city.

Colleagues in the University of Cincinnati History Department rendered valuable assistance. Saul Benison, Roger Daniels, George Engberg and Henry Shapiro commented upon all or portions of the work. Zane Miller did even more. He read the manuscript in various drafts and offered incisive comments that were instrumental in preparing the work for publication. Other historians, not associated with the University of Cincinnati, also gave important assistance. I benefited from discussions with Charles S. Olton and Billy G. Smith. Jesse Lemisch devoted countless hours to critiquing the manuscript in its various stages. His penetrating analyses, always offered in gentle but forceful terms, have helped give the work whatever merit it has. He alone can know how much I value his counsel and his friendship. My deepest debt is to another historian. June Granatir Alexander read drafts of the manuscript time and again, with a critical eye to both substance and style. Changes instituted at her suggestion have materially improved the final work. For all this I thank her, and I thank her as well for "living" with the poor of eighteenth-century Philadelphia far longer than I had

Preface

any right to make her do. I also wish to thank my friend Joel Havemann of the *National Journal* who offered encouragement and helpful editorial comments.

The financial burdens associated with doing the research for this study were lessened by grants from the University of Chicago and the Taft Fund of the University of Cincinnati. And my first extended stay in Philadelphia was made both easier and more enjoyable by two people who have nothing to do with the historical profession. As is often the case, my early research was conducted at a time when my funds were less than ample. In this situation, Ed Hunt, owner of John Barleycorn's, and his brother Jim often made sure that my dinner was something better than I normally ate. Ed and Jim, as well as others, reminded me that Philadelphia still is, in some ways, the City of Brotherly Love.

JKA

Render Them Submissive

Introduction

Over half a century ago, J. Franklin Jameson called upon historians to consider the impact of the Revolution on American society. Carefully noting that he was offering "only assertions" needing fuller investigation, Jameson suggested that major changes occurred in the nature of American society as "the transforming hand of revolution" swept over the colonies. Emphasizing reforms such as the attack upon slavery, expansion of the franchise, and redistribution of land, he maintained that this transforming hand brought forth a more open, more egalitarian society.[1] Since Jameson presented his views, analysts have devoted greater attention to the social aspects of the American Revolution and, despite continuing disagreement on the degree of democratization that occurred, most historians now accept the basic tenets of what is called the Jamesonian thesis.[2] But Frederick B. Tolles's 1954 claim that this thesis remained neither proven nor disproven is still valid. Too many large gaps yet exist in our understanding of the nature and evolution of American society during the late colonial and revolutionary eras.[3] This is especially true of poverty. Historians have produced valuable studies of poor laws and the history of poor relief. But most of these examinations give neither detailed analyses of attitudes toward poverty nor much information about the poor themselves.[4] We know little about what it meant to be

2   *Introduction*

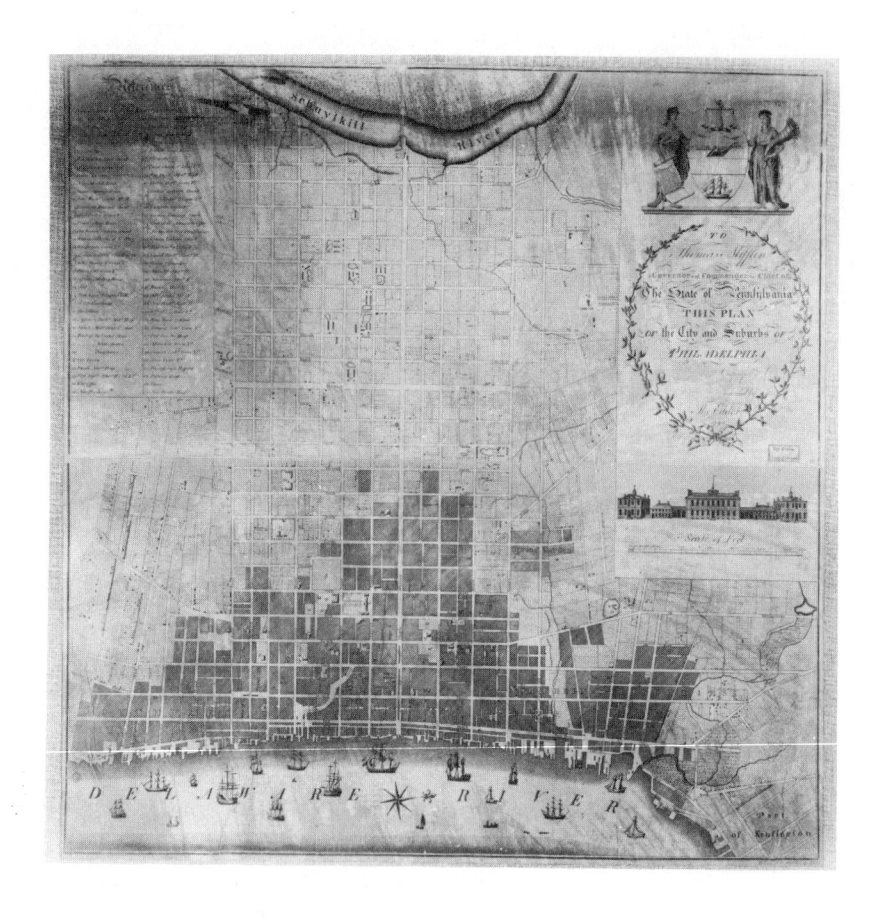

Detail from A. P. Folie, *A Ground Plan of the City and Suburbs of Philadelphia* (Philadelphia, 1794); supplied through the courtesy of the Geography and Map Division of the Library of Congress which holds the original.

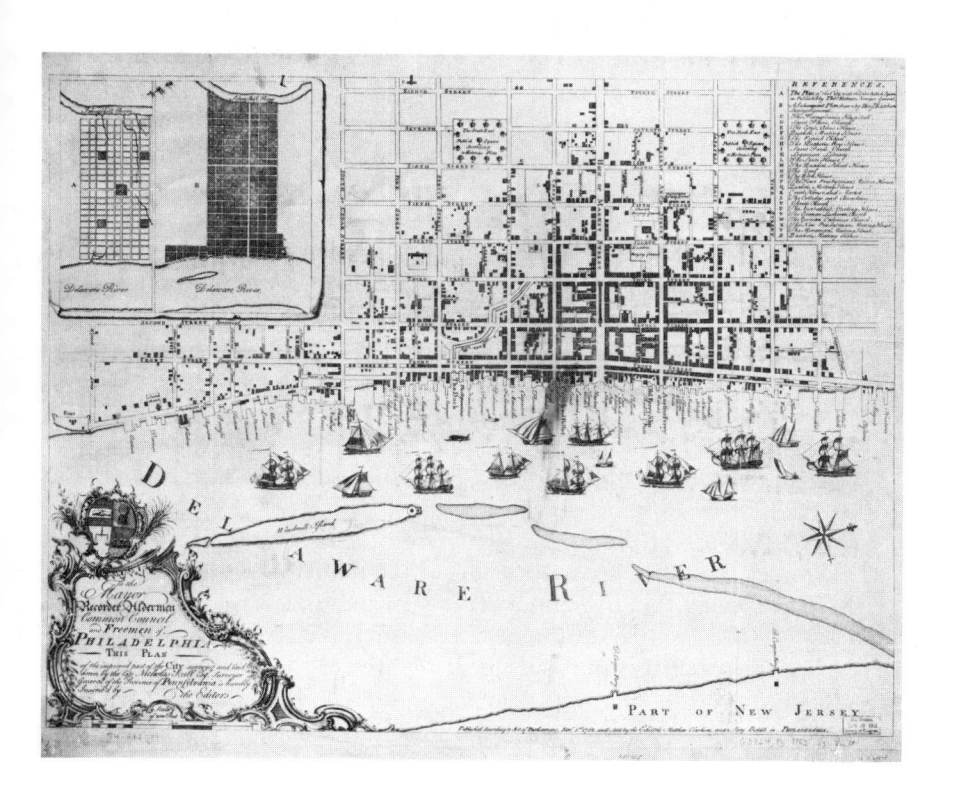

Introduction 3

Detail from Nicholas Scull, . . . *Plan of the improved part of the City* . . . *[of Philadelphia, 1762]* (Philadelphia, 1762); supplied through the courtesy of the Geography and Map Division of the Library of Congress which holds the original.

poor in early America or how attitudes toward the poor affected laws, institutions, or the actions of the poor themselves.[5] Until such gaps in our knowledge of the nature of poverty in early America are filled, our understanding of American society in the late colonial and revolutionary period will be not only incomplete but possibly misleading.

This study of attitudes toward the poor and responses to poverty in the Philadelphia of 1760–1800 endeavors to do two things. It attempts to expand our knowledge and understanding of urban poverty during the late colonial and postrevolutionary periods. And it offers one kind of test of the validity of the thesis that American society became more egalitarian as it underwent the transformations of revolution.

A study focusing on poverty in the Philadelphia of the late eighteenth century faces special problems because of the paucity of sources emanating directly from the poor. "Poverty," a perceptive Philadelphian said in 1796, "thou has no genealogies."[6] Since members of Philadelphia's lower classes left few of their own written accounts, we usually see these poorer founding fathers indirectly, often through governmental records, accounts of relief-dispensing agencies, and the comments of the more affluent. Because of the nature of the sources, this work primarily examines the attitudes and actions of the nonpoor in an attempt to reconstruct the institutional and attitudinal structure that often shaped the lives of the poor as a group. What follows, then, is not history from the bottom up. The work does seek to decipher what it meant to be poor; but, in the main, the poor serve as a kind of mirror reflecting the image of the larger Philadelphia society as it responded to the events of the revolutionary era.

When the Revolution broke over Philadelphia and the colonies, any transformation of society seemed possible. For some Philadelphians the coming of independence signaled the opportunity to translate American Enlightenment ideals into action: society could—would—be altered on the basis of rational reform rooted in the goodness and potential equality of humanity.[7] Thus, slavery came under attack. Major changes that most would call reforms occurred in the penal code and the practice of imprisoning debtors. The number of citizens eligible to vote

Introduction

expanded greatly. These and more reforms touching the poor occurred in Philadelphia during and because of the American Revolution. Yet, one may still ask, Did the sum total of reforms and changes wrought by the Revolution alter prevailing perceptions of the poor and significantly improve their position? This study demonstrates that *as an instrument for improvement*, the transforming hand of revolution fell rather lightly on the poor of Philadelphia, in large measure because many affluent citizens, deeply disturbed by the changes occurring in revolutionary society, worked vigorously to maintain or reestablish what they believed was the status quo antebellum, where the poor deferentially accepted their lower station in life.

For established Philadelphians, the Revolution did seem, as Alexander Graydon observed, to produce many "frightful evils" that destroyed the "so tranquil and so happy" world of the late colonial period.[8] The *Freeman's Journal*, in the politically volatile year of 1787, voiced the sense of concern that overcame many Philadelphians. "The American character," the *Journal* observed, is marked "with an over-drawn sense of Liberty. . . . This high sense of Liberty has, indeed, even in ruder minds, produced a fierce independent spirit, without which the Revolution could not have been effected; but it has also in too many created a licentiousness, at present very detrimental, and incompatible with good government."[9]

In the postwar years, many prosperous citizens thought licentiousness abounded—especially among the poor. By filling the air with profane and indecent language, the poor supposedly contaminated the children of higher rank. The poor seemed all too prone to engage in crime. Because of lack of education and political experience, the poor were, the argument went, the inhabitants most likely to support demagogues who, lusting after power, pushed talented men aside. And, after 1776, the poor had the vote. Moreover, as the population grew, the number of poor people increased. Thus, as many of the more prosperous citizens saw it, this group formed a growing and dangerous, or potentially dangerous, class.

Philadelphians embracing such views knew how they wanted the poor to behave: they should be hardworking, honest, nonaggressive, orderly, and content with their lot. In sum, they should deferentially accept their inferior place in society. These citizens did more than talk about the need for deference. They translated into action their growing fear of the poor and desire for deferential behavior. Especially in the period between 1785 and 1800, they assiduously and systematically worked to make the poor deferential. Dr. Benjamin Rush expressed a common attitude of persons holding such views when he asserted that "we have changed our forms of government, but it remains yet to effect a revolution in our principles, opinions, and manners so as to accommodate them to the forms of government we have adopted." Dr. Rush minced no words in reminding his fellow Philadelphians not to exhaust benevolent funds on medical aid to the poor, but rather to promote a religious, deference-supporting education for them, since "their morals are of more consequence to society than their health or lives."[10] This attitude too, as much as democratizing reform, marked the social change accompanying the American Revolution in Philadelphia.

For their part, the poor seemed to fear the power of the more prosperous. Driven by necessity, they faced a world over which they had too little control. The poor, as well as the near poor and even members of the middle class, feared the political power of the more affluent. The legal force of the government, especially as used by what came to be called trading justices, could thrust the poor into jail even if they committed no crime. The economic control exercised by the rich, and especially by rich members of the mercantile class, could at times drive the laboring part of the city to desperate acts.

Revolutionary Philadelphia, then, was something rather different from what recent historical studies have usually suggested. Prosperity was less than "commonplace" in the Philadelphia of the late eighteenth century. The city did not have a marvelous, unifying sense of community supporting the claim that the eighteenth-century town "suffered none of the communications problems of later Philadelphias."[11] In eighteenth-century Philadelphia, charity relief, both public and private, *was* utilized as an instrument designed to reform the behavior of the poor.[12] Despite any commitment to an experiment in republicanism, Philadelphians of the revolutionary era engaged in vicious and at times deadly battles to determine how republicanism should

Introduction

be translated into governmental structure and policy.[13] Indeed, a heightened sense of distrust and antagonism between the poor and the more prosperous increasingly became part of the atmosphere of late eighteenth-century Philadelphia. This distrust and antagonism, which led established citizens to seek to make the poor deferential, was a vital aspect of postrevolutionary Philadelphia society and of the change that accompanied the American Revolution.

Before turning to an analysis of these points, a basic question must be confronted: who were the poor and how many Philadelphians lived in poverty during the years 1760–1800? The sources needed to define the term "the poor" with precision and to determine accurately the number of poor do not exist.[14] Equally important, the problem of definition involves more than inadequate quantifiable sources. The views of a group of Philadelphians who wanted to establish a loan fund for the poor illustrate the complexities of the question. "Besides the absolute Poor, who *must be* supported," this group noted, "there are frequently many other Citizens in streightned circumstances; who from the want of small Sums are exposed to great difficulties, whereby they often suffer the loss of more than double the sum in which they are indebted." Clearly, "to many such the immediate supply of a few Dollars, would be the means of preserving them from absolute ruin and thereby prevent their becoming a public burden."[15] As these Philadelphians knew, it was hard, perhaps impossible, to draw a line between the poor and near poor.

Even if we fix upon some arbitrary figure to use in the definition of poverty, we miss the critical aspect of subjective individual perceptions and attitudes. A person or group might stand above any established poverty line and yet consider themselves poor or lacking in economic power. There is an attitude of poverty or powerlessness that can be something quite different from a statistically objective definition.[16] As we shall see, at numerous times Philadelphians who were probably not quantifiably poor felt themselves to be deprived and, as a consequence, joined forces with the poor.

Philadelphians of that day did not seem troubled by such considerations when discussing the issue. Most inhabitants confidently spoke of "the poor" or of a segment of "the poor" as if expecting those hearing or reading the comments to know who and what was meant. Nevertheless, it is possible to gain some understanding of what, to these late eighteenth-century Philadelphians, constituted poverty. The first dictionary printed in Philadelphia (1789) defined the poor as "those who are in the lowest rank of the community, those who cannot subsist but by the charity of others."[17] That seems clear enough. Certainly the almshouse inhabitants, those dependent on various charities, and many of the lame, the chronically sick, and the very old formed part of the group. But Philadelphians throughout the period also spoke of "the industrious poor." Such persons may have been in the lowest rank of the community, but they did not necessarily rely on charity for subsistence. Rather, they "depend on their daily labor, for daily supplies." Having "but a living by the work of his hands," the poor person "must either work or starve."[18] Applying these criteria, contemporary Philadelphians singled out certain groups as being among the poor or the working poor. Day laborers, those who lacked special skills and sold their manual labor on a day-by-day basis, were almost invariably included.[19] Many Irish immigrants, who often made up a sizable percentage of the day laborers, were poor.[20] Most free blacks, who often worked as sailors, day laborers, waiters, or servants, lived in poverty.[21] Common seamen were likely to be poor.[22] Although these groups formed the core of the working poor, Philadelphians believed that those who occupied the next rungs on the occupational ladder were often only slightly removed from the status of poverty. Because they too had to have daily work, many mechanics and even artisans had to face the fact that they could slip into poverty.[23] Indeed, the need for employment was such that violence might follow if work was not available. Benjamin Rush, when speaking of the effects of nonimportation, saw the problem and the danger with great clarity: "Our tradesmen begin to grow clamorous for want of employment. Our city is full of sailors who cannot procure berths, and who knows what the united resentments of these two numerous people may accomplish?" And, more than once, social disruption and protest did occur because of a lack of work.[24]

Philadelphians of the period rarely ventured useful guesses

Introduction

about how many city inhabitants lived in poverty. However, the records of two private charity subscriptions undertaken during harsh winters offer tantalizing if imprecise suggestions. During the winter of 1761–62, the Committee to Alleviate the Miseries of the Poor oversaw distribution of wood to "the poor." The committee's records reveal neither the total number aided nor their occupations, but Gary Nash, working from a list of those granted charity in the southern half of the city, estimates that, citywide, about 660 adults got help.[25] Counting each of the adults as members of a family and using a multiplier derived from a similar charity effort of 1783–84 yields an estimate that the 1761–62 subscription aided 2,150 poor people. This means that about one in ten Philadelphians received help from this private charity fund designed to aid the noninstitutionalized poor.[26] Of course, because of the very indirect production of these figures, the estimate is at best a general one.

The statistics on the number of people assisted by the subscription fund of 1783–84 are more reliable. The subscription committee reported aiding a total of 5,212 people living in approximately 1,600 families. By the committee's own account, it helped "a great many of the poor labouring people" in the city. If only poor laboring people received assistance, at least one in every seven Philadelphians obtained aid and can be counted among the working poor.[27] When the number of people relieved by public funds is added, almost one in six Philadelphians can be counted as having been poor in 1783–84. Moreover, this figure does not include the poor assisted by church charity, immigrant aid societies, and other established charities, or the poor who received no aid at all. Nor do these figures necessarily include the near poor.[28] Thus, following the views of eighteenth-century Philadelphians, it appears that in the Philadelphia of 1760–1800 at least 15 percent of the inhabitants were considered poor.[29] These figures, while revealing, are hardly definitive. Still, it is clear that, throughout this period, Philadelphians believed that a substantial number of the city's inhabitants lived in poverty and that the number of poor was growing. Many Philadelphians, especially once independence was established, became increasingly disturbed by this trend and took action to ameliorate the problems supposedly caused by it. These people, who were often from the ranks of the city's mercantile community, came to this position even though the material conditions of the poor changed but little during the last four decades of the eighteenth century.

1

"The Punishment of Dependence": Living Poor in Philadelphia, 1760–1800

Because Philadelphia's poor lacked economic power, only minor changes occurred in the material reality of how they lived and in what it meant to them to be poor in the city of 1760–1800. Facing a world over which they often had little control, they had only limited choices concerning such matters as selecting places of residence, making their livings, and, at times, how to conduct themselves. These forced decisions produced for the poor a way of life that remained strikingly consistent throughout the period. Thus, continuity rather than change marked the social realities of being poor in the Philadelphia of the late eighteenth century.

By the 1760s the distribution of wealth in the city was uneven, and it became even more highly skewed over time.[1] Fragmentary 1767 returns of the poor tax for Chestnut, Walnut, and Lower Delaware wards show this unevenness, although these wards contained fewer lower-class citizens than did the fringe areas of the city.[2] In these three wards, the bottom 25% of ratables who owned estates possessed only 5.5% of the taxable wealth, while the bottom 50% of ratables controlled merely 13.7%. In sharp contrast, the top 25% of ratables controlled 70.9% of the taxable wealth; the top 10% had 49.7% and the top 5%, 36.1%. The uneven wealth-holding pattern is dramatically shown by the fact that the top 1% of ratable persons owned almost as much ratable estate as the bottom 50%.[3]

The Revolution did not reverse this pattern. In 1800 there existed, at least in the city proper, what Richard Miller called a striking inequality of wealth. The top 0.5% of the city's taxpayers owned more taxable property than the bottom 75%. Only about one in four taxpayers possessed taxable property valued at more than $50.00, and 58.4% of the taxables were listed as owning *no* real property.[4]

This unequal distribution of wealth illustrates why Philadelphians asserted that the poor and near poor *had* to obtain regular employment: lacking economic reserves, these inhabitants had to work or starve. The simple fact was that "a labouring man, who has a wife and children, if he falls into sickness, or is by any means a short time out of employment, falls into distress."[5] And, said Philadelphians, the necessity of having constant employment normally dictated how the poor would act. When marrying, "the poor often meet with little more than will pay the Priest, and make them merry the first day, and rise content the next morning to drudge mutually for a comfortable subsistence." The poor might also have to work against their will. An "American Moralist" gave the example of a hairdresser who answered the call to work on Sunday. He violated the Sabbath because "the poor man himself, perhaps, dare not remonstrate, for fear he should be deprived of his employment for the rest of the week."[6] The spur of necessity also forced the poor to labor even if working endangered health and life. During hot summers, numbers of persons who worked hard, especially out of doors, died apparently from heat exhaustion.[7] When yellow fever struck, people were told to avoid all fatigue of body or mind and to avoid standing or sitting in the sun.[8] The poor porter, the poor laborer, the poor sawyer could not, if he had work, afford to follow these rules. The price of having to labor hard and constantly can be seen in the statement of "Phileleutheros" that "though persons who are used to easy labour, or some tradesmen, can follow their employments till forty or even fifty years of age and some longer, yet in this climate most who are used to hard labour without doors begin to fail soon after thirty, especially if they have been obliged to live on poor diet that afforded but little nourishment or was unwholesome."[9]

"The Punishment of Dependence"

One of the important realities of late eighteenth-century Philadelphia, then, was that the poor required work if it could be found. So too did the near poor, who also lacked economic reserves. Despite this obvious fact, a myth was created that, because of high wages, the poor and especially immigrants would find the Philadelphia region a veritable new Eden. Throughout the last four decades of the century, some persons, seeking to attract immigrants, maintained that scarcity of labor hindered the establishing of manufacturing enterprises because people supposedly demanded such high wages. Or, in a slightly different vein, the argument ran that, because land was so inexpensive, people would not work in manufacturing unless given high wages. According to another claim, since prices were low in America, high wages meant that poor people coming to America would fare better than in their native land.[10] Possibly Philadelphia's poor did fare better than their European counterparts, but making the leap, as promotional literature did, from a chance for a better life to the assertion that any industrious person could find prosperity was ridiculous.[11] Even accepting the questionable assumptions that all workers obtained high wages and that prices were low, the point remains: high wages meant nothing if one could not find regular employment.[12]

Literature promoting Philadelphia as a city where the industrious poor could find high wages and the good life came under serious, if unintentional, challenge by the calls to establish manufacturing enterprises. Some who promoted the Philadelphia area agreed that having employment constituted the critical ingredient in maintaining prosperity. They further conceded that finding work often proved difficult. Public pronouncements calling for expansion of Philadelphia's manufacturing persistently stressed that such enterprises would employ the poor and potentially poor otherwise unable to find work. This argument appeared time and again, suggesting that those promoting manufacturing expected such proposals to strike a responsive chord: as these promoters realized, many citizens believed that the poor required expanded employment opportunities for their own and for the city's good.

This theme of creating manufacturing to employ the poor was forcefully expressed in 1764 when a group proposed building a linen manufactory in Philadelphia because the number of poor in and around the city was great and increasing, "and as for want of Employment, many of them, especially in Winter, are reduced to great Straits, and rendered burthensome to their Neighbours." This enterprise would "alleviate their wants, by finding them Employment." In 1766 the city's grand jury urged the Assembly to support building an institution to employ the poor, because many "labouring People & others in low Circumstances" who had "flocked" to the city "willing to work" could not find sufficient employment to support themselves and their families."[13]

As the nonimportation of the early 1770s gave way to war, Philadelphians again heard that manufacturing must be expanded in order to lessen the number of poor, by giving employment to those who, without it, would be "begging bread." After the war, supporters of manufacturing continued hammering at the point that manufacturing would provide employment for several hundred "starving poor" who were without work "merely for the want of suitable objects about which they can be engaged." Nor were the obviously poor the only persons needing expanded employment opportunities. Manufacturers and mechanics pleaded for protection of industry, asking: "And shall those industrious citizens, who have so capitally contributed to the independence of their country, now be forgotten, and with their families become objects of the greatest distress, for want of employment in their respective branches [of manufacturing]?" When it seemed that too little was done to protect and promote their interests, these people readily asserted that mechanics and manufacturers "are everywhere languishing for want of employment."[14]

The same theme was voiced as the last decade of the century opened. Persons in the winter of 1790–91, who found "many willing to work, but destitute and starving for want of employ," emphasized that "It is said that our poor are indolent, and will not work: . . . [but] give the poor a sufficient compensation for their work; let the demand for their exertions be constant and steady, . . . and it will soon be found that the charge of indolence, is a calumny on the most destitute part of our fellow-citizens." Indeed, "as far as our experience extends, we have always found the people anxious for employment, and to perform it with fidelity. . . ."[15] Those trumpeting the glories of Philadelphia could boast as they tried to entice people to the city. Many already living in the city stressed the critical point that held true throughout the 1760–1800 period: "Citizens think these [are] good times, when all trades have plenty of work."[16] But in these years, Philadelphia could not always provide plenty of work.

One major barrier to full, constant employment for the poor rose from the city's geographic location. If the Delaware froze during the winter, as it often did, the poorer classes of citizens faced hard times when they were thrown out of work because of the interruption of navigation. As trade slowed or ground to a halt, some jobs often performed by the poor simply disappeared. Sailors could not get berths; calls for day laborers to unload goods or do other manual labor subsided; draymen were not needed to move a high volume of goods.[17]

When the Delaware did not freeze, the winter season still weighed heavily upon the poor and near poor as the economic life of the city grew lethargic. The seasonal nature of employment hurt more than the ordinary poor and those engaged in trade. In the winter the level of construction declined, and thus, the *Federal Gazette* maintained, "the mason, the carpenter, and other descriptions of artists (if heretofore improvident) dread the approach of want." There is no way of knowing if John Parker, a bricklayer and mason, was improvident before the winter of 1774, but he sought a ten-shilling-a-week loan from the St. George Society because, as his petition said, "he . . . cannot at this time of the Year get Employment in his Business and is therefore reduced with a Family consisting of a Wife & three Children to great Distress."[18]

Since Philadelphians knew that during the winter season the city had "little occasion . . . for the labour of the Poor," standard assertions held that the laboring poor should set aside earnings to tide them over the winter months, and that the poor were "frugal from necessity." The sad truth was that numbers of people who found some work during the milder months had to turn to the overseers of the poor for support in winter. Indeed, the managers of the house of employment, which sheltered some of the poor under public care, often found that "We have many here who Came in much indisposed and distressed, yet are so far Recovered as to be fit Objects to be removed, Yet We cannot deem it Consistent with the Principles of Humanity, to discharge them at this Season as we are fully Convinced that they Cannot procure Work, but (as several have lately) would soon Receive fresh Orders for Admission."[19]

The editor of the *Independent Gazetteer*, writing in 1785, emphasized the critical nature of seasonal unemployment, observing that "collections (time immemorial) have been made *every* winter, either by means of charity sermons among the different sects, or private subscriptions, for the poor." The scope of such aid reveals the difficulty of gaining employment during a harsh winter. The subscription of 1783–84, which aided only poor laboring people, gave assistance to about one in every seven Philadelphians. As the *Pennsylvania Gazette* observed during the difficult winter of 1790–91, "The numbers and sufferings of the poor in the City, and especially in the Liberties, are great; and perhaps if fully exhibited, would, to many, scarcely appear credible."[20]

Philadelphia's position as a major port of entry for immigrants added to the city's employment problems. Even skilled immigrants typically had a difficult time finding work. It was claimed that many fell into poverty; many became so discouraged that they returned home.[21] The *Evening Herald*, in 1785, revealed the pervasiveness of the problem by calling for the creation of immigrant aid societies, because the majority of newly arrived immigrants, even if they had financial resources, faced a "calamitous" or "awkward, irksome situation." In 1794 the Philadelphia Society for the Information and Assistance of Persons Emigrating from Foreign Countries depicted problems immigrants often faced. European immigrants, "although frequently endowed with talents and virtues the most valuable," arrived "on an unknown shore, bereft of the means of support, and destitute of friends" to advise or assist them, and therefore were "lost for a time to society and to themselves."[22]

Although numerous immigrant aid societies sprang into existence, new Philadelphians still found obtaining employment difficult.[23] The *Independent Gazetteer* emphasized the problem and placed the necessity of having work in sharp focus by printing a letter supposedly written by "Dennis K——y," an Irishman who came to Philadelphia in 1787. In the course of six weeks, he applied to about one hundred persons for work but could find none. Barely able to subsist, "K——y" heard that Pennsylvania had passed a law saying that thieves would be punished by hard labor but would also be well fed, clothed, and housed. "This was all I wanted," "K——y" wrote, "and I had no objection to working." Thus, he robbed, happily went to jail, and even urged his brother in Ireland to join him. The *Evening Herald*, speaking of this same law, asserted that "far from being considered as a punishment, it is viewed with desire by many poor wretches who are in want of work and subsistence." Although these reports overstated the case, they illustrate that for poor Philadelphians, and especially for immigrants, high wages became meaningless if jobs were not available.[24]

Philadelphia's poor, then, often had difficulty finding constant employment. Even assuming that work was generally available, Billy G. Smith's analysis of wages and the cost of living in the Philadelphia of this period suggests that the poor had to struggle merely to subsist.[25] For the great mass of the poor, economic mobility could be no more than an impossible dream.[26] Unquestionably, as demonstrated by the tax records previously examined, the poor lacked economic power. These intertwining factors reveal why many of the city's inhabitants, and certainly the poor, occupied an economically dependent position allowing little opportunity to compete with the city's elite for material prosperity.

Try as they might, the poor could not effectively hide their poverty; throughout the period they were visible. Their poverty normally became obvious by chance. But during the period 1718 to 1771, the legislature of Pennsylvania, seeking to ensure that only the truly needy received public assistance, attempted to render all receiving public poor relief instantly recognizable. In 1718 the legislature decreed that anyone receiving such assistance—as well as his whole family—must wear a large letter *P* and the first letter of his county or city name.[27]

Poorer Philadelphians who avoided public relief were probably just as visible, at least before the American Revolution.

The reminiscences gathered and analyzed by the nineteenth-century antiquarian John Watson indicate that, during the summer in prewar years, "poor labouring men" wore ticklenburg linen for shirts and striped ticking breeches. Tradesmen plied their trades in leather aprons, while "workingmen" commonly wore dirty buckskin breeches, check shirts, and red flannel jackets. For the more affluent, laced ruffles descending over the hand constituted a mark of gentility. Such persons felt that their winter coats and breeches should be made of broadcloth, and summer outfits ought to be of silk camlet. During the winter, as poor laboring men trekked about in gray duroy coats, "gentlemen" wore short-sleeved coats and utilized muffets to display their plaited linen sleeves, gold buttons, and other finery. In the days before the Revolution, the economic position of women was also distinguishable: hired women wore petticoats and short gowns of domestic cloth. The difference in clothing went right down to the ground, because only the "gentry" possessed calfskin shoes; servants wore shoes made of coarse neat's leather.[28] Thus, it seemed logical in 1760 to describe an escaped criminal's clothing as being "such as Servants commonly ware."[29]

Near the start of the Revolution, some of the obvious differences in patterns of dress apparently began to diminish. Observers asserted that many women of modest means tried to imitate the dress of the affluent and that apprentices and others in the lower orders were wearing more and more finery.[30] By the mid-1790s, it seemed to one analyst that "those in *high life* ape the fashions and manners of the English, French and other nations; the *middle class* those of the higher or more affluent . . . and the *poor* copy the example of the class above them." Thus, all lived beyond their means, "some to make an ostentatious shew of their wealth and others from a *false shame*, to conceal their poverty."[31] This writer, like others before him, overstated the case. Try as they might to ape those above them, the poor remained fairly visible even in the 1790s. As late as 1797, Charles Peale, in a newspaper comment, could describe a woman by saying "her dress bespoke that her wants were supplied by industry."[32] Still, if travelers' accounts are any indication, the middling and poorer classes dressed more nearly like their "betters" at the end of the century.[33]

"The Punishment of Dependence"

The limited change in patterns of dress was not accompanied by a change in the housing pattern of the poor. Throughout the period, houses rented, as contemporaries observed, "according to their situation for trade and other conveniences," and the prime sections for trade rarely extended beyond the areas bounded by Arch, Chestnut, and Second streets. This section also held appeal because it was the best cleaned, paved, and lighted area of the city. Accordingly, a small house in a remote part of the city rented for but one-tenth of what a large house in a "good situation" would bring. Because of these factors, the poor of Philadelphia normally lived together at or near the outer edge of the city.[34]

The poor tax levied in 1767 for the centrally located Walnut, Chestnut, and Lower Delaware wards, none of which extended west of Second Street, illustrates the fact that the poor rarely lived in the core areas. Although the taxables of these wards included people pursuing more than forty different occupations, persons identifiable as having occupations often followed by the poor were not listed. For example, not one day laborer, porter, or sawyer was reported as living there. In sharp contrast, merchants made up 25.9% of all persons in these wards for whom occupations were listed.[35]

Examination of the situation among day laborers, a group universally numbered among the poor, reveals that this housing pattern had not changed by the early 1780s. In the western portion of Mulberry ward, which in 1780 was a fringe ward, 104 out of 527 taxables were laborers. In 1781 in Southwark, which lay beyond the city limits and which had a high concentration of sailors, 101 of the 723 taxables were laborers. The centrally located core wards in 1780 had a far different structure. Chestnut ward had 103 taxables, only 1 of whom was a laborer; in Lower Delaware ward, only 3 of the 104 taxables were laborers; High Street ward had 175 taxables, only 4 of whom were laborers.[36] If the poor did live in the central wards, they normally were bunched together; in 1780, for example, 3 of the 4 laborers residing in High Street ward lived together or next to each other.[37]

The federal census of 1790 shows the persistence of this housing pattern. Of the 827 residents of Southwark whose occupations were listed, 200 (24.2%) held menial jobs, working as laborers, porters, helpers, and so on. In the more centrally located area between South and Race streets, only 239 (8.7%) of the 2,758 residents whose employment was noted followed such occupations. Considering only people whose occupations were listed in the 1790 census, the ratio of residents in the central area to those in Southwark was about 3.5 to 1. But the ratio of doctors was 12 to 1; the ratio of merchants and dealers was 13 to 1; the ratio of lawyers was 12 to 1. Southwark obviously had a small share of greater Philadelphia's professional people.[38]

Similarly, Richard C. Miller's analysis of the housing pattern of the city in 1800 shows that the middle and poorer socioeconomic groups most often lived in the peripheral wards. Moreover, few laborers lived in the city proper: only 592 (8.8%) of the 6,765 residents of the city whose occupations Miller could identify were unskilled laborers.[39] Laborers were far more likely to reside in the suburbs. In 1800 in the eastern Northern Liberties, 378 (21.8%) of 1,734 taxables were laborers. In the western Northern Liberties, laborers accounted for 469 (26.2%) of the 1,788 taxables. Laborers comprised only about 10% of the taxables in eastern Southwark, but seamen, many of them members of the lower class, made up about 26% of the area's taxable population.[40]

The poor were most likely to live in the suburban areas and in fringe districts away from the core wards because these areas were remote from the central business district and thus were less desirable sections of the city. But, at least in the eyes of many of the nonpoor, more than mere distance from the heart of the city made the peripheral regions undesirable. As these more affluent inhabitants saw it, disorder flourished in the areas where the poor predominated. Newspaper essayist "Casca," speaking of Southwark, called it "the *wrong end* of the city." Part of Southwark's northern section, known as Irish Town, had the reputation of being a center of prostitution, and the whole area below South Street seemed dangerous because it was the part of the city "most infested with sailor taverns." In 1787 a black was convicted of running a disorderly house in Southwark as a "resort for all the loose and idle characters of the city"—a conviction that prompted one newspaper to comment, "These facts are laid before the public to prove the growing nuisance of the cabins in the suburbs of the city, occupied by free negroes." A decade later, a committee formed to seek out and reform disorderly free blacks visited the southern parts of the city and suburbs.[41] John Watson, although writing later, probably summed up the feelings of many contemporary Philadelphians when he claimed that "the south-western part of the city was always a *wooden town*, with a surplus population of the baser sort." While the most derogatory comments focused on the southern extremes of the city, which developed more quickly than the Northern Liberties, the environs of Philadelphia were generally viewed as being the far too disorderly haunts of the poor.[42]

The outskirts of the city, where the poor were most likely to live, also struck contemporary observers as the most offensive, unhealthy parts of the city. The air was impure and, in summer, filled with flies. Dead dogs, cats, and other putrifying bodies strewed the ground. Ponds of stagnated water emitted "noxious effluvia," making them, according to the conventional medical wisdom, not only "sinks of filth" but also "*hot beds of disease.*"[43] Dr. Benjamin Rush summed up one price the poor paid for living in these areas when he observed that "it is from these ponds, and masses of putrid water, that those fevers are generated, which prevail every autumn, particularly among the poor, in the suburbs of the city."[44]

Because they usually inhabited the city's alleys, those poor living in the heart of Philadelphia did not automatically escape the health hazards of the suburbs.[45] In 1765 the city government said that garbage would be removed from the paved streets, lanes, and alleys between South and Vine. The promise was never really kept. In 1769, "Tom Trudge," a self-proclaimed "poor fellow," charged that regular cleaning occurred only on those streets "honoured with the residence of the gentry." He found that situation understandable, since paving was laid down in areas housing the "opulent merchants and gentry." Because the dung-cart never visited the alleys and by-places where the poor resided, they were forced to wade through refuse. Others agreed with "Trudge" that the city government disregarded the physical environment of the poor citizens. The city did do a better job of cleaning the city as then legally defined in the 1770s, but the improvement was short-lived.[46] As late as 1798, "A Citizen" protested that "the dirt remains on our streets," asking rhetorically, if the streets remained filthy, "what must be the state of narrow alleys?" They were, as "A Philadelphian" noted, quite simply "too generally neglected and filthy—and too many of the houses within them are in the same state."[47] The board of health in 1798 tried to rectify the situation by urging that strict attention be paid to cleansing the narrow alleys and lanes as well as the large streets. But throughout the period, the alleys where the poor of the central city tended to cluster were not so different from the environs in being "the common receptacles of filth."[48]

The homes of the poor were not much better, often being "huts," "sheds," or "mean low box[es] of wood" that themselves seemed so shabby as to present a hazard to health.[49] Benjamin Rush shuddered in remembering that, when he visited the abodes of the sick poor in the early 1770s, he "risqued not only taking their disease but being infected with vermin." "A Clergyman" reported that ministers and doctors visiting the dwellings of the poor "often observe nuisances as offensive to the senses as dangerous to health. Among other things the reservoirs of putrid excrements are truly pestilential." Another citizen concerned about cleaning up the city observed that many cellars, as well as the streets, presented hazards to health. This citizen, emphasizing that he spoke from personal observation, asserted that the poorer classes of people often made cellars the depositories of much filth. There tainted provisions purchased at a low price, untanned and uncured hides, and other dangerous things rotted in the hot seasons.[50] As these contemporaries viewed it, you could smell the housing of the poor even if it was out of sight.

Lack of economic power dictated more than how poor people dressed and where they lived. It also gave them little choice but to treat some of the prosperous citizens with at least pretended respect, civility, and deference. The poor had to behave this way because, throughout the period 1760–1800 and especially after independence, it was essential to be able to obtain a recommendation from a "respectable" person.[51] One often needed such a recommendation to gain employment or to obtain a license as a huckster or, on a higher plane, as a tavernkeeper.[52] Private charities of all kinds typically investigated to see if a person was "worthy" unless that person produced a "proper Recommendation from respectable Inhabitants."[53] Overseers of the poor also checked to determine if the needy were "suitable Objects" and in doing so often showed as much concern for reputation as for a legal right to assistance. A poor person wanting the services of the Philadelphia Dispensary, which opened in 1786 as an agency specifically designed to help the sick poor, had to get a recommendation from a contributor.[54] Individual dentists and physicians often offered to assist the poor gratis, but some also said that the poor must be "well recommended."[55] For a poor person in jail, the ability to have someone attest to his or her good previous reputation could be the key to receiving assistance or freedom. Indeed, the recommendation system became so deeply rooted in Philadelphia that even during the chaos of some yellow fever epidemics, a person applying for assistance had "to produce a recommendation from respectable citizens."[56]

Although the recommendation system weighed heavily on the poor, the *Philadelphia Minerva* probably exaggerated when it had "A Miser" say: "In the evening took my maid to the tabernacle, and afterwards debauched her; I threatened to refuse her a character [reference] if she did not comply." Still, the *Minerva* correctly emphasized that the recommendation system could dictate the actions of the poor. The Philadelphian who observed that "we must bear with those that are above us" because "it is the punishment of dependence" was correct.[57] A 1785 newspaper advertisement depicting a thief as having "a servant-like address" is suggestive in this regard, for such a description would be valuable only if servants had a distinguishable and probably deferential manner of speaking.[58] Even if a poor person did not have a servant-like address, taking a properly deferential stance could enhance the chances of receiving a recommendation or of receiving charity. It is thus not surprising that many Philadelphians and charity-dispensing groups expected and received "a becoming deference" from the poor.[59]

Throughout the years 1760–1800, the poor faced "the punishment of dependence." The American Revolution did not alter the fact that, because of limited economic power, the poor often had little control over their lives. Throughout the period, they had little choice: they required regular employment to subsist and they had to work even if doing so endangered their health. Throughout the period, they lived in the least desirable areas and housing of Philadelphia because that was all they could afford. And throughout the period, at least some manner of deference marked them, because they often *had* to be able to obtain recommendations from "respectable" citizens.

One at least partial change in the reality of living poor did occur during the period. By the eve of the Revolution, the poor probably began dressing more nearly like Philadelphians of means, a trend that seems to have continued to the end of the period. The responses to this change are illuminating. In 1774, "A Merchant" sent to the *Pennsylvania Journal* a clipping from an English newspaper that called for laws limiting what apprentices could wear. Their hats should be of wool without any silk; their shirts should not have ruffles or any fine needlework; their shoes should be of neat's leather. In short, the "upstairs" should "once more, be humbled." But later accounts suggest that apprentices and the lower orders were not humbled. In 1787 a Philadelphian, speaking of women's clothing, claimed that "in former times, dress was deemed one of the most palpable distinctions of rank. Ladies then took their precedencies, and understood their respective stations, by what they wore and their manner of wearing it. This ancient and easy mode of discrimination is no longer known in society. The very servant not only apes but rivals her mistress in every species of whim and extravagance." Thus, "all sorts of people are . . . melted down into one glaring mass of absurdity or superfluity. The lower orders are intirely lost in a general propensity to mimic the finery of higher; and every woman we meet would seem by her gesture and apparel to possess at least an independent fortune: and no difference at all in this respect is left to tell the mere spectator, whether her circumstances be narrow or affluent." Yearning for the seeming order of that earlier day, he warned that "it is dangerous to tamper with truth or decency in any case." Thus, he advised parents to "proportion . . . the dress of your daughters to their situations in life."[60]

The matter of proper dress was deemed important enough that a convention of the United States Abolition Societies urged free blacks to "be simple in your dress."[61] Issac Weld, an Englishman generally very complimentary about Americans, asserted that such concerns about keeping one's place were not to be taken lightly. In 1795 he observed that, "amongst the uppermost circles in Philadelphia, pride, haughtiness, and ostentation are conspicuous; and it seems as if nothing could make them happier than that an order of nobility should be established, by which they might be exalted above their fellow citizens, as much as they are in their own conceit."[62]

Weld may have been overly harsh, but he did not miss the mark. If the example of the dress of the poor is at all typical of how the more prosperous viewed them, certain points emerge. Throughout the years 1760 to 1800, most affluent Philadelphians thought that the poor should stay in their place. At some former time, the poor had supposedly accepted this state of things. But in postindependence Philadelphia, the poor shed some of the trappings of deference and behaved less and less as they were expected to do. That could not be tolerated. The American Revolution played a vital role in leading the more prosperous to this conclusion, for it helped weaken systems of control that had worked to keep the colonial poor in check.

2

The Context: Change, Anxiety, and
The Desire for Control in the City

Although the material reality of living poor in Philadelphia held markedly consistent in the years 1760–1800, change was a hallmark of the city. Social, economic, and political transformation came at such a rate, especially after 1775, that Philadelphia seemed to many a city cut loose from moorings that had supposedly made the colonial city peaceful and tranquil.[1] More and more it seemed that the lower orders were no longer controlled by institutional and attitudinal controls that flourished in colonial days. Such changes caused tension and anxiety to mount and helped convince many established Philadelphians that strident efforts were required to bring the city safely back under their domination.

A vital element of change was the not so simple matter of numbers. Partly because Philadelphia was a major port of entry for immigrants, its population increased from about 20,000 in 1760 to over 30,000 by the eve of the Revolution. The war years, which temporarily halted the waves of immigrants, cut into the city's growth, but by 1790 over 42,500 lived in the urban area. Despite yellow fever outbreaks that killed thousands, phenomenal growth occurred in the 1790s: in 1800 the city contained almost 70,000 inhabitants.[2]

Some citizens, believing that people are the wealth of the state, gloried in this growth and labored to increase Philadelphia's size and power by extolling the marvelous opportunities awaiting those who moved to the area.[3] But the increase in population, especially when caused by immigration, also created tension and anxiety. Philadelphia wanted immigrants, but only the right kind of immigrants.

Concern about the effects of immigration became especially prevalent in the years after independence.[4] The *Evening Herald*, expressing the typical view, warned that unless aided in finding employment, immigrants could become a "useless, and perhaps dangerous acquisition."[5] Tench Coxe, one of the city's leading boosters, pointed out that, after the Revolution, the state received all "sober" immigrants with open arms. The *Pennsylvania Journal* agreed by proclaiming its hope that Pennsylvania would always be "the asylum of peac[e]able and honest emigrants."[6] Thus, when French peasantry began arriving in large numbers in 1790, they usually found a ready welcome because of their "sobriety, honesty and industry."[7] But many Philadelphians agreed with Charles Biddle, who, as vice-president of Pennsylvania, claimed that the state needed a system to admit "the industrious and honest" while excluding "the idle and profligate" immigrant.[8] Nor was it only the supposedly poor, weak, or idle who caused alarm. During and after the Revolution, Irish and French immigrants, even when industrious, often came under attack for their political views. In a time of great political stress, the Philadelphians who feared that these two national groups would rarely be their allies depicted the Irish and French as bloody Jacobins thirsting to subvert order and stability.[9] Thus, the very numbers that produced Philadelphia's spectacular growth created tension and division within the society.

Developing a way to bar undesirable immigrants seemed all the more essential because the institutions of slavery, apprenticeship, and indentured servitude, which allowed masters to regulate and control their unfree laborers, declined over the period. Slave labor, an important if declining element in colonial days, virtually disappeared from Philadelphia by 1800.[10] And because indentured servants and apprentices served for limited periods, there slowly built up over the century an ever-increasing pool of free wage earners. The Revolution accentuated this process; virtually all persons bound as indentured servants before 1775 had gained their freedom by 1783, and very few people were bound as indentured servants during the war.[11] Although there was no precise point when a free-wage system replaced bound labor, Philadelphia was far closer to utilizing a free-wage system in 1800 than in 1775.[12]

The increasing supply of free laborers made it easier for some Philadelphia businessmen to change both their organization and their goals by the 1790s. Employing as many as twenty-five workers, some shoemakers became manufacturer-wholesalers; several carpenters became contractors. These entrepreneurs needed the flexibility that the free-wage system offered to expand or contract their labor force as business warranted, and they wanted to keep wages low to increase profits. These changes helped foster union activity in the last years of the century. In the 1790s, work stoppages, especially by journeymen shoemakers and carpenters, became increasingly commonplace, although only journeymen shoemakers maintained a permanent labor organization between strikes.[13]

When considering the poor of Philadelphia, it is essential to note that the limited eighteenth-century labor union activity involved skilled laborers who possessed the best opportunity to establish themselves in business. Some of these skilled workers may have been poor, but the beginnings of the Philadelphia union movement in the 1790s typically did not embrace the poor. The days of an organized workingman's labor and political movement that significantly included the poor lay ahead in the nineteenth century. Still, by the 1790s some labor groups and employers were embroiled in economic struggles, as workers, no longer bound and controlled by masters, aggressively pursued their individual economic goals.[14] The social and economic stability that accompanied an extensive unfree labor system was crumbling under an emerging economic system that increasingly pitted independent, free wage earners against employers.

The world of colonial politics was also built upon legal and social controls designed to keep political power in the hands of the affluent few. Suffrage laws limited the vote to those worth fifty pounds or to those with a freehold estate. These requirements were not always strictly enforced, and some persons lied about their wealth to gain the vote. But at least one-third of Philadelphia's adult males, including the mass of the poor, were effectively excluded from the franchise and from running for office. Even many who could vote and thus were legally qualified to run for office could not hope to seek a place in the legislature; the low pay of representatives made it most difficult for those without independent wealth to run for the Assembly. And because the principal municipal powers rested in the self-perpetuating Philadelphia Corporation, even those able to vote and possessing some wealth could exert only a limited and indirect influence on how the city was governed. Although many inhabitants detested the city's Corporation government, elite citizens maintained that the lower orders did not mind being excluded from the electoral process by arguing that the poor embraced the ideal of deference, which held that politics should be directed by the talented, rich few.[15]

The assertion that the poorer commonalty gladly embraced deference was a self-serving claim and a caricature of politics. The suffrage requirements worked to force the people into this deferential posture. And political skill, rather than a willing deference, often may have determined who served in elective offices. In 1770 a Philadelphia essayist who signed himself "A Brother Chip" claimed that this was the case. He observed, "It has been customary for a certain Company of leading Men to nominate Persons, and settle the Ticket for Assembly-men, Commissioners, Assessors, &c. without even permitting the affirmative or negative Voice of a Mechanic to interfere. . . ."[16] Social forces, as well as the skill of leading men, also worked to enforce seeming deference. As we have seen, the poorer commonalty, including some mechanics and even artisans, had to be able to obtain recommendations, and a proper display of deference, or at least seeming deference, might well enhance the chances of getting those recommendations. Conversely, the supplicant might endanger his chances of obtaining them if he failed to remember that *"We must not be self conceited, nor aim at honours which we were never designed for."* And active political involvement by the poor of the city would, given the views of many elites, constitute aiming for honors not designed for the commonalty.[17]

As the colonial era gave way to revolution and independence, these structural and attitudinal supports designed to keep political control safely in the hands of the affluent few came under increasing attack. In the decade and a half before independence, heated public debates on the proper political organization for Pennsylvania and the British Empire produced an increasing volume of political literature, which often depicted the warring elites as vile, untrustworthy people and suggested, however unintentionally, that political leaders might not be worthy of deference. In the 1770s master craftsmen, who were not numbered among the poor, rejected deference and struck out for a greater voice in politics. The start of war brought greater reliance on the militia, which included large numbers of apprentices, indentured servants, and free, poor Philadelphians. Organized and raised to a position of power, the militia quickly demonstrated that it was anything but deferential. The rank and file claimed and got the right to elect most militia officers, and the militia entered the general political scene demanding both independence and a restructuring of government that would extend the vote to include the poor.[18]

Under these circumstances, Philadelphians realized that the suffrage requirements meant a great deal in practical and symbolic terms. Many shuddered when the state's constitutional convention of 1776, which had a high proportion of radicals drawn from the lower ranks of society, proposed throwing the franchise open to every free, adult, male citizen who paid any public tax.[19] When expansion of the franchise came under consideration, essayist "Peter Easy" offered a revealing defense of the restrictive colonial voting requirements. "I cannot perceive," he declared, "the propriety or prudence of putting *these inhabitants* [those worth fifty pounds] upon a level with the indolent or prodigal, who have not acquired such a small sum as *fifty* pounds." Because all other rights depended absolutely upon the "great right of election," extending the vote to those without property would be dangerous. "Generally the most illiterate and ignorant" members of society, "Peter Easy" contended, these propertyless people, "having nothing to lose, and a prospect of gaining by public convulsions," were ever ready to follow wicked, demagogical leaders or to engage in tumultuous and seditious actions.

"Peter Easy" was afraid, afraid that votes in the hands of the poor would bring chaos. To avoid this horror, he wanted only the propertied to vote, for "*it will ever be their* INTEREST *to keep things quiet, and to have officers go on with regularity*; and if the other class grows turbulent, the whole force and dignity of government can be exerted to keep them in order." Prizing quiet, order, and regularity, "Peter Easy" spoke from the heart as well as the mind when he plaintively asked: "Can[']t the liberties and happiness of *Pennsylvania* be trusted to those men in it, who are worth *fifty* pounds each?" As he looked at the proposed liberal franchise, he had nightmares. His anxiety was heightened because others looked at the possibility of a wide franchise and had dreams. "Orator" proclaimed, "Now *all men* will be put on a level with respect to THIS GRAND RIGHT OF VOTING AT ELECTIONS, and that may in time bring them to a level *in every other respect.*"[20]

To the chagrin of "Peter Easy," the Constitution of 1776, enacted in September, did grant the vote to free, adult males who paid any public tax. It also presented a bold, egalitarian theory claiming that all men possessed the right of "Acquiring, Possessing and Protecting Property and pursuing *and obtaining* happiness and Safety." The Constitution asserted that all power was derived from the people and that therefore all public officers "are their Trustees and Servants, and at all times accountable to them." It followed that "Government is and ought to be Instituted for the Common Benefit Protection and Security of the People, Nation or Community, and not for the particular Emolument or advantage of any Single man, Family or set of Men, who are a part only of the Community."

To implement these ideals, the structure of government gave strong voice to the will of the people. The office of governor with the power of veto was abolished. A unicameral legislature vested with effective power to curb the judicial branch was created. Save for emergency measures, bills introduced into the legislature in one session could not be enacted until the following session, and the preamble to a bill was to state why the bill was needed. Finally, all regular sessions of the legislature were opened to the public.[21]

Benjamin Rush, who thought the Constitution of 1776 replaced "one of the happiest governments in the world" with a "mob government," confidently asserted that "the most respectable" Whigs detested the Constitution and would destroy it. Thus, Rush, "Peter Easy," and their respectable Whig friends wanted to dismember the empire without allowing fundamental change in the internal political structure of the city and state.[22] That proved impossible.[23]

By allowing the poor into the electoral process, the Constitution of 1776 helped change the tone and substance of political debate in the revolutionary city. In colonial days, especially when the issue of taxation was involved, Philadelphia politicians were occasionally denounced for ignoring or supposedly abusing the poor.[24] But once the poor had the vote, such pronouncements became a staple of Philadelphia political life. Examinations of the major issues of the day emphasized the attitudes, needs, and potential actions of poorer Philadelphians. During election campaigns, individual politicians regularly faced attack for purportedly gouging the poor or gained praise for their accessibility to and concern for the poor. Political factions vied with each other in denouncing their opponents as aristocrats who haughtily disdained the interests of the poor.[25] Some elections themselves caused complaint because, it was charged, the poorer and even middling classes were deprived of their votes by manipulation, fraud, or intimidation.[26]

In the years after 1776, Philadelphians often heard rhetoric emphasizing the difference, especially the difference of power, between economic classes. "Wealth begets power, and power too oft leads to usurpation." "Rich men enjoy too great a share of power at all times even without the addition of governmental powers. Do not rich men oppress you, says the Apostle?" "A dangerous aristocracy is forming" which believes "it is necessary to keep the *people* poor and dependent, in order to render them submissive." "If the humble are to be exalted the lofty should be lowered." And "however dirty, ragged, poor and despicable, an injured people may appear, they always have one species of revenge left to them, which they rarely fail to make

The Context

the most of, viz. the power and privilege of cursing their oppressors."[27]

This rhetoric spoke to more than the destitute. By focusing on relative differences in power, such pronouncements were aimed at Philadelphians of any rank who felt themselves threatened by the economic and political power of the elite. Political rhetoricians utilizing this style realized that a person could live above poverty and yet perceive himself as politically weak and, at least on political issues, display the attitude of poverty. For example, a tradesman who in 1784 could pay forty-five pounds a year as rent for a house was not in a strict sense poor. Yet he labeled himself "a poor tradesman," saying that his forty-five pounds procured just a shell of a house. "Robert Slender" (Philip Freneau) might not have been poor by a material definition, but in 1799 he declared, "I stand unnoticed among the swinish herd, as the poor are generally called by the great and *well born*."[28] As these statements suggest, because persons living above poverty could, at times, feel themselves united with the poor on political questions, nowhere is the difficulty of defining "the poor" harder than in politics.

The new brand of political rhetoric that flourished in the revolutionary city invited citizens to believe that politics typically operated on the basis of class differences and antagonisms. And the politicos who used such rhetoric obviously expected to touch a sensitive spot in the minds of either the poorer or the more affluent Philadelphians. Thus, many Philadelphians *believed* that the political actions of one economic class often harmed other economic classes and that there often existed among different economic groups a mutual distrust and anxiety about the power and actions of other groups. Less affluent Philadelphians, including citizens who would not normally be called poor, often felt that the economic and political power of the rich was being marshaled against them. The more opulent thought that the poor, no longer properly deferential, would use their new voting power to assault the needs and interests of the affluent. Or the poor might even embrace violence, as "Peter Easy" forecast, and reduce the city to anarchy. Such beliefs and the anxiety that accompanied them were not animated merely by the power of empty rhetoric. Revolutionary Philadelphia experienced spasms of political warfare rooted in class division, which gave the new political rhetoric the ring of authenticity.

One of the most traumatic and influential instances of such political battles occurred in 1779.[29] At the start of the year, Philadelphia's poor faced hard times, as the price of bread and other necessities soared under the pressure of monopolizers and forestallers. In mid-January, 150 seamen went on strike for higher wages, and it required troops to quell their protest. Two days later, the Supreme Executive Council said that this "most heinously criminal" manipulation of prices, which was "ruinous to the industrious poor," would be halted.[30] In April the General Assembly pledged the same thing. But council orders and legislation proved ineffective, and prices continued to rise.

Angered by more than high prices, the patience of the First Company of Philadelphia Militia Artillery quickly wore thin. On May 12 the militiamen demanded that the Supreme Executive Council stop the manipulation of prices and force those who refused to serve in the militia to do so, or fine them according to their wealth. Unless such actions were taken, "the Mid[d]ling and poor will still bear the Burden" of "fighting the Battles of those who are Avariciously intent on Amassing Wealth by Destruction of the more virtuous part of the Community." Although the militia implied that they would, if need be, use weapons to obtain relief, their memorial produced no action at that time.[31]

Many Philadelphians shared the militia's view that prices had to be lowered, and on May 25 a town meeting was held to decide on a course of action. Daniel Roberdeau, a militia officer who chaired the meeting, railed against those "getting rich by sucking the blood of this country" and asserted that under the circumstances "the community, in their own defence, have a natural right to counteract, . . . and to set limits to evils, which affect themselves." The meeting agreed and a committee was appointed to force prices down.[32]

In late June of 1779, the militia company that had memorialized the council in May issued a strident public statement supporting town meeting actions. "We have arms in our hands and know the use of them," the militia proclaimed, "and are ready and willing to support your Honorable Board in fully executing the righteous and equitable measures for which you were appointed; nor will we lay them down till this is accomplished. We wish not to have the preeminence; but we will no longer be trampled upon." And "if by reason of the obstinacy and perverseness of individuals, your Committee find themselves inadequate to the task, *our drum shall beat to arms.*"[33]

Despite town meeting and militia efforts, by late September price regulation had failed. The militia, true to its threats, took action. After two meetings where leaders of the radical party of Pennsylvania tried to forestall violence, the militia, 150 to 200 strong, took to the streets on October 4. They arrested four men seen as opposing price regulation and paraded them through the city to the beat of the rogue's march. As this was occurring, James Wilson, fearing that he too would be arrested, gathered friends; they barricaded themselves in Wilson's home. The militia's line of march suggests that no special effort was made to pass Wilson's home, but, after winding through the city, the militia crowd did move up Third Street toward Wilson's house.

As the militiamen approached Dock Street, a mere half block from the Wilson house, they were stopped by Colonel Grayson, a member of the board of war. Speaking to Captain Ephraim Faulkner, who was at the head of the militia, Grayson expressed fear that the militia intended to attack Wilson's house. Faulkner assured him that the men "had no intention to meddle with Mr. Wilson or his house, their object was to support the constitution, the laws and the Committee of Trade. The labouring part of the City had become desperate from the high price of the necessities of life."[34] With this, the crowd of militiamen passed up Third Street toward the Wilson home. When the main body of the militia passed the house, nothing happened. But as the last section of the crowd passed, windows in the house opened. Words, then shots followed. Several people, all save one a member of the crowd, died; many were seriously wounded.

The Fort Wilson Riot, as it came to be known, alarmed many and especially those who held positions of power. Major Samuel Shaw, a merchant in civilian life, wrote: "There has been hell to pay in Philadelphia. . . . It is hoped that a spirited interposition of the executive powers of the State will prevent a renewal of the tragedy." Henry Laurens, merchant and past president of the Continental Congress, proclaimed, "We are at this moment on a precipice, and what I have long dreaded and often intimated to my friends, seems to be breaking forth—a convulsion among the people." Samuel Patterson reflected the mood in the city when he cried out: "God help us—Terrible times. . . . The poor starving here & rise for redress. Many flying the city for fear of Vengeance." "It is not over," he warned, asserting that the militia "will have blood for blood."[35]

The Supreme Executive Council and the Assembly apparently shared such fears, for they quickly took out riot insurance. By October 10 it had been decided to distribute one hundred barrels of flour in the city, with a preference being given to the families of militiamen. It was also decreed that henceforth persons not serving in the militia would be fined according to their wealth. Moreover, if a complaint was lodged against anyone whose general conduct seemed to show opposition to the war effort, that person would be arrested. Capitulation to the threat of violence seemed complete when the Supreme Executive Council, on October 26, told merchants that the late tragic events offered a "useful lesson." The council warned that monopolizers and forestallers bringing distress on the public forfeited any right to the support and protection of the government.[36] Crowd action to protect the poor and the laboring part of the community against greedy merchants—and the threat of a renewal of that action—had struck home.

The Fort Wilson incident cast a long shadow across Philadelphia. In the years after 1779, it stood as a reminder that the poor might embrace "mob" violence as a political tool.[37] And the events of 1779 dramatically suggested to respectable Philadelphians that the good old prewar days of deference—if they had ever existed—were gone. Less than four years later, yet another example of what Benjamin Rush called "mobocracy" burned the fear of Fort Wilson-style incidents even more deeply into the city's conscience.

In June of 1783, members of the Pennsylvania Line were angered by the belief that they would be discharged without pay. Soldiers stationed in Philadelphia, augmented by troops who marched into the city from Lancaster, decided to force the issue on June 21. Two to three hundred armed soldiers proceeded to the State House, demanded that the Supreme Executive Council authorize a settlement of the soldiers' accounts, and informed the council: "You have only twenty minutes to deliberate on this important matter." Although the council refused to act, no violence occurred. Over the next three days, negotiations took place, and, in the end, after five hundred militiamen had been called out in a show of force, the mutineering soldiers stopped pressing their position with the threat of armed force. Despite the peaceful ending to the mutiny, the Continental Congress, feeling that it had not been properly protected during the days of threatened violence, left the city and never again met in Philadelphia.[38] "Mob" action spilled blood in 1779; now the "mob" had driven Congress away and thereby reduced the influence and political luster of Philadelphia. Worse yet, in each incident elements of the last line of defense against domestic insurrection—the militia and the army—had engaged in riots to redress grievances. Where would it end? Would only a "mobocracy" where "all laws breathe the spirit of town meetings and porter shops" satisfy the "common people?"[39]

Fear of lower-class "mob" violence, nourished by actual crowd actions, haunted Philadelphians who yearned for a deferential, stable society. It reinforced their commitment to the ideal that electoral politics had to be safely lodged in the hands of respectable gentlemen who would not cater to the prattlings of the poor and their allies. The horrors of the French Revolution, by raising the specter of possible political chaos and class warfare, deepened that commitment, as Israel Israel's efforts to become a state senator graphically demonstrated in 1797–98.

Israel Israel, a baptized and practicing Episcopalian, owned the Cross Keys Tavern and was a leader in the Democratic Societies. He became well known during the yellow fever outbreak of 1793 for heading the subscription fund that distributed necessities to the needy. Using this relief work as a major campaign point, Israel ran for the Pennsylvania legislature in 1793 and 1795, losing both times. The election of 1797 was a different story. Starting in August 1797, yellow fever again ravaged Philadelphia. Aware of the dangers of yellow fever, up to one-half of the population, including most of the wealthier citizens, fled the city. A number of citizens chided the rich for not properly helping the poor they instead left to their fate. Once again special committees assisted the poor and distressed. Once again Israel Israel helped distribute relief.[40]

In this situation, Israel launched yet another attempt to become a state legislator by running for the Senate seat of Benjamin R. Morgan, Esq., a federalist lawyer who had been in the state legislature for five years.[41] On October 9, the *Aurora* proclaimed its support for Israel, saying that "the *well born*" of Philadelphia would oppose him because he was a tavernkeeper. "But as the right of suffrage is fortunately *not yet* confined to the *gentlemen* of the *learned professions*," the *Aurora* said, "it is not to be imagined that this objection will have any weight with the generality of voters." Indeed, "the great body of our citizens, the useful classes among us, the artisans and mechanics have too much respect for them selves to object to ISRAEL ISRAEL because he is not a merchant or a lawyer."

Morgan's supporters also rushed endorsements into print, arguing that it would be wrong to turn out a talented, experienced gentleman in favor of a person with no governmental experience. Moreover, since many of the citizens had fled the city, it would be "ungenerous" to vote out the old ticket: to do so would constitute taking undue advantage of those who were absent. Indeed, such an election could not be represented as being the true voice of Philadelphia's freemen.[42]

When the voice of the freemen who remained or who returned to vote was heard, Israel Israel won—but just barely. Out of a total of 4,010 votes cast in the election, Israel's majority was a scant 38. An analysis of the areas from which he fashioned his majority demonstrates his strong support among the poor. Israel carried only two of the twelve city wards, North and South Mulberry, and these wards held a high percentage of lower-class residents. Victory came only because he won slightly more than 83 percent of the vote in the Northern Liberties and almost 87 percent of the vote in Southwark, both lower-class districts.[43]

Morgan's forces denounced the election and argued that Israel won because yellow fever drove "the freeholders and other respectable inhabitants" away, allowing "the citoyens of Irishtown [in Southwark] and the Northern Liberties" to elect him.

Only Israel's appeal to the "deluded masses" and chance gave him the victory. William Cobbett, the virulently anti-Republican editor of *Porcupine's Gazette*, noted Israel's ownership of the "Cross-Keys Grog Shop," which prompted him to lash out: "This is a step towards perfection in the representative way which we had not before taken. A public house is a most excellent stand for collecting the sentiments of the sovereign people, who never speaks his mind right freely, except when he's half drunk."[44]

Israel's opponents did not stop at denouncing him and his supporters in print but petitioned the Senate and demanded that the election be overturned because of procedural irregularities. A Senate committee agreed that a new election should be held; it was scheduled for February 22. Once the Senate ordered a new election, essays and announcements of endorsement meetings inundated the press. Charges and countercharges were liberally hurled about as both sides claimed that the opposition would use fraud, intimidation, and dark schemes to win.[45]

The Israel group presented a variety of arguments, many of them aimed at the poor. "A Republican," and others, charged that Israel's election was not put aside for irregularities; Israel's opponents objected to "his being a zealous defender of, and advocate for liberty and equality amongst men, disapproving of all distinctions, titles, excises and stamp acts, with every other political measure which lays a burden on the common poor people for the benefit of the rich." Clearly, those "who are naturally enemies to the liberties of the common and poor people" would align themselves with Morgan.[46] Other supporters stressed that Israel was a true republican and a friend to the poor, as his relief work indicated. Using such appeals, the pro-Israel group hammered at the theme that the rights and interests of the ordinary people would be destroyed if Israel were not reelected.[47]

The Morgan forces zealously countered these claims as essay after essay defended the actions that had declared Israel's seat vacant. Morgan's backers also took the political offensive by comparing the education, talents, and governmental experience of the two men and proclaiming Israel no match for their candidate. Examining Israel's patriotism, they found him too much a friend of France when war with France seemed imminent.

But above all, the Morgan camp called up the specter of the French Revolution's excesses by depicting Israel and his backers as riotous Jacobins. Time and again the charge appeared that Israel's forces used violence to disrupt or take over Morgan endorsement meetings.[48] Thus, while Israel played upon his concern for the poor, the Morgan camp played upon the fears of the more affluent. At times the appeals had at least some pretense of subtlety. "Those who are opposed to the general administration of the established government," one argued, "are commonly persons, who have little or nothing to lose, except their time, which hangs heavy on their hands, unless employed in mischief." Better men "will labour and toil for years to acquire property— . . . but alas! when this is done, they leave the out posts unguarded, and, the enemy enters while they sleep, and ere they are aware, the fruits of their industry is wrested from them by the lawless sons of anarchy and misrule." "Foresight" attempted no circumlocution. "The hour of danger is come," he cried out. "Our country is struggling in the deadly gripe [i.e., grip] of disorder and rapine, and the contest is doubtful." Government and laws tottered under "the unremitting exertions of ruffians panting for tumult, plunder and bloodshed," who "in hellish anticipation view your property as already their own."[49]

On February 22, citizens flocked to the polls; when the votes were counted, Morgan had won by a majority of 357 out of 8,723 votes cast. Israel won just one-third of the votes cast in the city wards, and as in the first election, the only city wards he carried were North and South Mulberry. He again won handily in the lower-class suburban areas by gaining 69 percent of the vote in the eastern Northern Liberties, 76 percent in the western Northern Liberties, and just less than 75 percent of the vote in Southwark.[50] Clearly his strongest support came from the areas where the poor predominated. Not without reason did William Cobbett claim that many of the indigent voted for Israel because of his relief work.[51]

With the victory for Morgan assured, Cobbett gloated that the Morgan backers "have proved themselves not only the most rich and the best informed, but also the most *numerous.*" Still, he conceded that Morgan won only because the Quakers, who normally did not vote, supported him. Had the Quakers, as a group among the most prosperous Philadelphians, not supported Morgan, Philadelphia would have had "the mortification to see a grogshop man fixed in the Senate." With special relish he related an election story that revealed the deep class divisions in the election. A Quaker, on his way to vote, asked a man walking along the road if he wanted a ride, but also asked the man for whom he would vote. When the man said Israel Israel, the Quaker told him to walk. "This," Cobbett noted, "is a good example. Let no one give them a lift. —Let them trudge through the dirt, without shoes and stockings, 'till misery and pain bring them to their senses."[52]

The pro-Israel *Aurora* agreed that the vote divided along class lines. And, said the editor, the closeness of the election "must strike terror into the hearts of the aristocrats." Indeed, Israel had done well, considering that all the influence of wealth was marshaled against him. Morgan was put in by threats and promises and by "the indirect and direct bribery of a faction that stick at nothing to carry their ends." Hired carriages transported the sick and lame to the polls. The Morgan clique paid people's taxes, which constituted indirect bribery. Employees were threatened with the loss of their jobs; tenants faced eviction; Morgan supporters told people in debt that they faced ruin; industrious tradesmen heard that they would no longer be frequented. All this was threatened if these people refused to "sacrifice their right of suffrage." And, the editor continued, many other equally infamous actions helped defeat Israel.[53]

Morgan's forces also leveled charges of election wrongdoing. It was asserted that, in the week before the election, many taverns remained open and free drinks were poured for all Israel supporters. Worse yet, on election day, "lawless mobs . . . tyranically beat up the quarters of the peaceable federalists" and threatened, with the French code of club law, every man favoring Morgan. At one polling place, a man, armed with a drawn sword, paraded all day long; on his cap was a huge label inscribed *"Israel or Death,"* and beneath these words was depicted the rawhead and bloodybones resting on a coffin. All this was done, said the Morgan people, to intimidate the weak; in short, violence and the foulest kind of corruption supported Israel.[54]

The charges presented by each side are, whether true or not, revealing. Morgan's people supposedly utilized superior economic power to influence the election. Save for the charge of providing free alcohol, the Israel group reportedly used physical violence, physical intimidation. It takes money to hire a coach; the poorest person can pick up a club. Thus, the charges of corruption mirror the appeals made before the election. From start to finish, the election seemed to pit the rich against the poor.

Israel Israel's bid to become a state senator in 1797-98 confirmed the views of the "Peter Easys" of Philadelphia. The poor, having gained the vote, were far from deferential. They attended endorsement meetings and, according to Morgan supporters, used violence to carry the election for their candidate. Given the choice of supporting a gentleman lawyer with five years of governmental service, the poor preferred the unqualified, demagogical tavernkeeper because he claimed to have helped them and to represent their interests against those of the selfish rich. In the golden age of colonial politics, with its restrictive franchise, the likes of Israel Israel could not have hoped to win by seeking the support of the poor. But when the liberal franchise of the revolutionary era combined with a lack of deference, he came dangerously close to winning because of the votes of the poor.

Dramatic political confrontations, such as Fort Wilson, the "mutiny" of 1783, and the case of Israel Israel, offered influential support to the new political rhetoric which emphasized that politics often operated on the basis of class differences. In less dramatic fashion, the long-running battle over the governance of the city demonstrated the truth of the claim that politics in independent Philadelphia had a marked tendency to fracture along class lines and that older institutional and attitudinal controls no longer kept the lower orders in their place.[55]

When the aristocratic, self-perpetuating Corporation that dominated colonial Philadelphia's government stopped functioning in early 1776, the governance of the city fell to a number of separate agencies whose officials were often elected by the voters. In this way, save for the period of British occupation when the old charter government was revived, the Revolution allowed the voters of Philadelphia, including the eligible poor, far more voice than ever before in how the city would be governed. Some citizens, especially those who detested the democratic tendencies of the Constitution of 1776, found this arrangement unacceptable. They wanted a vigorous, unified city government that could control the city and that, ideally, would be structured in such a way as to dilute the power of the newly enfranchised masses. Thus, not surprisingly, the conservative Republican Society, which was founded to overturn the Constitution of 1776, made the reincorporation of Philadelphia a central part of its program to alter the nature of revolutionary government.[56]

Between 1781 and 1786, three unsuccessful efforts were mounted to have the legislature again incorporate Philadelphia.[57] One such effort was rooted in a memorial written by the grand jury of Philadelphia in late 1785. This memorial presented the basic arguments used in the reincorporation campaigns. Crime and immorality were on the rise; vagabonds were flocking to the city; the streets were cluttered and dirty. And the vast increase in the population of the city compounded these evils. In short, Philadelphia was becoming unmanageable, ungovernable. The only answer, as the grand jury saw it, was to "restore Philadelphia to the dignity of a city (which it now only enjoys in name) by granting an act of incorporation."[58]

An analysis of the members of the grand jury that offered this ringing endorsement of reincorporation provides a suggestive comment on the segments of society that most favored a change in the way the city was governed. As a group, the members of the 1785 grand jury overwhelmingly represented Philadelphia's mercantile community. Ten of the seventeen grand jury members were merchants; one was a sea captain-merchant; four were grocers. Only two of the men, both carpenters, came from the ranks of the mechanic-artisan group. And, as a group, the members were, at a minimum, substantial inhabitants of the middling rank. Only three of the eleven members who could be traced in the tax records were rated for less than two hundred pounds. But two of these three rented houses worth one thousand pounds or more, and the other owned a pleasure carriage. The eight others were all worth more than a thousand pounds ratable estate, and the average tax rating of all eleven was just over seventeen hundred pounds. The fact that seven of the eleven owned pleasure carriages illustrates that these men were indeed among the affluent.[59]

The reincorporation efforts backed by the Republican Society and the mercantile members of the grand jury produced vigorous counterattacks couched in class-conscious rhetoric. An antiincorporation petition of 1783, signed by approximately fourteen hundred inhabitants of the city, argued that reincorporation would "subject us to an aristocratic police."[60] An essay by "One of the Little Folk," which appeared less than three weeks after the grand jury memorial was printed, voiced a similar theme by commenting that "the great people among us" desired incorporation and adding that "I have always been alarmed at the strides of power, . . . intended for no other purpose than to draw a line between the *Great Folk* and the *Little Folk*. . . . We well know how high people are apt to look, when they get into office, and have power in their hands."[61] Clearly, many Philadelphians feared the possible reinstitution of the old-style closed corporation, which would return control of the city to the aristocratic few.

The fourth attempt to incorporate the city, begun in November 1788, went virtually unchallenged, and on March 11, 1789 an act incorporating Philadelphia became law. The new form of city government significantly diluted the voting power of less affluent citizens. Freemen meeting normal franchise requirements could vote for the thirty-member common council that joined with the fifteen aldermen to pass laws, ordinances, and regulations. However, only freeholders could vote for aldermen, who selected the mayor and recorder from their own number. The power and prestige of aldermen were further enhanced by a provision giving them seven-year terms, while the common councillors served three-year terms. Further, aldermen automatically became justices of the peace and, accordingly, acquired both legislative and judicial powers.[62] Because of this mix of power and the two-tiered voting system, the battle over incorporation did not end in 1789; it merely took on new forms.

The first election held under the new charter showed the class antagonisms and fear of an aristocratic city government that the opponents of incorporation had long exhibited. "No Freeholder" urged those in his station of life to elect common councilmen "who will not *betray*, but *feelingly support*, your interest." This was necessary because the incorporation act "not only *deprives* the *poor* of a *vote* in the election of *Aldermen*, but it places the *Aldermen* in a state of *dependence upon the rich only*." He warned, "This dependence may induce them to *disregard and oppress the poor*, who may have the misfortune to contend for *their rights with the rich*."[63] "An old Mechanic" concurred, saying that aldermen would surely be "the most wealthy and opulent citizens"; therefore, mechanics had to attend to their true interests by voting for "*worthy reputable mechanics*" as common councillors.[64]

Despite such pleas, the men elected were not only wealthy, they were also old-line conservatives. Samuel Powell, who had been the last mayor under the prewar Corporation, was again selected by the aldermen to fill that post. Even the common council had a familiar look. Rather than consisting of mechanics, it represented the old Quaker and conservative merchant element.[65]

The actions of these newly elected city officials, who were drawn from the upper ranks of society, produced yet more acrimony and nondeferential class-conscious rhetoric. Essayists argued that the Corporation possessed arbitrary power to decide which areas to pave and light and that the lighting and paving policy of "our worthy Corporation . . . savors strongly of partiality somewhere." The city government's regulation of wages and failure to stop market abuses that harmed the laboring poor led "A Drayman" to charge that the government protected "the *well-born*" while neglecting "to hinder the rich from oppressing the poor." The enactment in June 1790 of an ordinance designed to keep items offered for sale from obstructing the sidewalks produced angry cries. Goods could not impede movement on the sidewalk, but much greater obstructions, such as stone steps and trees, were tolerated before the doors of the rich. "If the wealthy were to have been affected by this regulation," one essayist maintained, "it would not have disgraced the city code." In 1795 efforts to ban the construction of wooden buildings in the heart of the city produced a mass meeting that proclaimed the ordinance "particularly oppressive to the mechanic and poor man." The meeting pointedly told the city fathers that "the ordinance, however favorable to the interests of the opulent, is fatal to the exertions and comfort of the poor."[66]

Such attacks on the new city government's actions added weight to claims that the act of incorporation had to be rendered more democratic. In November 1792 "a numerous meeting" of Philadelphians called upon the legislature to alter the act. The unanimous declaration of the meeting argued that "civil liberty can only flow from a free and republican government, pure in its principles and guarded in its structure." The meeting then denounced the fact that freemen could not select the aldermen who voted taxes on the citizens. This and other evils had to be remedied.[67] "A native of Philadelphia" voiced similar themes, asserting that the "unequal and unjust" act of incorporation denied two-thirds of the people a vote for aldermen, thus "depriving the taxed of a vote in the choice of the office that is to lay the tax." Doubtless, few missed his reference to a stated cause of the Revolution. If the people needed reminding, a newspaper reported that at a July Fourth party, officers of the Pennsylvania militia drank to the toast: "The City of Philadelphia—May the aristocratic act of incorporation experience that revision that will secure to the citizens an Equality of rights."[68]

In 1796 the Pennsylvania legislature admitted that the original act of incorporation was faulty and amended it. Henceforth, Philadelphia freemen annually balloted for twenty common councillors. The freemen also elected twelve selectmen, who served staggered terms, so that one-third of them would stand for election each year. The common and select councils possessed exclusive legislative authority. The governor of the state appointed one recorder and fifteen aldermen, who held office during good behavior. These officials exercised all powers, save legislative powers, that aldermen had had under the original incorporation act. The common and select councils annually chose one of the aldermen as mayor; he supervised and executed the ordinances of the city. Finally, the law decreed that the meetings of the city councils would be open to all peaceable and orderly persons.[69]

The extended debate over the governance of Philadelphia illustrated vital changes occurring in the politics of the revolutionary city. Biting rhetoric proclaiming the existence of division based on economic classes became commonplace. That rhetoric accurately reflected the fact that the needs and desires of the af-

The Context

fluent often differed from those of the poor and even the middling classes. Equally important, when the poor and their allies felt abused, they did not quietly defer. This became especially obvious as mass meetings and memorials denounced the creation of sharp distinctions in voting rights based on wealth. Philadelphia's less affluent citizens successfully fought to retain their suffrage rights in city elections. In the new order of politics, the voice of the commonalty could not easily be ignored.

The new political world wrought by the Revolution, like the movement toward a free-wage labor system, suggested to established Philadelphians that institutional and attitudinal controls that flourished in the colonial city were no longer keeping the poor and lower classes quiescent. In independent Philadelphia, less affluent individuals seemed to pursue their own goals in ways that challenged the needs and interests of the more affluent and disrupted society. Faced with such disturbing changes, many Philadelphians altered their perceptions of the poor and groped for ways to defuse what they perceived as the potential danger from below.

3

*Perceptions of "The Other Half":
The Increasing Quest for Control*

In 1767 a Philadelphian, describing the plight of a poor soldier, claimed, "No Observation is more common, and at the same time more true, than That one half of the world are ignorant [of] how the other half lives."[1] Although many essays in eighteenth-century Philadelphia newspapers were penned by foolish or ignorant people, this author, even if he overstated his case, was neither foolish nor ignorant. But he was only half right. It seems doubtful that Philadelphians realized the full extent of poverty in their midst, and it is certainly possible that many, especially the prosperous, did not and could not appreciate the wretched state in which many others lived. Yet eighteenth-century Philadelphians believed that many of the city's inhabitants lived in poverty. The abundance of references to the poor that appeared in print during the period 1760-1800 attests to Philadelphians' awareness of the poorer element among them.

An analysis of commentaries on the poor reveals that *general* attitudes toward the poor were not altered by the Revolution: thoughout the years 1760-1800, the poor were told to accept deferentially their low station. However, by the time independence was secured, a subtle, yet vital, change was occurring in the way in which articulate citizens perceived the poor. From the mid-1780s to the end of the century, Philadelphians felt the compulsion to analyze the nature, meaning, and causes of poverty far more fully and precisely than ever before. This examination led the articulate to draw sharp distinctions between segments of the poor, based on moral considerations. As these writers explored the meaning of poverty in the postwar era, they offered a stream of arguments supporting the view that the poor should passively accept an inferior place in society. The new analysis and the arguments for quiet acceptance of poverty amounted to a moral crusade designed to make the "other half" behave as the more affluent wanted them to behave.

This crusade occurred because many Philadelphians came to believe that deference and industrious poverty were no longer the norm. Many of the poor, it appeared, had gone sour and become dangerous. This seemed especially true in the new political world that sprang from the Revolution, in which the poor, having the vote, behaved without the old respect toward the wealthy. The moral crusade offered an antidote to nondeferential behavior. If the poor could be convinced to accept the ideal of passivity, they would not use their potential political power in an effort to alter the nature of society. Rather, they would allow those from a higher station in life to direct politics. If only the poor could be convinced that they should embrace industrious poverty, with its ready acceptance of deference, the supposed order and tranquility of colonial society and politics could be resurrected. The moral crusade of the postindependence era was designed to help produce that resurrection.

During the years between 1760 and the winning of American independence, articulate Philadelphians typically divided the poor into two categories. One segment, the "labouring" or the "industrious" poor, were people who understood that, since the poor man must either work or starve, "necessity" often supplied the most satisfactory guide to finding employment. The industrious poor man, accepting this fact, "makes the best of his lot; works cheerfully, and enjoys the fruit of his honest labour."[2] One could, in fact, smile at the "happiness" that accompanied the hardworking industry "of an honest man of plain common sense, [who] jogs contented in the road of life."[3]

Such happiness, the argument went, typically eluded the more affluent. Yes, "if all made the improvement they ought . . . there can be little doubt but the higher and more leisurable stations would be upon the whole the happiest." But "they rarely prove so," as multitudes of the wealthy became unhappy because "their wishes have increased in proportion to their acquisitions." Thus, "the discontented Rich are poor."[4]

The message contained in such pronouncements seemed clear: the wise poor person would work hard and accept a low station. Indeed, if those in "poverty and illiteracy" rose above "obscurity" to "a higher sphere of life," they often lost their goodness by becoming "forgetful of the happiness" they enjoyed when they lived in poverty. This made them haughty and, in the end, probably miserable.[5] Young Miss Sarah Eve, writing in her diary, sounded the common theme when she said: "At the worst what is poverty! it is living more according to nature[;] . . . a person that is poor could they divest themselves of opinion is more independent than one that is not so, as the one limits his wants and expectations to his circumstances. . . . Poverty without pride is nothing, but with it, it is the very deuce!"[6] The moral tale of "The Bee and the Fly," published in 1772, summed up the whole case. The bee haughtily reminded the fly that bees made "nothing but the most delicious honey," while flies "live upon nothing but ordure and excrement." "We live as well as we can," responded the fly, adding, "Poverty is no vice, but I am sure passion is." Of course, soon thereafter the bee killed himself by stinging someone. Reflecting on the bee's fate, the poor industrious fly sagely observed that *"one had better have less considerable talents, and use them with discretion."*[7]

Perhaps because such moral pronouncements appeared only infrequently in print during the years before independence, the publicly sketched picture of the happy, industrious poor and the unfortunate rich went virtually unchallenged in these years. In 1767 an essayist did maintain that, "while the slightest inconveniencies of the great are magnified into calamities; while tragedy mouths out their sufferings in all the strains of eloquence, the miseries of the poor are intirely disregarded." This was the case even though "some of the lower rank of people undergo more real hardships in one day, than those of a more exalted station suffer in their whole lives." Still, this commentator then proclaimed that "he who, in the vale of obscurity, can brave adversity; who, without friends to encourage, acquaintance to pity, or even without hope to alleviate his misfortunes, can behave with tranquility and indifference, is truly great."[8]

In this preindependence period, Philadelphians offered no praise at all for that segment of the poor "inclined to live in Sloth and Idleness." Such "idle" poor danced blindly along "the Road of pleasure" until they found "Misery" or "Despair." It seemed obvious that the idle poor, unlike the industrious poor, were doomed to a life of failure. In 1781 a commentator attempted to articulate what distinguished the idle from the industrious poor and to assess their relative prospects. He claimed that "a man may be suspected of being deficient in industry, temperance, or honesty, (the first virtues in a commonwealth) who is not possessed after a certain number of years, of a moderate share of property."[9]

Certainly the writer who called for establishing manufacturing enterprises partly to excite "a general and laudable spirit of industry among the poor" expected that articulate Philadelphians agreed on the importance of this spirit. "A Shepherd," calling for the creation of woolen manufactures, worked the same theme by proclaiming that "encouraging Industry among the Poor . . . has ever been the Policy of wise Statesmen."[10] "Industry" was the ideal, and at least some Philadelphians argued that citizens and government must strive to make the poor industrious.

In the postwar years, these general perceptions and attitudes held steady, while the articulate began diagnosing much more precisely than before what caused a poor person to be industrious or an idler. In doing so, these citizens significantly refined the descriptive terms normally used for different segments of the poor. In the postwar years, Philadelphians became more and more likely to call the idle poor the "vulgar" or the "vicious" poor. Their poverty, the argument went, stemmed from moral weakness, which endangered the peace of society. Such people were, of course, idlers. Certainly it seemed logical for "Sunday Monitor," when speaking of some of the afflictions that "rise directly out of our sins," to say that "poverty springs from idleness." Indeed, as others noted, idleness was "the Devil['s] cushion" because "there are few who know how to be idle and innocent": "the slothful mind as naturally turns to vice as the untilled land turns to weeds."[11]

As the more prosperous Philadelphians probed for the root causes of vulgar poverty, they came in this period to place great emphasis on the evils of alcohol. Some even proclaimed spirituous liquors "the parents of idleness and extravagance, and the certain forerunners of poverty, and frequently of gaols. . . ." The tie of alcohol, idleness, and moral weakness produced the claim that the "Dram-Shop" was "Penury's cause," because

> IT Tempt th' unfeeling idlers from their home.
> Domestice [sic] cares, and business must give way,
> 'Till drams of "liquid fire" illume the day;
> And yet these sots will murmur and repine,
> And charge their wretchedness to trade's decline,
>
> .   .   .   .
>
> A few short years, this tipling course they run,
> While rags, disease and infamy come on—

When death took such people, it "rids the world of useless lumps of clay." The vulgar poor, it seemed, failed to realize that "without *Temperance*, there is no Happiness."[12]

The vicious poor were not only idlers who often drank to excess; many of them also exhibited "a fondness for loose and idle companions" and sought only "pleasure." They gambled and engaged in immoral behavior, eschewing "frugality," "oeconomy," and "foresight." In the end, these poor found not only "poverty" but "disgrace and ruin." One became a "worthless," "vagabond" type who could be dismissed as a "Drunken; Rioting, Sulking[,] Lazy fellow."[13]

The growing disdain for the idle poor was reflected in the terms the postwar citizens increasingly used to describe the industrious poor, who were routinely labeled "honest," "deserving," "virtuous." In the mid-1780s this group was openly called "the better sort of poor"—precisely because they avoided the immorality of the vicious poor. "The better sort of poor," of course, displayed industry and were also identifiable by their sobriety, frugality, and honesty. Indeed, in the postwar period, the terms "industrious poor" or "labouring poor" typically carried the connotations of sobriety and honesty.[14]

In the years after the achievement of independence, Philadelphia essayists hammered at the point that the wise, the moral, poor person would be industrious. In fact, these writers engaged in a veritable celebration of the moral value of industry. "The blessed effects of honest industry" became the key to success for all, not just for the poor. Thus, "useful and skillful industry is the soul of an active life," and "virtuous habits of industry . . . only are productive of happiness." The value of hard work was so great that it formed "an antidote to almost all evils." The moral tone associated with attitudes toward constant labor was simply, yet sharply, offered in the claim that "idleness is disgraceful. Industry is the ornament of wealth, the support and consolation of poverty."[15] Of course, if a spirit of industry was good for all, it was essential for the poor.

The more precise postwar definition of types of poverty and the celebration of industry made the distinction between the "idle" and the "industrious" poor sharper, clearer than ever before. Idleness was not only bad; it was immoral and likely to lead to criminal acts. Conversely, industry was a badge of moral goodness, because *"virtuous* poverty is no crime." The *Aurora* stressed this point in 1795 when it published a "Useful Biography" lionizing a common laborer because he had displayed "unwearied industry."[16]

In the postwar years, many articulate citizens painstakingly labored to convince the poor that they should and must be industrious, and one of the methods was that of turning the prewar trickle of general comments on the happy, industrious poor and the unfortunate rich into a torrent. In the postwar period, such comments were refined and presented in a far more sophisticated and systematic form, and they were presented often. Some persons who argued this case no doubt expressed sincerely held beliefs and offered sage advice, seeing the miserly or extravagant rich as morally weak, and judging that idleness and love of alcohol among the poor could well ruin lives. Nevertheless, the moral crusade stemmed also from a desire to keep the poor from challenging the basic order and structure of society at a time when the poor seemed to have a greater freedom of action than in colonial days.

One goal of the crusade was to prove systematically that "Riches bring Cares." The simple fact was that "Wealth, pomp, and honor are but gaudy Toys;/Alas, how poor the pleasure they impart!" Indeed, the "nymph" of contentment "seldom makes her home/In proud grandeur's gilded dome." As those already liberally endowed with worldly goods reached for more, they found that "prosperity debilitates instead of strengthening the mind. —Its common effect is, to create an extreme sensibility to the slightest wound." Perhaps some such sensibility was inescapable, since the wealthy could not count on friends being real friends. In addition, the rich, to be happy, felt a need for the security of a guard. Thus, even if "the higher departments of life" yielded more pleasure, they also produced more pain.[17]

Riches could also be debilitating because love of fancy foods and wines often caused the more affluent to fall prey to the doctor and surgeon. Great wealth could be devitalizing: with it there "is more room for the freaks of caprice, and more privilege for ignorance and vice; a quicker succession of flatteries, and a larger circle of voluptuousness." Truly, "he whom the wantonness of abundance has once softened, easily sinks into neglect of his affairs; and he that thinks he can afford to be negligent, is not far from being poor." Trying "to live in Stile," bowing to "every fashionable folly," was "to be as unthinking and as irrational as possible—to get into debt—and at last—to die like a dog." Supposedly, given these dangers, the "great" were "ever anxious."[18]

In 1787 the *Pennsylvania Evening Herald* summarized the case against "Riches." When "the desire to wealth is taking hold of the heart, let us look around and see how it operates upon those whose industry, or fortune has obtained it." Just a little reflection would show that "when we find them oppressed with their own abundance, luxurious without pleasure, idle without ease, impatient and querulous in themselves, and despised, or hated by the rest of mankind, we shall soon be convinced that if the real wants of our condition are satisfied, there remains little to be sought with solicitude, or desired with eagerness." For

"Beneath those fine trappings" of "dress, pomp, and grandeur," "we oftentimes find/The pangs of remorse and despair."[19]

Having wealth might produce a life of misery, pain, despair, but not so for the understanding poor person. Of course, facing "extreme poverty" and living as a "poor neglected wretch" was hardly desirable. Some degree of wealth was necessary so that one could be exempt from the grip of necessity. Still, "a mediocrity of circumstance is what will give us the greatest felicity, and make our path through life smooth."[20]

Those living in poverty always knew some form of adversity. Yet that was good, even ennobling, for "Prosperity best discovers Vice, but Adversity, Virtue!" Indeed, "all the treasures of the earth, are not to be compared to the least virtue of the soul." "To be good is to be happy," since "Virtue alone, has that to give which makes it joy to die or live." The virtuous man "is rich amidst poverty, and no one can deprive him of what he possesses." The rich were less fortunate:

> Many unjust grow rich, the pious poor—
> We would not change our virtue for their store:
> For constant virtue is a solid bass—
> Riches from man to man uncertain pass.[21]

The poor, precisely because they faced adversity and lacked fine possessions, not only found virtue; they avoided many of the problems and dangers of riches. The rich, often caught up in "The Curse of Avarice," lost sight of life's true meaning. And

> What man in his wits had not rather be poor,
> Than for lucre his freedom to give.
> Ever busy the means of his life to secure,
> And so ever neglecting to live.

Poverty actually protected the poor "from nameless griefs and toils." The poor did not have to fear the thief; they retained their health while the rich often fell victim to sickness through extravagant living. A poor man's friends, unlike those of the rich, were trustworthy, true. In short, "he that is voluntarily poor, possesses nothing, and nothing possesses him."[22]

The poor found the real happiness in life, in no small part, because of their training and station. For if the poor met with inconveniences, most of them were "removed by the very labor they are obliged to take; and which from their infancy they are inured to. They find pleasure where pain might have been expected: And in what they are necessitated to undergo consists their happiness; and, in true thinking, where the happiness of all finally consists." Thus, for the poor, "labor is ease, and ease is labor." "True Happiness" surely awaited those who understood that "the wants of my nature are cheaply supply'd, and the rest is folly and care."[23]

Of course, the poor should work, and work hard, to obtain the minimum wealth that would make their lives "calm," "clean," and "neat," even if their houses were "mean." But they must not aim too high. Failure often awaited one who, "brought up to follow the manual employment of the field," aimed at "a life of ease and affluence." Truly, "it is a great misfortune to be born high-spirited and poor: A soul of this make has much ado to submit; but necessity forces nature, and the encounter is severe. People of this temper seldom make their fortune; they have not still the power to subdue their own inclinations. . . ." It certainly seemed obvious that by raising expectations "too High," one found misery, not happiness.[24]

Even misery offered its benefits because it made accepting death much easier for the poor than for the rich. "Death seems to enter a cottage only as a gentle deliverer from the miseries of human life; but in seats of grandeur with insult and terror." "The Friendless Orphan" could welcome death as it signaled "the end of all his woes." One could even "rejoice" at the death of a beggar for "here his sorrows cease,/ . . . Where Death, the Leveller —restores to peace/The wretch who living knew not where to rest." Certainly with death the "storms [of pain] can never threaten more. . . ."[25]

The mortality of man also insured that the poor would find a certain equality: "Death . . . to one common doom brings kings and peasants, conquerors and slaves." The equality of the grave might even allow the poor to turn the tables on "luxury," which so often "cast on poverty a scornful eye." The poem "Equality" offered an excellent example of this argument:

> I dreamt, that, burried with my fellow clay,
> Close by a common beggar's side I lay;
> And, as so mean an object shock'd my pride,
> Thus, like a corps of consequence, I cried:—
> Scoundrel! be gone, and henceforth touch me not,
> More manners learn, and at a distance rot.
>
> Scoundrel! —then with laughter tone cry'd he,
> Proud lump of earth! I scorn thy words and thee:—
> Here all are EQUAL, now thy case is mine—
> This is my rotting place, and that is thine.[26]

If death brought only an end to woe and the equality of rotting, it would give little solace to the poor. But death offered much more by signaling a chance to rise into heaven, where "all is endless joy" and "where no distinction shall be known." Most important, the "everlasting life" of heaven could "neither be bought or sold." Indeed, "Pow'r, wealth, and beauty are a short-liv'd trust: 'Tis virtue only blossoms in the dust." "In the world to come,/ . . . no distinction shall be known./But what proceeds from worth alone." Thus, "in this world honours are under no regularity: true quality is neglected; Virtue oppressed; and Vice triumphant. The last day will rectify this disorder, and assign to every one a station suited to the dignity of his character. Ranks will then be properly adjusted, and precedency set right."[27]

Because virtue turned the key to the gates of heaven, the unkind rich could be locked out. "*A poor old* horse" (and a poor old servant, one assumes) could knowingly predict the fate of a master who abandoned him when he became too old to work. "My master's woes begin where mine shall end—/In pastures green I shall forever dwell/While cruelty sinks into its native hell." On the other hand, "a poor, but Honest MAN," whose breast was filled with "Strict virtue" and whose "coat of arms [was] a spotless life," faced bright prospects.

> In the great day, though pride
> Now scorns his pedigree;
> Thousands shall wish the'd been ally'd
> To this *great family*.

This was so because only those of "virtuous and humble mind" could hope to gain heaven. "And when they die, Heaven will receive them to that world where sorrow never comes, and their Humility, when on earth, will give them a place at God's right hand, where flow pleasures forevermore."[28]

Although the crusade presented a variety of themes, they all stressed one basic argument: "Be content with your lot"; "content makes any lot a prize." This was the wise course, because "by raising our expectations too high" we increase our miseries rather than finding happiness. Contentment provided its own reward, for "to be content only, is to be rich." Surely "we ought not to measure the wealth of a man by what he enjoys, but by what he has learnt not to want." Thus "The Contented Man's Soliloquy" correctly held that

> My portion is not large indeed,
> But then how *little* do I need,
> For nature's wants are few;
> *In this* the art of living lies,
> To want *no more* than may suffice,
> And make that *little* do.

The wise man faced injury and suffering with patience, resignation, and courage, for it was only logical to suffer "willingly what we cannot avoid."[29]

Such reasons for accepting one's lot paled into insignificance before the argument that "the best resolution we can make is, to suffer what we cannot alter, and to pursue without repining, the road which Providence, who directs every thing, has marked to us." The "Idea of a Happy Man" included urging people to perform the duties "their different stations in life exact of them." The "Ode to Adversity" properly proclaimed:

> Then, till life's latest sands are run,
> Oh, teach me, power divine,
> To cry my God, they will be done,
> Whate'er becomes of mine.

Surely, "happy are they who attend to the precepts of their Creator, For his language is, my children be contented, repine not under your afflictions, but remember that you experience them in order that you may be prepared for the joys of immortality."[30] The essence of the crusade to keep the poor content, then, came to this: "Persuade yourselves, the favor of God and the possession of virtue, form the principal happiness of the rational nature. Let a contented mind and a peaceful life, hold the next place in your estimation."[31]

It might seem that the evidence presented to support the existence of a public crusade to teach the poor and all members of the lower classes to accept their lot deferentially proves little. After all, some Philadelphians *must* have rejected the views expressed. True enough. But the shocking fact is that an examination of the postwar sources uncovered only two publicly printed items questioning the basic arguments presented.[32] In late 1784 an essayist seemingly challenged the idea that "Riches bring Cares" when he said that "high birth gives great privileges, and a great ascendance over those of a lower rank." Still, those of such "high birth" did not rest secure: "The great degrade themselves from their authority, by abusing it, and pressing too hard upon those below them." Moreover, this writer apparently accepted a basic tenet of the crusade: "We must bear with those that are above . . . ; but we must bear without dastardy and baseness." Indeed, any supporter of the crusade would have applauded this essayist's claim that "persons of an inferior rank may come up to a level with others, by the greatness of their souls."[33] This was less than a frontal assault upon the usual position.

In 1786 there appeared one uncompromising attack upon the assertions of the crusade. The author of "Reflections on Prosperity and Adversity," obviously sensitive to the existence of the crusade, asserted that "it is a common remark; it is almost a proverb, *That it is more difficult to bear Prosperity than Adversity*. For this observation we have to thank the inattention and barbarity of mankind, whose observations are, in general, superficial; and who seem strenuous to promote insensibility to the condition and to the merit of the poor." Indeed, "the rich are not satisfied with being often industrious to obtrude on the minds of the miserable a melancholy comparison . . . ; they must likewise aggravate their calamities with insolent nonsense, which hypocritically assumes that garb of primitive and apostolic consolation: They tell them, that they have an easier part to act in life than themselves. With equal propriety might they assert, that it is more agreeable to wear a chain than a bracelet...."[34]

This one bold denunciation of the ideal of the poor rich and the rich poor virtually disappears amid the myriad of items that formed the moralistic crusade of the postwar period. It stands alone and lonely and, in its loneliness, offers eloquent testimony to the pervasive public display of the ideas that "Riches bring Cares," but the "contented" poor person has the best of both worlds—here and in the hereafter.

Although this message was directed at the poor, it spoke to the middling sort as well. All people should accept the position God designated for them; none should aim for stations not intended for them. In this way, the moral crusade presented a picture of how the whole society ought to function: each person has a ranked place in society; everyone should know that place; and each should stay in it. As the moral crusade had it, society, when functioning properly, was orderly, stable, and characterized by a flow of deference from those in the lower ranks of society. Persons who held this view could sincerely, and without any ulterior motive, argue that all would benefit from such a system. The poor would gain happiness and quite possibly heaven. In a time of need, the argument went, the rich actually owed relief to the laboring poor. Industrious persons in the lower range of the middling rank, when in need, had a similar right to expect aid from the more affluent. By giving such assistance, the rich not only had the pleasure of performing their Christian duty, they also helped preserve the order and stability of society.[35] And it was the desire for order and stability that, above all, fueled the rise of the postwar moral crusade to recapture what was perceived as the tranquil, deferential prewar world. Articulate Philadelphians were not content merely to anchor their quest for deference in a rhetorical campaign. In the postindependence era, they arrived at new perceptions of social disorder, crime, and punishment. These new perceptions helped produce more action designed to reinstate the supposed deferential world of bygone days.

4

Social Disorder, Crime, and Punishment:
Reform and the Quest for Control

In the colonial period, Philadelphians, knowing that social disorder often accompanied urban living, worked to suppress the forces seen as supporting disorder, vice, and crime. However, they evidenced little concern about why crime occurred or who committed it. During the revolutionary era, Philadelphians began examining the issues of social disorder, crime, and punishment far more closely than ever before. Embracing Enlightenment humanitarianism, some reformers maintained that the system of justice must be rendered more evenhanded and humane.[1] These reformers could, in the postwar years, rejoice when debtors and the innocent poor were no longer routinely tossed into a miserable existence in jail. Enlightenment ideals did not, however, dominate the new analysis of crime and punishment that flourished in the revolutionary city. Considering the nature and supposed perpetrators of crime, many inhabitants concluded that the poor increasingly threatened social order and stability. They did not argue that the dignity of mankind and the ideal of social progress made reform of the social justice system necessary. Rather, emphasizing themes presented in the moral crusade, discussed in Chapter Three, they stressed that ways had to be found to control or reform the potentially dangerous poor, lest vice and crime plague the city. Only after these views were forcefully presented to the legislature in the mid-1780s did the legislature move to revise the penal code. And the revisers reflected the views and concerns articulated in the moral crusade both by trying to make criminals emulate the industrious poor and by trying to stop the evil of idleness associated with imprisonment for debt.

Philadelphians of the prewar era believed that tippling houses presented a special source of concern. As early as 1744, the city government cried out against the vast number of such houses, arguing that they lowered the city's moral tone. The problem persisted. In 1764 a legislative committee observed that "public Houses and Dram-shops have increased to an enormous Degree, to the great Corruption of Morals in the Populace." In the decade before the war, the mayor's court of Philadelphia worked diligently to stamp out disorderly houses and to control the number of taverns. The effect of these actions is not clear, but even if the court improved the situation, that improvement covered only the area between Vine and South streets. The mayor's court jurisdiction did not extend to the suburbs, and as "A Citizen" asserted in 1772: "The environs of this city very much abound" with "abominable [tavern] houses." By the eve of the Revolution, Philadelphians still sought an effective way to control taverns and disorderly houses.[2]

Philadelphia produced better results in providing the colonial equivalent of a police force. Beginning in 1749, the wardens of Philadelphia could hire night watchmen to stop social disorder and prevent crime by capturing nightwalkers, malefactors, rogues, vagabonds, and disorderly persons who disturbed the public peace. According to Carl Bridenbaugh, the night watch that developed soon set the colonial standard. By 1772 the watch patrolled seventeen separate beats from 10:00 PM to 4:00 AM in summer and from 9:00 PM to 6:00 AM in winter. During the day, over twenty constables performed similar duties to maintain the peace.[3] As with the mayor's court, the power of the watch ended at Vine and South streets, and the environs therefore lacked a police force. Still, by the eve of the Revolution, the city proper had developed what was for the times a reasonably effective police system.

In the decade and a half before the Revolution, residents of Philadelphia made surprisingly few observations on crime in the city. James Hamilton, deputy governor of the province, suggested in 1761 that the poor perpetrated most crimes by asserting that legal fees would not maintain the attorney general, since the people prosecuted were, "in general, the most indigent of Mankind, and consequently unable to pay." Records proving or refuting Hamilton's claim have not survived, but a fragmentary piece of evidence from 1766 supports his contention. In that year, ten men escaped from the city jail. Included in that breakout were two laborers, two persons with no occupation listed, and one each of the following: joiner, shipwright, tailor, sailor, shoemaker, rope maker. At least five of the eight escapees with listed occupations were, if typical of their occupational groups, probably numbered among the poor.[4] Save for such general comments and bits of evidence, the questions of who committed crime and why escaped systematic analysis in prerevolutionary Philadelphia.

Persons convicted of criminal acts during the period 1760-76, whether poor or not, faced harsh penalties. By 1760, Pennsylvania followed the English practice of emphasizing corporal punishment, including the death penalty, rather than imprisonment. Diverse crimes, including rape, highway robbery, arson, counterfeiting, and burglary, carried the death penalty. A person convicted of a capital felony for which the laws of Great Britain allowed benefit of clergy could use that rule and be branded rather than executed. In addition to being branded, such a criminal might, at the court's discretion, be incarcerated at hard labor for from six months to two years. If convicted a second time on a similar count, the criminal faced the death penalty. Simple larceny was punishable by a sliding scale of retribution. In all cases, the convicted thief had to restore the goods or pay their full value to the rightful owner. In addition, the criminal was to pay the government the following amounts: for the first such conviction, the value of the goods taken; for the second, twice the value of the goods taken; for the third, three times the value of the stolen goods. Until these sums were paid, the thief underwent confinement. Further, public whipping with stripes well laid on their bare backs awaited all convicted larcenists. First offenders received not more than twenty-one stripes; a second conviction drew twenty-one to forty lashes;

and the third offense brought thirty-nine to fifty stripes. At the discretion of the court, third-time offenders could also be imprisoned and there set at work and "corrected" for a period of one to four years.[5]

As in England, the intent of this criminal code was the prevention of crime by means of the threat of death or other corporal punishment. Imprisonment constituted a mere supplement to this system, which featured punishment rather than reformation of criminals. Thus, the jails of colonial Philadelphia housed few convicted criminals.[6] This does not mean that the jails were thinly populated during these years—far from it. Because imprisonment for debt existed throughout the prerevolutionary period, many poor persons found themselves in jail.

During the colonial era, the predicament of indebted Philadelphians who could not pay their creditors was indeed bleak. The basic law on insolvent debtors and imprisonment for debt, passed in 1730, established a complex and expensive procedure for gaining freedom once imprisoned for debt.[7] The legislature realized this fact by saying that the procedure required to gain freedom would work a very great hardship upon a poor prisoner confined for a small debt. To avoid this potential problem, persons in debt for not more than forty shillings, besides the cost of the suit, could petition for release. In addition, such poor persons could retain clothes, bedding, and tools to a value of twenty shillings for a single person and fifty shillings for a married person.

This law had two major flaws. The government made no provision for providing imprisoned debtors with *any* necessities of life—save the prison roof over their heads. Thus, persons in jail because they could not pay their debts, which could be quite small, were expected to pay for their own food, clothing, and fuel. Nor did the law allow court and prison fees to be included in the cancellation of debts totaling less than forty shillings. Given these regulations, many poor persons languished in the debtors' prison for long periods.[8]

The difficulty of getting out of jail once imprisoned for debt significantly increased a year later. The legislature, believing that some persons used the law for insolvent debtors to avoid paying bills they could afford to pay, materially altered the law.

Disorder, Crime, and Punishment

Henceforth, childless persons in debt for less than twenty pounds could not take advantage of the provisions of the 1730 act. Instead, they must surrender all their material goods. If the value of these did not cover their debts, the residue had to be paid by servitude if the creditor demanded it. Single persons under the age of fifty-three could not be forced to serve more than seven years; married men under the age of forty-six could not be made to serve more than five years. Within these limits, the court decided upon the length of servitude required. A person owing less than forty shillings could be freed by the order of two magistrates if he was willing to pay his debt by servitude. This 1731 act remained in force until at least 1765 and quite possibly after that.[9]

The poor were thus caught in a web of legal entanglements. If they owed less than forty shillings, they could escape prison by serving a period of servitude worth the debts they could not pay. That provision certainly was not onerous. But people owing forty shillings to twenty pounds faced a potentially lengthy period of servitude to cancel their debts. A person jailed for a debt of more than twenty pounds was hard pressed to use the legal procedures to free himself.

In 1765 the legislature attempted to ease the burden of imprisoned debtors by decreeing that creditors must pay for the maintenance of imprisoned debtors, or they would be freed. Such maintenance was not to exceed five shillings a week for a single person and seven shillings and sixpence for a person with children. However, this act did not eliminate the jail fees and court costs that could keep a poor person in jail, and, as the legislature noted in 1770, the law decreeing that creditors must pay for maintenance was not fully effective.[10]

Despite the efforts of the legislature to reform the laws, many persons imprisoned for debt in Philadelphia between 1760 and 1776 found it hard to subsist, since they had to pay for food, clothing, and fuel. Fortunately for the debtors, a wide variety of private actions, sometimes undertaken at the request of poor debtors, helped them subsist; but such aid was given only sporadically.[11] Realizing "the miserable situation of numbers confined in jail (particularly during the inclemency of the winter)," a group of Philadelphians banded together in February

1776 to form the Philadelphia Society for Assisting Distressed Prisoners. Members of the society began by assessing themselves ten shillings each and by establishing a group of managers to administer whatever relief they thought necessary. This organization apparently functioned well for about nineteen months but dissolved when the British occupied Philadelphia in 1778.[12]

In the decade and a half before the Revolution, then, Philadelphia's government combated social disorder and crime by maintaining a watch and by trying to reduce the number of disorderly houses and regulate the number of taverns. The ventures for controlling taverns appear to have been less successful than the endeavors to create an effective watch system. Philadelphians of this period expended little effort in analyzing why crimes were committed, but they apparently believed that a large number of criminals were poor, as probably was the case. The criminal code of the day sought to prevent crime through fear of death or other corporal punishment rather than through reforming offenders. Persons who could not pay their debts faced imprisonment. There were attempts to reform the system of imprisonment for debt, but few meaningful improvements materialized before the Revolution.

By 1800, the situation was, in most respects, quite different. And the American Revolution helped produce significant changes in the perception and handling of social disorder, crime, and punishment. As in politics, the Constitution of 1776 proved a vital instrument for bringing about such change, especially in the criminal code and in the system of imprisonment for debt.

The Constitution of 1776 pointed the way to reform of the system of imprisonment for debt by directing the legislature to enact laws enabling an honest debtor who delivered his real and personal property to his creditors to remain free. Despite repeated revision of the laws on insolvent debtors, the Constitution's suggestion was still not implemented by 1787. The pre-revolutionary problems persisted, as even people who owed only small debts continued to suffer confinement for long periods. Persons found innocent of criminal charges but unable to pay the costs of prosecution were still clamped into jail as debtors, and they had to pay all the costs of their maintenance. The number of people who faced these problems was indeed large.[13]

For the period 1780–90, when criminals were more likely than in colonial days to be incarcerated, the number of debtors in the city and county jail of Philadelphia actually outnumbered criminals, 4,061 to 3,999.[14]

Not all people imprisoned for debt in the postrevolutionary period were poor. Some swindlers went into debt purposely to obtain and transfer goods, and then used the insolvent debtors act to gain freedom.[15] However, the number of people following this course could not have been a significant portion of the imprisoned debtors. Further, according to "A Citizen of Philadelphia," writing in 1787, those who owed fifteen pounds to fifty thousand pounds had, besides the statutes for freeing insolvent debtors, "fifty different ways of escaping the horrors" of jail. "Consult its archives," he flatly asserted, "and you will find it is the poor, the ignorant, and the most miserable who are most found upon its records." "Justice in Mercy" agreed and offered precise data for 1785 to prove the point. Citing the reports of the head jailer, "Justice" noted that about one-half of the 151 prisoners then confined were debtors. Of that half, not more than 15 could support themselves, and the other 60 were "so *miserably poor*, that they must *perish* with *hunger* and *cold*, unless fed and cloathed by the charitable inhabitants of the city!" Such assistance was, however, at best a stopgap measure.[16]

The continuing problems of persons imprisoned for debt led in 1787 to the creation of the Philadelphia Society for Alleviating the Miseries of Public Prisons. This group, like the earlier prison society, assessed its members 10 shillings a year and elected a committee to visit the prison each week. The committee was to distribute relief, watch over the morals of the prisoners, and report any abuses they discovered to the officers of government authorized to redress them. In addition, four physicians from the society would visit prisons as needed to give advice on matters of health.[17]

The society immediately began helping prisoners in all of the city's houses of confinement. It arranged for a man to stay at the jail at all times to receive food offered as benevolent donations. Old clothes were advertised for, collected, and given to those most in need. Wood and soup were distributed on an irregular basis until February 1789, when it was decided that soup would be delivered weekly during the winter season. The society also petitioned the Assembly and the city to correct various evils.[18] It is not clear if the society was directly responsible for the major reform bill of 1792, but in that year the legislature acknowledged its duty to aid those confined for debt in Philadelphia who were so poor that they could not procure food, fuel, or clothing. It was, said the legislature, "inconsistent with humanity to suffer them to want the common necessaries of life." Correspondingly, inspectors of jails, as well as county justices of the peace, were to begin inspecting the debtors' prison. Fuel and blankets would be distributed at county expense to all who could not afford them. The creditor whose complaint had put the person in prison was to supply seven cents per day so that the inspectors could buy food for the prisoner. If the creditor proved unwilling to provide the required sum, the debtor would go free.[19]

This improvement in the living conditions of debtors marked a significant victory for the society. But it was only half the battle. The original prison relief society founded in 1776 had decried the fact that many whose labor might be useful to society had to endure imprisonment because they could not pay fees. This charge was well founded: Pennsylvania law required that even a person found innocent must pay court costs. Despite repeated attacks on this practice, it still existed when the Society for Alleviating the Miseries of Public Prisons was formed.[20] To combat the problem, the society announced in 1787 that it would work for the release of "proper objects" held in jail only for fees. It soon found itself inundated with petitions. Elizabeth Donnovan, signing with her mark, proclaimed that she lived "in the greatest distress" in "this place of dreadfull distress, the Work House, . . . for my fees which I shall never be able to pay while kept in here, being a poor old Woman unable to earn even a subsistence for myself, notwithstanding the heard [sic] hearted Keeper will not discharge me until I pay for my Bread & his fees." William Leslie pleaded: "No Man can be more unjustly kept here [in jail] than I am—I was tried last City Court for a Larceny, and acquited . . . , & have been confined about 9 weeks, every [sic] since my Trial for My Court Charges, which I can never pay if kept here."[21]

In addition to the innocent but poor, the debtors' prison also housed many held merely for nonpayment of insignificant debts. One investigation of the prison in 1786 revealed that seven prisoners owed debts totaling not quite as many pounds.[22] The society, also having pledged to help free "proper objects" held for such small debts, after investigating the reputation and character of the various petitioners, began paying the fees and trifling debts of many of them. From January to July 1788, the society secured the release of at least fifty-two prisoners by paying fees or debts. In all of these cases, save one, the cost per person was four shillings and sixpence (sixty cents), which was a jail fee. In 1789 the legislature admitted that the practice of long confinement for small debts, fines, or forfeitures still existed for persons incapable of making satisfaction. Arguing that this punishment "tends to the distress of their families as well as to the public injury by the burdens created and idle habits contracted thereby," the legislators took action. Henceforth, any person owing less than five pounds in debts, fines, or forfeitures would be freed after having served thirty days.[23] Here was a major change and a major reform, called forth as much by a growing desire to control the evil influence of idleness as it was by a humanitarian concern for the plight of the poor. However, this law did nothing to eliminate the problem of jail fees.

In December of 1790, the society petitioned the legislature and requested that the jail fees of people incarcerated for debt be dropped, seeing that these persons frequently faced many months of confinement because they could not pay fees. The petition also urged that the keeper of the debtors' apartment be made a salaried officer, since his fees, even if collectable, would not equal a living wage. In September 1791, the legislature moved to remedy these problems. Now the costs of indictments thrown out for lack of evidence would be paid by the city or county, and persons found innocent of alleged crime would not pay costs. Anyone held only for costs could use the various acts for the relief of insolvent debtors to obtain freedom. Finally, if the court imposing costs believed that the person could not pay, he was to be discharged. Six months later, the legislature made the keeper of the debtors' prison a salaried officer.[24]

The society was so pleased with the actions of the governmental inspectors and the April 1792 law ordering that debtors be provided with the necessities of life that it decided to curtail its activities in July 1792. Henceforth, the meetings of the society would be less frequent, and the cost of joining the society was reduced to seven shillings and sixpence a year.[25]

Despite the society's substantial achievements, its victory was not complete. People could still be confined for small debts. The *Philadelphia Gazette*, complaining that 287 persons were locked in prison for such debts in 1793, maintained: "Let fraud be punished when proved, as a crime, but let the state no more be the collector of tavern debts, or the arbiter of tipling house disputes." The *Gazette* further urged that no one be imprisoned for a debt of less than forty shillings. But, in 1795, it was still possible for a gentlewoman to pay a debt of twenty-four shillings and thereby secure the release of a person who had been in prison for several weeks.[26]

Nor could all innocent people automatically avoid jail. Calling forth the image of the noted Enlightenment reformer, "Beccaria" charged in 1796 that "scarce a session of any of our inferior courts of *justice* passes over, without many people being thrown into prison for no crime at all, unless we should rank poverty under this head." "Many poor wretches," he thundered, "are suffering all the miseries of a jail for no other crime than —POVERTY!" Citing a list of legal fees that could be charged, he argued that such fees sent innocent but poor people to jail, and he offered specific examples to prove this assertion. Such complaints apparently had validity, for, in 1797, the legislature noted that a person indicted and then acquitted by a petit jury frequently had to pay for the prosecution. Calling this an injustice and a punishment to the innocent, the legislature ordered counties to pay all the trial costs of persons found innocent.[27]

"Beccaria" also attacked the procedure that allowed those held only for costs to use the laws for insolvent debtors. He correctly noted that, to use the insolvency laws, a person had to attend a quarterly court. The person could, therefore, if unable to pay costs, be jailed for up to three months. Despite "Beccaria's" plea, the situation remained. This and other charges of improper treatment of imprisoned debtors continued to be voiced, but imprisonment for debt had not been completely eliminated by 1800.[28]

Disorder, Crime, and Punishment 71

Still, in the postwar period, the gross abuses associated with imprisonment for debt were greatly reformed. The charge of the Constitution of 1776 had been taken up. Although the desire, associated with the moral crusade, to attack idleness was a vital force for bringing about reform, at least in the area of imprisonment for debt, Philadelphia's poor did feel the transforming hand as an instrument of improvement.

The reform spirit and concern for the poor that marked the work of the Philadelphia Society for Alleviating the Miseries of Public Prisons was evidenced even more forcefully in attacks upon trading justices. The magistrates with whom the poor most likely dealt derived their income from fixed fees for services rendered. Such a magistrate might, in dealing with the unwary and uninformed, charge higher fees than the laws specified or multiply the legal papers issued. Persons employing such practices gained the name of trading justices.

Complaints that legal officers gouged the people by overcharging on fees existed before the war. In January 1767 the legislature, after considering petitions from persons imprisoned for debt, established a committee of grievances to hear the complaints of those who believed they had been aggrieved by any public officer taking exorbitant fees.[29] Still, "A Federalist," writing in 1788, claimed that before the Revolution there had been only one trading justice and that the abuse was thus a limited one before the 1780s.[30] If public complaints are an accurate index, this writer was correct in claiming that few abuses existed before and during the war. But from 1785 to 1789 the actions of trading justices became a pressing issue; essays and comments on the unethical practices of magistrates appeared in the press with great regularity.[31]

Philadelphians who attacked the practice of retailing justice in the year 1785 clearly raised a legitimate grievance. In October, Alexander Carlisle, high constable for the city and county, was found guilty of extorting fees and fired.[32] Once he departed, complaints of trading justices subsided for half a year. When the issue again surfaced, it involved questions about the type of person who should be a magistrate. "A Wellwisher to the Community" spoke for numerous Philadelphians when he warned that some of the candidates for justice of the peace "are canvasing for themselves; of these latter gentlemen beware! they will grind the faces of the poor to support their imaginary dignity." Such essayists wanted only men of established wealth and reputation as justices of the peace.[33] It is therefore possible that some Philadelphians attempted to raise the specter of trading justices to keep as many positions of power as possible in the hands of the wealthy.

Although some citizens speaking against the retailing of justice probably did so for political reasons, many others attacked trading justices simply because they were evil.[34] Some urged publishing lists of fees so that the people would at least not be overcharged by magistrates, and a few essayists did publish fee schedules. Other reformers sensibly urged that putting magistrates on a fixed salary would stop trading.[35] Also, an attempt was made to establish a subscription fund and a lawyer's association to help the poor in dealing with the law. Such actions seemed necessary to prevent the retailers of law from acquiring fortunes by gouging their fellow inhabitants. The fact was that "the poor, whose labor is scarcely sufficient to support them, cannot be supposed able to obtain redress in the courts by law. Every extortion from them is sunk in oblivion for want of power to bring forward their complaints."[36] These actions and comments show that attacks on trading justices were more than political ploys, and it does appear that trading justices vigorously practiced their trade in the late 1780s.

Philadelphians who spoke out against the retailers of justice realized that any city inhabitant might be victimized. As "Civis" said, Philadelphia magistrates too often were "rapacious wolves, who look on all classes of their fellow-citizens as their common prey." But the rich and powerful were hardly the wolves' favorite target. They much preferred to prey upon the poor, since such actions "pass un[n]oticed." Clearly, "the common people," the "poor and friendless," were most likely to fall into "the clutches" of those "monsters," the trading justices.[37]

When Philadelphia was reincorporated in 1789, the direct election of justices of the peace stopped. Instead, the aldermen of the city served as justices of the peace. Although this revised system did not stop all complaints about trading justices, it appears that the worst abuses, which affected primarily the poor, abated in the 1790s.[38] But again, for a large portion of the period under study, the poor had ample reason to fear the power of the law. It was not just trading justices; it was not just going to prison if innocent but unable to pay court costs; it was also lacking the resources to have recourse to the courts. Certainly, during the years 1785 to 1789, the poor of Philadelphia were subjected to the arbitrary power and criminality of at least some of the city's legal officers. Ironically, in this same period, more prosperous Philadelphians came to believe that the disorder and potential criminality of the poor had reached dangerous new heights.

During the war years, Philadelphians, as they had done in colonial days, occasionally voiced concern about social disorder and crime.[39] In the fall of 1785, such passing references gave way to an anguished outpouring that decried the degree of vice and crime flourishing in the area. The *Pennsylvania Packet* sadly found that it could sketch *"The Picture of an insignificant Fellow."* He "gets drunk every day, and revels at bagnios every night. He joins in mobs, beats down the watchmen, breaks open doors, takes off knockers, and disturbs the quiet of honest people." "Honestus" agreed, proclaiming it "next to impossible in the crouds of vice, to preserve the morals of children, not under the immediate eye of faithful guardians."[40]

The grand jury of the city, at its quarter sessions held in October 1785, drew a yet more foreboding picture. In a memorial to the legislature, the grand jury recorded its concern over the great and increasing degree of vice and immorality in the city. Contrivances for gaming did great injury to the morals of many, and the uncommonly high number of bills for assault, larceny, keeping tippling houses, and the like offered "melancholy proofs of the depravity of morals which too greatly prevails." Moreover, there was reason to believe that many of the criminals were poor, because the city faced a constant influx of vagabonds, "who, encouraged to hope for a more plentiful harvest of plunder in this metropolis, resort here, where they may also be better concealed in their villanies, by wretches as abandoned as themselves." Asserting that such vagabond types dread hard labor more than a thousand stripes, the grand jury maintained that many such people had probably been driven to

Philadelphia because the city of New York had abandoned whipping criminals and had substituted hard labor while chained to wheelbarrows. Although the grand jury did not call for a similar mode of punishment in Philadelphia, the general import of this point was surely understood by the legislature.[41]

"A Native of Philadelphia," writing in mid-November, agreed that the situation had gotten out of hand. Youths were frequently being seduced by the vicious allure of the billiard table and the brothel. The list of criminals apprehended in the city was, in size and content, simply too unpleasant to be described. Even given the corrupting effect of any large city, he continued, Philadelphia had to be considered the harbor and refuge of numerous criminals, since the number of offenders annually convicted in the city and suburbs probably equaled half the number sentenced in the rest of the state. In addition, he added, at least half as many more criminals probably eluded capture. A group of Philadelphians who petitioned the legislature in late December concurred by bemoaning the great increase of vice, immorality, and crime. Something *had* to be done, they argued, to strike at the causes of these evils, which this group felt could chiefly be found in the numerous houses devoted to gaming, drunkenness, receipt of stolen goods, and concealment of criminals.[42]

This outpouring of concern and anguish was probably not lost on the state's legislators when they began considering a bill to alter the nature of the criminal code. But, according to the legislature, the new code that became law in September 1786 was prompted by two other considerations. The legislature first cited the Pennsylvania Constitution of 1776 as a basis for action by observing that it had directed the legislature to reform the penal code. As the lawmakers noted, the Constitution indicated that punishments should be made more proportional to the crimes and that visible punishment of long duration at hard labor should, where appropriate, be used to deter crime more effectually. The second reason offered in support of a change in the penal code asserted that the old punishments sprang from the wrong philosophy. Indeed, the prewar emphasis on death and other corporal punishments did not answer the principal goals of society, which were "to correct and reform the offenders, and to produce such strong impression upon the minds of others as to deter them from committing the like offenses." Furthermore, "it is the wish of every good government to reclaim rather than to destroy." Here then was a major social change produced by the revolutionary Constitution and by an increasing belief that a better method of controlling crime had to be found.

The new penal code severely limited the use of the death penalty and corporal punishment. Now, persons convicted of robbery, burglary, or sodomy or buggery, or convicted as accessories to such crimes, had to forfeit to the state all the lands, tenements, goods, and chattels they owned. Having been reduced to poverty, these criminals faced jail sentences of not more than ten years. Persons convicted of a simple larceny where the value of the stolen goods was less than twenty shillings were to restore the goods or the full value of goods, pay a like amount to the state, and undergo imprisonment for not more than one year. The same penalties held for a simple larceny where the value of the goods taken was twenty shillings or more, save that the maximum period of servitude was three years. Other crimes previously punished by branding, mutilation of the ears, whipping, or imprisonment for life now brought fines and incarceration for up to two years.

The legislature firmly believed that continued hard labor, publicly and disgracefully imposed, would "correct and reform" criminals. Accordingly, prisoners were to work in the streets while chained to wheelbarrows. To guarantee that criminals did labor, for every day of work missed without good cause, two days would be added to the sentence. For their efforts, the prisoners received shelter and coarse, wholesome food provided at public expense. To insure that criminals would be shamed, their uniforms were made of rough materials, bearing on the outer garment some visible mark designating the nature of their crime, and males were to have their hair and beards close shaven every week. In this way, escape would be made more difficult and the prisoners could be marked for public censure. Thus, shame, hard work, and fear of long sentences would supposedly combine to deter crime and reform criminals.

This legislation also aimed to reduce criminality by distinguishing between the different classes of offenders. The lawmakers, in terms similar to those of the moral crusade, maintained that many young offenders committed crimes "from habits of idleness and intemperance and from want of pious education." Persons not "so hardened as to be void of shame or beyond the hope of being reclaimed" needed help. To save "the remaining seeds of virtue and goodness in the young and unwary," it would be best to separate them from old and hardened offenders.

This 1786 criminal code held out special hope for those who modeled themselves after the industrious poor lionized in the moral crusade. If prisoners "laboured faithfully . . . and evidenced a patient submission," they could be pardoned without serving their full sentence. This policy was inaugurated "to encourage those offenders in whom the love of virtue and the shame of vice is not wholly extinguished to set about a sincere and actual repentance and reformation of life and conduct." The Assembly expressed its hope that such prisoners, once freed, would become useful members of society.[43]

From 1786 until 1790, when it was significantly altered, this act helped draw Philadelphians into an extended analysis of the new penal system and also of criminality in general. Parts of the act, such as that section separating youthful offenders from hardened criminals, drew praise. But the wheelbarrow section of the law seems to have produced havoc. Apparently, numerous Philadelphians offered alms and sympathy, rather than shame, to prisoners working in the streets. And having criminals do work that honest laboring people could do evoked the wrath of many of the city's laboring persons. Worse yet, when out of doors, prisoners proved hard to control and, it was claimed, often escaped.[44] In July 1789 the *Universal Magazine* of London offered a biting analysis of the problem by asserting that wheelbarrow convicts escaped in such large numbers that no person dared to venture upon the streets after eight in the evening unless the night watch was nearby. The danger was such that the Supreme Executive Council was forced to have militiamen patrol the streets. This fear of wheelbarrow men may have been excessive, but Philadelphians had good reason to be concerned about crime: it appears that criminal activity was quite high between 1786 and 1790.[45]

As the level of criminal activity and the attack upon the wheelbarrow law increased, Philadelphians engaged in a more extensive public discussion than ever before of what caused crime and who perpetrated it. Most analysts suggested a lack of moral strength as the cause. Some perceived this weakness as inevitable, since "Vices, like diseases, are often hereditary. The property of the one is to infect the manners, as the other poisons the springs of life." Whether inherited or not, as this group saw it, habits of "indolence and dissipation" led people to rob even when work was available. "Idleness . . . will be found the source of every vice, and consequently the cause of every crime." Others who focused on moral weakness considered it unnecessary to look beyond the tippling houses: spirituous liquors led persons to perpetrate crimes that rendered their confinement necessary for the safety and repose of society. Philadelphians holding this view rejoiced in 1789 when the number of taverns in the city was significantly reduced. They argued that this reduction laid the foundation "for a *restoration* of sobriety, industry and morality among the lower orders of the people." Closing a number of taverns, it was maintained, protected society "from midnight plunderers and strolling vagrants, by striking at the very root of vice." Some commentators believed that all these weaknesses worked in combination, since the principal causes of vice and crime supposedly were "spirituous liquors, a love of ease or laziness, and a fondness for loose and idle companions."[46]

A second group of people writing in the 1786-90 period maintained that the poor were especially prone to fall into crime, but only if they could not find work. The *Independent Gazetteer*, in urging creation of a city manufacturing enterprise, asserted that this step would "make our poor more sober and moral by employing them in honest industry instead of fixing them on loose and idle habits, or temp[t]ing them by want of bread to pilfering and still greater crimes." Dr. Enoch Edwards, who joined with other Philadelphians in promoting agriculture and domestic manufacturing, held that only by providing the poor with constant employment could one bring "security to government": when the poor "are depressed for want of employment, they become idle, lazy, indolent and necessitous—and it is from the starved part of every community, that we may look for danger; their idleness gives time to invent, and their necessities push them forward, with a courage sharpened by despair, to perpetuate acts of the most daring criminality."[47] The *Evening Herald* voiced a similar position but placed special emphasis on the plight of immigrants. A society to help industrious immigrants find employment was needed, lest bad fortune and an insufficient knowledge of America cause these new arrivals to become a discouraged, "useless, and perhaps dangerous acquisition." In describing the alarming increase of robberies occurring in Philadelphia in the fall of 1787, the *Herald* maintained that the crime wave stemmed from the new penal code, which punished criminals by hard labor rather than by inflicting corporal punishment. This new law proved ineffective because, "so far from being considered as a punishment, it is viewed with desire by many poor wretches who are in want of work and subsistence."[48]

"The American Moralist," in the spring of 1789, agreed that the poor could be forced into crime, but he apparently did not blame them. Noting that some people who were not in need committed crime, he asked, "What may not be expected from him, who is pushed forward into sin by the impulse of poverty, who lives in continual want of what he sees wasted by thousands in negligent extravangance, and who[se] pain is every moment aggravated by the contempt of those whom nature has subjected to the same necessities with himself, and who are only his superiors by that wealth which they know not how to possess with moderation and decency?" He answered his own question with the comment, "How strongly may such a man be tempted to declare war upon the prosperous and the great!"[49]

These analysts, despite their differing opinions about the causes of crime, agreed that the poor were the people most likely to commit criminal acts. If the extant sources, which cover the years 1794–1800, accurately reflect the situation in the last decade and a half of the century, this view was firmly rooted in fact. Joseph Gale, editor of *Gale's Independent Gazetteer*, observed in January 1797 that "the most afflictive and accumulated distress" in Philadelphia existed "amongst the *Irish Emigrants* and the *French Negroes*; and it may not perhaps, be unworthy of public attention," he commented, "to enquire how these people are generally supported, and whether many acts of depredation, and many scenes of horror which have occurred in this and neighboring States, may not, in some degree, be traced to the extreme poverty of this distressed class of people. . . ."[50] Gale was strikingly perceptive. In the preceding year, people born in Ireland accounted for 38.9 percent of all the convictions in the mayor's court.[51] Blacks represented at least another 28.2 percent of those found guilty. Slightly more than 70 percent of all people convicted in the mayor's court in 1796 were born outside the United States. Nor was 1796 an abnormal year. Of the persons convicted in the mayor's court from 1794 to 1800, 31.8 percent were blacks and 31.7 percent were born in Ireland. As we have seen, the vast majority of blacks in the city were poor, and, as Joseph Gale and others noted, Irish immigrants were very likely to be numbered among the poor. Considering just these two groups, it seems clear that those people convicted in the mayor's court came predominantly from Philadelphia's "other half."[52]

The occupations of the criminals convicted between 1794 and 1800 also attest to their poverty. Of the convicts whose occupations were noted, 27 percent were laborers. The next highest group, mariners, accounted for only 7.9 percent of the total. Equally significant, the mayor's court convicted few people whose occupations indicated possibly high income.[53]

The nature and extent of the criminal activities of these convicts also point to their poverty. Although the court tried a wide variety of crimes, the great majority of convictions, over 80 percent, were for robbery. Some fairly spectacular robberies occurred. Three blacks from Cape Francis stole $500, and another three men stole $160 in paper currency and $160 worth of silver; Joseph Wyatt, a silversmith working with an accomplice, embezzled five hundred ounces of silver from the U.S. Mint.[54] Slightly more typical was the theft of watches and other small items of high value that could be pawned. However, in a great number of cases, the items taken indicate that a pressing need for clothing pushed people into crime. Oliver O'Hara, Joe Martin, and John Baston stole one pair of boots or shoes each. James Fisher, John Thomas, and Hugh McDowell each pilfered five or fewer pairs of stockings. John McNeil, who could not work during his confinement because of a lump on the right shoulder, shoplifted a coat. Esther Green, John Williams, and Thomas Divine each took one piece of cloth. Others apparently needed food. Richard Butler absconded with a salmon, and Joseph, a black man, snatched two loaves of sugar. William Beemery(?) purloined two shillings and sixpence worth of mutton. James Barry tried to meet both his food and his clothing needs at one time when he filched two baskets of poultry and some clothing.[55]

However examined, the detailed records from the mayor's court confirm that Philadelphians convicted of criminal acts were likely to be poor. This was not, of course, a new phenomenon produced by the Revolution. What was new was the effort in the years 1786–90 to understand why such poor people became criminals.

The Philadelphians who denounced the wheelbarrow law and maintained that crime sprang from the worst evils associated with idle, vicious poverty had to be pleased with the revisions of the penal code enacted in the spring of 1790. The legislature, conceding that the practice of having criminals work in the streets had proven a debacle, said that convicts would now labor only in houses of correction. The legislature also expressed its hope that "the addition of unremitted solitude to laborious employment . . . will contribute as much to reform as to deter" crime. To insure that all prisoners did labor, the law required that they work eight hours a day from November to January and ten hours a day from February to October, Sundays excepted.

This new penal code repealed the 1786 law and thus eliminated the possibility of an early release for those who worked hard and behaved well. The 1790 code did, however, offer a new incentive to criminals willing to labor with diligence "as an evidence of reformation." If the labor of the convict, after the costs of maintenance and work materials were subtracted, produced a surplus, the convict received one half of that sum. This law also gave special attention to segregating prisoners in the Philadelphia jail. Cells, six by eight feet square and nine feet high, were to be built in the yard and separated from the common yard by walls high enough to prevent all external communication. These cells would house "the more hardened and attrocious offenders." This action reaffirmed the legislators' efforts to reclaim persons who still had "remaining seeds of virtue and goodness."

The Philadelphians who had since 1785 vigorously railed against the increase of vagabonds and social disorder in the streets could also applaud this new act because it gave the legal officers of Philadelphia strong powers to keep undesirables from infesting the streets. Henceforth, any vagrant or idle and disorderly person, once convicted, faced a jail sentence at hard labor of up to thirty days. The city had gained the power to sweep the vulgar riffraff off the streets.[56]

Five years later, the legislature voiced approval of this major change in the penal code by saying that the act, as slightly modified, had evidently diminished the number of crimes and been highly beneficial in reforming offenders. Philadelphians agreed.[57] But despite such applause, residents of the city in the 1790s remained deeply concerned about the evils of vice and social disorder; some believed that governmental action, even with the new penal code, did not effectively suppress these evils. Correspondingly, a new social institution—the citizen association that aimed to attack and control vice, social disorder, and crime—came into being.[58] The Association in Southwark for Suppressing Vice and Immorality, the first such Philadelphia agency, apparently began functioning in 1790. It sought to close gaming houses and every other house "of bad character." The *Federal Gazette* praised this effort and called for more such groups to protect the rising generation and to save it from "destruction." The paper also suggested that such organizations could work to educate youths "in habits of virtue and industry."[59]

Concern for the morality of the youth of the city played a vital role in the creation of the second association to combat vice. In 1791 three of the city's newspapers printed and reprinted articles denouncing the "brigades" of "low idle boys" who roamed the streets looking for mischief to do.[60] The antisocial actions of youths reached such heights that in June 1795, Matthew Clarkson, the mayor of Philadelphia, published an essay calling for "*the better government of youth.*" Citing the "disorderly practices of ungoverned boys" in the streets, the mayor claimed that "our youth are becoming generally corrupt." He urged all parents to govern carefully the activities and moral training of their children on the grounds that the worst and most daring crimes could usually be traced to youthful mischiefs. Although Clarkson spoke of the corruption of youth in general, he emphasized the "present . . . loud and general complaints of the insubordination of apprentice youth, as well as servants of other descriptions."[61] The special attention Clarkson gave children from the lower strata of Philadelphia society is revealing; it suggests that he may well have believed that the children of the poor were the ones most likely to engage in youthful mischiefs leading to adult crime.[62]

Mayor Clarkson's presentation struck a responsive chord among residents of Southwark, who held that "virtue and good government are the ornament and stability of Society, while vice and disorder procure its misery and destruction." Believing this and spurred by Clarkson's address, the group formed the "Association of the district of Southwark, for the suppression of vice and immorality" in August of 1795. Their goal, broadly stated, was to aid the civil officers in bringing disorderly persons to punishment and to halt the spread of immoral and vicious practices. The haunts of drunkenness and debauchery, violence in the streets, and Sabbath lawbreaking would all come under their watchful eye. Association members indicated whom they believed most likely to need regulation and assistance by pledging that the group would "endeavor to afford advice to the stranger and distressed, to procure employment for the destitute and to join in the establishment of free schools for the children of the poor, for apprentices and orphans in which they may be taught to read and become acquainted with the principles of morality."[63]

Possibly following the lead of the Southwark association, citizens in Philadelphia in late 1797 or early 1798 established their own Society for the Suppression of Vice and Immorality. But, at least in the view of William Cobbett, the ultraconservative newspaper owner, the problems of stopping social disorder seemed overwhelming. While wishing the society well, he feared that the successful suppression of vice and immorality was impossible "where the abominable vices of *whoring, drunkenness, swindling, fraud,* and *daring impiety* abound to the extent they do in this city."[64]

Records do not reveal how effective the associations were. But it is essential to note that they began functioning in the 1790s in response to a perceived increase in immorality, especially immorality among the poor. As we shall see, their work was augmented by that of private poor relief groups, which often made moral reform of the poor an integral part of their activities. But all such efforts together were not, at times, strident enough for some citizens, whose anger over vice and immorality led to extralegal actions. In early August of 1800, a quarrel occurred between two men who had met in the China Factory, a house of ill fame in Southwark. As a result of the fight, one of the combatants died. According to the *Daily Advertiser*, a group assembled on the night of August 12 and proceeded to demolish houses of prostitution in Southwark. The work reportedly went on, without interruption, until the fourteenth. The results: "Scarce any thing but the chimnies of six houses, are now left standing." The police made "but few and feeble (if any) efforts" to stop this "Riot." The *Advertiser* added that such efforts would have been useless and voiced tacit approval of the "tumult and destruction," saying that the buildings in question had long been "the subject of regret by all well-disposed Citizens of Southwark." Clearly, "the eagerness with which this opportunity was seized for their destruction, is sufficient proof of the detestation in which their infamous occupants was [*sic*] held by the public."[65] This "riot" was apparently an atypical event for Philadelphia, but it illustrates a basic point: in the postwar years, Philadelphians became increasingly disturbed by the supposed vice and immorality that seemed to abound, especially among the poor. And Philadelphians worked as never before to find ways to attack vice and immorality.

A comparison of prewar with postwar Philadelphia suggests that the American Revolution produced significant changes in how social disorder, crime, and punishment were perceived and acted upon. Of course, some things did not change. It appears that, throughout the period 1760–1800, the convicted criminals of Philadelphia were likely to be poor. And while the gross abuses of trading justices that occurred from 1785 to 1789 were halted, throughout the period 1760–1800 the poor apparently found it more difficult than did the affluent to utilize fully and benefit from the legal system. Still, the changes that did occur were quite impressive. In the prewar years, one could be imprisoned for very small debts. Even if found innocent of criminal charges, the poor might land in jail because they lacked the money to pay court costs or jail fees, and persons imprisoned for debt were, nonetheless, required to pay for their food, clothing, and fuel. Spurred by the call of the Constitution of 1776, by persons espousing Enlightenment ideals of prison reform, and by a fear of idleness, the state government had by 1800 instituted major changes: (1) food and other necessities were provided for imprisoned debtors; (2) persons acquitted of criminal charges no longer faced imprisonment because they could not pay court costs; (3) the number of people confined for small debts declined significantly. Imprisonment for debt still existed in the Philadelphia of 1800, but the changes just outlined marked a major reform effort.

Reform ideals, as well as a growing concern for controlling crime, were also instrumental in helping to produce the dramatic postwar alteration of the criminal code. By the dawn of the nineteenth century, only murder in the first degree carried a death penalty; for all other crimes, corporal punishment had been outlawed. Thus, the prewar efforts to prevent crime by fear of death and other corporal punishment gave way to an emphasis upon rehabilitation of criminals, which utilized (1) the attempt to reform criminals by confining them at hard labor and (2) physical separation of criminals into different classes to protect young offenders from older, hardened criminal types. All of these changes illustrate that the American Revolution helped produce transformations in the area of criminal justice that affected the poor.

Although the directives of the Constitution of 1776 were instrumental in bringing about alterations in imprisonment for debt and in the criminal code, it must be noted that the major reforms just outlined occurred in the period 1785–1800. Why was so little done from 1776 to 1785? Why was so much done from 1785 to 1800? One plausible explanation is that, during the war years, the pressing need of winning independence deflected people and government from undertaking the reforms they wished to pursue. There is merit in this argument. But it is only part of the answer. The mid-1780s were, as we have and shall see again, important because they marked a new awareness by Philadelphians of the poor and more especially of the seeming danger the poor posed for society. It was in the period 1785 and following that Philadelphians began to distinguish more precisely between the "industrious" and the "idle" poor. It was in this period that Philadelphians put greater emphasis on the fact that "idle" poverty constituted "vicious" and "vulgar" poverty. It was in 1785 that Philadelphians began to analyze the nature of social disorder and crime to a far greater extent than before, coming to the conclusion that the poor often caused social disorder and were likely, because of supposed moral weakness, to engage in crime. The fear of and anxiety about such social disorder and crime led to a social innovation. By the 1790s, groups of citizens became convinced that the efforts of governmental agencies could not stop what was perceived as the rise in vice, immorality, and crime, and they responded by creating private associations to suppress these evils.

Thus, the increasing effort to transform the city's system of criminal justice stemmed from more than the philosophical desire for reform usually associated with the Enlightenment ideals flourishing in revolutionary America; it was rooted as well in an increasing fear of the potential for vice and criminality among the poor. Philadelphians evidenced a marked concern for training or forcing the poor in general to conform to the ideals of industrious poverty only when it appeared that the poor as a group posed an imminent danger to the peace, order, and stability of society. The general perception that special exertions were required to control the poor did not reach major proportions until the 1780s. But the city officials charged with administering public assistance to the city's needy faced what they believed was a crisis as early as the 1760s. Their efforts to resolve this crisis produced major changes even before the Revolution and fomented a long bitter debate over the proper goals for the city's public poor relief system.

5

*Public Poor Relief, 1760–1776: Turbulent
Innovation before the Revolution*

Philadelphia's system of public poor relief changed markedly in the decade and a half before the American Revolution. Burdened by an ever-increasing number of poor, the city attacked the problems of public poor relief in a bold and novel way by creating a corporation that blended public and private power and controlled public poor relief in an area extending well past urban Philadelphia. However, by the eve of the Revolution, it was obvious that this experiment had created more problems than it had solved. The city's suburban areas rebelled against the new system and tried to destroy it. One group of public poor relief officials, who represented the Quaker mercantile elite, wanted to use public poor relief primarily to reform the poor. The other officials, who were typically drawn from the middling ranks of the mechanic-artisan element of Philadelphia, believed that relief should seek to aid rather than reform the poor. These differences in status and philosophy became mutually reinforcing and led the two groups into protracted institutional warfare over the issue of what public poor relief should and should not attempt to do.

In 1760 public poor relief in the city proper was administered by the overseers of the poor. These officials, appointed for one-year terms by the justices of the peace each March 25th, helped determine the amounts needed to maintain the poor and assessed and collected the poor tax. The sums obtained, augmented by fines and forfeitures, paid for a wide range of activities. The overseers ran the city almshouse, granted outdoor relief, and worked to rid the city of persons who received public poor relief or were likely to become chargeable but did not have legal settlements in the city. Overseers of the poor in the suburban areas performed similar duties, although none of the suburban areas maintained an almshouse.[1]

The city overseers, even before 1760, experienced real difficulty in raising the sums necessary to maintain the poor. By the 1760s the nagging problem of meeting the costs of public poor relief reached crisis proportions.[2] According to the overseers in office in 1764, the number of people maintained by the city had about doubled between 1755 and 1764.[3] The increasing number, said the overseers, made financing public poor relief most difficult, and the problem was likely to worsen since the overseers could not, with all their duties, guard against the daily influx of poor newcomers. Indeed, the number of persons under public care had so increased that the almshouse had become appallingly overcrowded: five or six beds were stuffed into rooms ten or eleven feet square, and even the church area had been converted into an apartment with fifteen beds. Despite these makeshift arrangements, many poor still lacked proper lodging.

The overseers attacked these problems by asking the legislature to create a new institution where the able-bodied poor could labor. The claim was offered that three-fourths of the publicly maintained poor could earn enough in the summer for winter needs if properly set to work in a well-regulated workhouse or house of employment. To strengthen their case, the overseers asserted that similar institutions had achieved success in Great Britain. The legislature established a committee to consider this plan, but no legislation was forthcoming.[4]

On January 15, 1766, the overseers again petitioned the legislature and again complained that the number of poor increased daily despite the overseers' strenuous efforts to prevent that increase. The cost of maintaining the poor was so high and the general economy so bad that the established poor tax system could not support them. In fact, of the nearly £3,100 spent on poor relief in 1765, just less than £816—over 25 percent—came from donations. Even with all this effort, the amount expended proved insufficient to support the poor in the almshouse and the 150 outpensioners. Once again the overseers urged that establishing an institution to provide work for the poor would prove the best way to reduce the cost of their maintenance.

The Grand Jury of the City of Philadelphia supported the overseers' plan by personally presenting a memorial to the legislature. The grand jury observed that for several years the economy had provided full employment for laboring people and others in "low circumstances." These good times attracted many poor people to the city, and, because of a belief that they could support themselves, the overseers did not always take care to establish their proper places of residence. By 1766, with trade so stagnated, many willing to work could not maintain themselves or their families. "Many others, inclined to live in Sloth and Idleness," could not procure even enough to subsist. Given these facts, a new method of relieving the poor had to be found, and the answer was, as the overseers had said, the creation of a house of employment based on the English model. Such an institution would give proper employment to the industrious, while "subjecting the Indolent and Supine to the Necessity of labouring for their Support." Building a house of employment would also allow the Pennsylvania Hospital to aid its "proper Objects" by eliminating the need to expend funds on "many Idle Poor."[5]

The movement for a house of employment was obviously well orchestrated. When the grand jury retired, the managers of the Pennsylvania Hospital informed the legislature that their institution faced financial ruin because the number of distressed poor who applied for relief had increased dramatically. Moreover, many poor people, once cured but still in a weak state, could not find proper employment to tide them over until fully recovered. What was needed was a house of employment, and that could be established only with the aid of the legislature.[6]

Public calls to establish a house of employment were apparently supplemented by private assurances that, if the legislature created a special corporation to erect and run it, the institution could be paid for by private funds.[7] Here was an attractive offer. If the legislators merely authorized formation of a corporation,

Philadelphia's system of public poor relief could become more humane and yet less costly.

This offer struck a responsive chord. On February 8, 1766, the legislature enacted a law "for the Better Employment, Relief and Support of the Poor within the City of Philadelphia, the District of Southwark, the Townships of Moyamensing, and Passyunk, and the Northern Liberties."[8] Philadelphia's suburban areas were included in this organization for two reasons. First, combining these areas would supposedly aid the poor by preventing disputes about removals based on legal area of settlement. It was claimed that, because they moved from place to place in the urban area, many persons did not have legal settlements in either the city or suburbs. Yet these people were Philadelphians and had "an equitable Right to a common Support from all." Second, it was also asserted that the cost of maintaining the poor could be reduced if one agency controlled public poor relief in all of greater Philadelphia.[9] To meet these ends, the law established the Contributors to the Relief and Employment of the Poor within the City of Philadelphia. To become a contributor, one had to donate at least ten pounds toward building the new facility.[10]

The house of employment was, by law, really two institutions in one. The east wing, or almshouse portion, housed those incapable of working. The west wing, or house of employment section, held the poor deemed able to labor. This category included all persons who offered to work for their maintenance at wages that would advance the goals of the contributorship.[11] The house of employment section was also to house people whose "disorderly conduct" gave "disturbance" to their neighborhood and who appeared likely to become public charges. From the start, then, this institution designed to employ and relieve the industrious poor was also a place of punishment for the "idle" or "vagrant."[12]

In establishing the contributorship system, the legislature significantly diminished the power of the overseers. Under the system inaugurated in 1766, the twelve managers of the house, elected annually by the contributors from their own number, determined the amount to be raised by taxation. Although the overseers still collected the poor tax, they legally could spend tax money only for removals of those who lacked legal settlements and for immediate, short-term relief. By law, the rest of the tax funds went to the managers. In this way, the poor relief system in Philadelphia blended private and public power. The contributorship, a private corporation, was to be the chief instrument of public poor relief and hence was to receive most of the poor tax.[13]

Although based on an English model, the contributorship system signaled a bold, innovative attempt to support greater Philadelphia's poor at a reasonable cost. But the new system malfunctioned almost from the start. Problems began when construction of the new house of employment began, for it cost over £11,750 to erect the structure, and at least £6,750 of that sum was borrowed. Thus, the contributorship fell deeply in debt even before the house opened its doors on October 16, 1767.[14] It was hardly an auspicious beginning for an institution that was intended to lower the cost of public poor relief.

The financial difficulties of the contributorship helped foment conflicts in the prewar years. Between 1768 and 1776, citizens of the Northern Liberties, Southwark, and Passyunk made five separate attempts to break away from the greater Philadelphia system. As presented in petitions to the legislature, the crux of the suburban areas' argument was that their sections now paid more than ever for public poor relief and, given the number of suburban poor, more than they should.[15] The contributorship challenged these claims, and the prerevolutionary legislators accepted the contributors' position.[16] Although the greater Philadelphia system of poor relief created in 1766 remained intact on the eve of the Revolution, dismemberment remained a real possibility.

The financial woes of the prewar public relief system also helped provoke battles between the managers of the house and the overseers. Under the mixed public/private system of the contributorship, the overseers collected poor taxes, while the managers determined how the monies would be spent. The overseers wanted to use significant amounts of the poor tax for outdoor relief, but the contributorship went deeply into debt building and running the house. Moreover, because tax revenue usually fell short of anticipated income or came in late, the contributorship's financial position quickly deteriorated. Faced with this plight, the managers resented the overseers using large portions of the poor tax monies on outdoor relief, and in June 1769 the managers ordered outdoor relief stopped.[17]

The managers wanted the poor forced into the house not only to lower costs, but also so that those who were idle could be reformed: the managers took to heart the ideal that the house could be, as it often was called, a "bettering house." This policy was clearly and publicly stated in 1770 in a listing of the virtues of the institution. The managers claimed that many paupers in the house were people "of dissolute manners committed by the Magistrates, as Nuisances to the Community; with Constitutions, in a number of Instances, Emaciated with Diseases, the Effect of their Vicious Courses, After having been a time subjected to the Rules and Orders of the House, kept to such Labour as they have been capable of, and deprived of the use of Spiritous Liquors, have been in a good degree restored to the Vigour of Health." A large number of these people were "so remarkable Altered as to become subjects of Surprize to many of the Inhabitants who had known them in their former Condition."[18] Such reformed people, once discharged, were not likely again to become public charges; therefore, their reform would help lower the cost of relief. Of course these impressive results could not have been achieved unless the poor were in the house.[19] For both economic and philosophical reasons, the managers wanted outdoor relief stopped.

The overseers vigorously opposed elimination of outdoor relief by arguing that many poor persons unable to labor in the house could be maintained out of doors on a small pension; it would markedly raise the cost of poor relief to insist that such people move into the house. And it would be "a Piece of Cruelty," said the overseers, to push people into the house when a small amount of outdoor relief would soon allow them to become self-supporting. Also, forcing a man and wife who had maintained "an Honest Sober Character" into the house would be especially cruel, since they would be required to live apart.

Building upon the example of worthy families being separated, the overseers presented the managers with a scathing attack on the house. Poor people found the regulations of the house so unacceptable that many, when urged to go in for relief, "declared in a Solemn manner that they would rather perish through want" than enter the house. Withdrawal of outdoor relief would induce the "Wicked & Profligate" to rob and steal, while reducing the "most Religious & Sober" to extreme "misery & want." Or both groups might go begging, which would be "Offensive to all & . . . disturb the peace & good Order of the City."[20]

The managers disagreed. "Many Difficulties and impositions" arose from outdoor relief, with the chief problem being pensions that gave regular fixed sums to the poor. Out pension relief was "inconsistent with and subversive of the Nature and Design" of the house, and so no outdoor relief should be given "except in cases of extreme Sickness, Age & of which the Managers shall have cognizance." If, upon examination, persons were entitled to the benefit of the bettering house, they would "be obliged to remove therein, and be subject to the Laws and Ordinances made for the government of the same."[21]

The antagonism between the managers and overseers, which became quite bitter, sprang from a complex set of interrelated factors. Part of the problem may well have been that the managers and overseers of this period came from very different segments of Philadelphia society. The managers were, almost to a man, Quakers; the overseers represented a wider range of religious affiliations. Just less than 75 percent of the managers were merchants; over 80 percent of the overseers were mechanics or artisans. And, while slightly more than 65 percent of the managers were rated at one hundred pounds or more on the 1769 tax list, less than 5 percent of the overseers were so rated. The differences in the occupational and economic position of the two groups are also seen in the fact that while thirteen of the twenty-four managers signed the 1765 nonimportation agreement produced by the merchants and traders of Philadelphia, only one of the twenty-four overseers was a signatory. The political experience and power of the two groups was also markedly different. The twenty-four managers could boast of having among their number four who had served as commissioners, surveyors, or regulators of streets; one warden of the lamps; one or possibly two members of the Philadelphia common council; a treasurer of the county of Philadelphia; a sheriff of the county of Philadelphia; a speaker of the Pennsylvania Assembly; and one or possibly two members of the Pennsylvania Provincial Council. Not one of the overseers had held any of these posts.[22] Thus, the managers were representatives of the dominant Quaker mercantile elite; the overseers came from the mechanic-artisan groups of the city and were, at best, members of the city's middling rank.[23]

These differences probably made it easier for each group to believe that the other was acting from unacceptable motives. The managers, as leaders of Philadelphia society, seemed to expect the overseers to realize that the right of control and leadership, by tradition as well as law, rested with the contributorship. The overseers, who had originated the call for a house of employment, seemed to find it galling that the managers, representatives of the city's status elite, were using their power to try to reduce the traditional prerogatives of the overseers and thereby to make them little more than servants of the managers.

The divergent socioeconomic stations of these officials also helped foment the deep philosophical disagreement that divided the two groups. The managers, although they had acquired great wealth, were not necessarily insensitive to the plight of the poor. But the managers lived in a world where the immediate horrors of poverty did not often touch them in a direct, personal way. Equally important, the managers typically dealt with the very bottom segment of those receiving public poor relief. These facts led them to conclude that the poor needed reformation. Thus, they stressed that the poor should be pressured into the bettering house, where they would learn habits of industry and sobriety. On the other hand, the overseers, as members of the middling rank and of the mechanic-artisan community, lived in a world where poverty was more likely to touch them or their acquaintances personally. Certainly the overseers came from that segment of the city's population which was constantly reminded to work regularly and be frugal in order to avoid the sting of poverty. The overseers also, because they dealt with those who refused to go into the house as well as with those who did enter, saw a wider range of poor than did the managers.

Certainly the overseers drew sharper distinctions among poor people than did the managers. The overseers wanted the "good" poor who detested the house to receive aid out of doors, as they had traditionally done.

These differences in socioeconomic status and in philosophy, real as they were, probably would not have led to battles had the finances of the contributorship been sound. The managers and overseers each could have compromised enough to avoid vicious infighting. But the managers, faced with large debts, a high overhead, and slow collection of poor taxes, naturally wanted to retain as much of the tax monies as possible. They sought greater funds by following their philosophy to its ultimate conclusion: the poor needed some reformation and so should be forced into the house. This the overseers would not accept. They argued for outdoor relief not only because of a philosophy of poor relief, but also because they wanted to serve in an office that gave them discretionary power. If outdoor relief stopped, they would become mere tax collectors and enforcers of the settlement laws.

The differences between the managers and overseers went beyond possible desires for personal power. The regulations of the house *were* demeaning to the poor, for, in many ways, it resembled a prison. House rules decreed that the doorkeeper keep the gates well secured, and no one was allowed in or out without the permission of the steward.[24] Inside, life was regimented. People got up when the bell rang; they went to bed by nine o'clock in the summer and by eight o'clock in the winter. Even the eating process was tightly regulated: the steward or another appointed official was to "attend at all mealtimes and see the People under their care mess together, according to the order or classes settled by the Managers; that they do not directly begin to eat, or to help one another, but that they wait in silence, that the pious or devout among them may have opportunity of saying grace, or returning thanks for the mercies bestowed on them; and that they behave with decency & good Manners towards each other."

The poor able to work were also to be strictly controlled. Most picked oakum, while those with skills useful to the house, such as tailoring or shoemaking, labored at their trades. All girls deemed of a proper age learned things that would "qualify them for service." Whatever their assignments, all workers had to keep diligently at their tasks, and a variety of punishments awaited any who "shall neglect to repair to their proper places for work, or being there, shall refuse to work or shall tatter, be idle, or shall not well perform the task of Work set them, or shall waste and spoil any of the Materials or tools of the several Manufactures." Anyone avoiding work by feigning sickness also faced punishment.

The managers revealed their own feelings toward the poor in these rules. The poor who could work had to do so "as well to inure them to Labour, as to contribute to their support." Proper social conduct, as well as industry, was expected. Not only should the poor "behave soberly, decently, and Courteously to each other," they must behave "submissively to their superiors & Governors." The poor, who were clearly inferior, had to be reformed so that they would no longer be the dangerous class. To help this reformation along, the managers promised some rewards to those who worked hard and obeyed the rules.

The house rules held out far more possibility of punishment than of reward. Actions calling for chastisement included such obvious evils as breaking windows, fighting, bringing in liquor, stealing, or following "wanton & lascivious behavior." But the poor could also be disciplined for behaving "disrespectfully to their Governors." Submission was not only expected; it was demanded. Punishments, which the managers normally had to sanction before they were inflicted, included forcing the offender to wear a chain and iron ring around his leg. City magistrates had to authorize any corporal punishment or addition of labor to the tasks assigned, but the steward had full power to discipline "unruly, disorderly, or stubbornly preverse [sic]" inmates by ordering their confinement in the "dark room" on a diet of bread and water for up to forty-eight hours. The steward could not himself, in all probability, be stubbornly perverse, since he had to give the managers a list of those confined in the dark room, along with a notation of their transgressions.[25]

Given the rules of the house, it is not hard to believe that the poor avoided it if at all possible. But the overseers willingly sent some persons to the house; it was the poor of "Honest Sober Character" they wanted to keep outside it. The overseers worked to make their claim that such people refused to enter the house a reality by often carefully checking on the characters of those who applied for relief and then granting outdoor relief to those considered industrious.[26]

As an immediate result of the first fight over outdoor relief in 1769, the overseers stopped appointing committees to visit the house, on the basis that the visits served "no good Purposes."[27] This stance constituted a form of blackmail, because the overseers determined the legal residence of poor people. Unless the overseers acted, the managers could not evict persons who lacked legal settlements in greater Philadelphia; this inability to evict drove up the cost of running the house. After further acrimonious wrangling, the managers agreed to allow outdoor relief in February 1770.[28] Knowing that the managers might again try to eliminate it, the overseers turned to the legislature, which was scheduled to reexamine the poor laws in 1771. Offering petitions arguing the case for outdoor relief, the overseers sought a guarantee that they could continue to aid the poor out of doors.[29]

The revised poor law, enacted in March 1771, dismayed the overseers, for it reduced their power. Now they could spend tax monies only for receiving and removing poor people as the settlement laws directed and to pay for collecting the tax; the fines, forfeitures, and donations the overseers had used for outdoor relief became the contributorship's. Nor could the overseers easily vent their anger by a lackadaisical collection of the poor tax. If they failed to produce the tax monies within two months of receipt of a collection warrant, they faced a fifty-pound fine. Overseers using public monies for purposes not stated in the law had to repay that sum from their own pockets. This act made the overseers mere tax collectors and shufflers of poor people. The only part of the legislation they could view with pleasure was the section saying that the law would last just five years.[30]

The managers did not immediately move to eliminate outdoor relief when the 1771 law was passed. But in February 1772 they complained of receiving numerous requests from residents of Southwark for outdoor relief. Proclaiming such relief inconsistent with the design of the house, the managers said that the rule of June 10, 1769, eliminating all outdoor relief, must be "strictly observed," at least for Southwark. Despite this statement, outpensions were granted from February to at least October of 1772, although, after February, the amount expended for outdoor relief dropped significantly. Thus, it appears that while residents of Southwark received no outdoor relief, outpensions were given at a reduced level in the other areas of the city.[31]

In early 1774 the issue of stopping outdoor relief again surfaced. Until that time, the managers allowed the overseers to use fine money for outdoor relief. Because these sums proved insufficient, the overseers asked if they could use tax monies for this purpose. The managers responded that the tax money proved insufficient to maintain the poor in the house and that the overseers should therefore spend tax monies only for removal of nonresident paupers. Because the managers continued to allow some outdoor relief, this action did not cause the antagonistic feelings produced by the elimination of outdoor relief in 1769. But the overseers, though apparently not bitter, refused to become mere tax collectors. They began searching for a way to grant outdoor relief as they saw fit.[32]

In November 1775 the managers went a long way toward helping the overseers in their struggles with the contributorship. Probably as part of an effort to have the city cancel a £750 loan, the managers presented a history of the house to city officials. This account admitted that the contributorship was basically a failure. The managers began by noting that few arrived at the house except those who were sick, naked, old and superannuated, or helpless infants. Thus, before a person could be useful to the house, he had to be nursed, cured, and clothed, at considerable expense and trouble. At this point he was often discharged as able to maintain himself. Even if a man lacking a trade remained in the house after being nursed and clothed, his labor picking oakum could not pay his maintenance. When a man had a trade, he normally refused to stay and work in the house unless paid a wage.

The ingratitude of such men was, as the managers saw it, incredible. If the managers refused to pay them wages or to discharge them, they ran away. Worse yet, they "stay out as long as they please, and when they think proper, procure fresh orders and return, mostly as sick naked and burthensome." Because both men and women did this, the house constantly lost resources without getting the labor of the poor in return.

The situation with women working at spinning was just as bad. Many, although seemingly industrious, could not spin even their assigned task of four dozen of flax yarn per week. If the women produced more than the required amount, it helped but little, since the rules of the house said that for each dozen produced above the assigned amount, the women received fourpence worth of food or clothes. Those able to spin more than four dozen typically spun six or eight dozen per week "for a short space only, to obtain clothing &c, then generally run off." Numbers of women also worked as washers, cooks, seamstresses, drudges, and attendants in the house. Their labor was essential but turned no profit. Still, "if a penny saved is a penny earned, those Women are of the most profitable kind of any we have."

Given these facts, it became clear why only one-fourth, or at most one-third, of the total number of residents in the house could engage in manufacturing, and most of these were invalids. Since so many of the house's residents were "entirely dead Weight," "all is done that can be reasonably expected" to have them labor. Having detailed this state of affairs, the managers rhetorically asked: "Where now is to be the great profits of manufacturing, carried on only with such people . . . ?"

As the managers viewed the situation, the labor of the poor could not be expected to pay the costs of the house, "especially if the Poor, are to be relieved when admitted, which we hope is the intent." Thus, Philadelphians should not disparage the lack of profit from the house. Rather, they should rejoice that the labor "of these few poor helpless old people" provided clothing for poor people throughout the city as well as in the house.

The problems inherent in the labor supply were matched by the contributors' financial problems. If the funds of the institution were unencumbered and at all considerable, the house could engage in some manufacturing of consequence. But because of the advanced price of goods, virtually all available funds went merely to maintain the poor. Although this want of capital supposedly made significant manufacturing impossible, the managers claimed that they were making headway with thread manufacturing. Further, because this work required more flax than could be spun in the house, the managers gave out flax for spinning in the hope that this would keep even more people from becoming public charges in the house. Still, no matter what the state of manufacturing, only negligible returns resulted, because even the excellent goods produced in the house could not be sold at their proper value.

Having admitted that the original plan of the house was ill conceived, the managers turned to their own defense. They had undertaken "this disagreeable Service to the public, without Reward or Emolument," and therefore the "ungenerous and illiberal Reflections and Insinuations against our Management and Oeconomy" were especially galling. Nor was the house really a failure. "Surely such great numbers of helpless—destitute poor people, comfortably supported or casually and properly relieved in so easy a manner, ought, one should think, give rise to the most pleasing reflections, to the Supporters of the House of Employment &c., in this City." Indeed, the house was more than an asylum for the poor; it also functioned as a hospital "in every sense of the word, and perhaps more extensively so than any other Institution on this Continent." The full range of afflictions, including mental diseases, received treatment there. In addition, the house served as a lying-in hospital, aiding upwards of thirty poor women per year, and also as a foundling hospital and charity school, where more than fifty children, on the average, were cared for and kept until they could be bound out.

The noble results achieved by the house were not, as some ill-informed people said, achieved only at an exorbitant price. It did cost more to maintain the poor than before the house existed, but this rise stemmed from the great increase in the number of poor, the rise in the price of provisions, and the failure of levied taxes to produce anticipated revenues. Considering all factors, the proportional cost of maintaining a poor person was much less than before the house was founded. The managers went so far as to claim that, if they were not burdened with old debts and if taxes were collected fully and quickly, one sixpenny tax a year would come very close to maintaining the poor of the city and suburbs.

The managers' carefully worded defense of their actions also sounded a note of civic pride. They alleged that a close investigation of the best information about relief houses in European cities similar to Philadelphia revealed that "there is not one such Institution . . . that does not annually expend vastly greater Sums . . . in proportion to numbers on their poor[']s maintenance." And, despite the greater expense, the poor in the comparable European institutions "are treated with much greater Rigour and Severity and do not live near so comfortable as our Poor do." The contributors claimed that they had every right to hope for the "advice, assistance & Support" of the city officials "in behalf of the Public and the Poor."[33]

Although the managers unquestionably pictured their efforts in the best possible light, there was much truth in the presentation: both the number of poor and the cost of provisions had increased dramatically, while tax collection was less than perfect. But the basic problem lay in the conception of the contributorship. The original hopes for a house of employment were simply too sanguine. The poor, willing or forced to go to the house, could not be expected to pay their own way by laboring. Moreover, the cost of building the house proved so much greater than anticipated that it faced financial woes no matter how well managed. These financial troubles forced the managers to try to reduce expenses by periodically attacking outdoor relief. Such action antagonized the overseers who collected the tax and probably made them less concerned about vigorous collection. This situation pushed the contributorship deeper into financial trouble. It was a vicious cycle. This system of divided authority—half public, half private—could not last forever.

In February 1776, the overseers attempted to end the system of divided authority in public relief. Aware that the 1771 poor law was about to expire, they urged the legislature to make a sweeping revision of the law to eliminate the split authority in poor relief by eliminating the contributorship. In its place, the overseers proposed an organization of twelve overseers or managers of the poor who would run the house and have authority to give outpension or other outdoor relief at their discretion as long as two magistrates authorized it. But the lawmakers again sided with the managers by making the 1771 legislation perpetual and thus continuing the contributorship's effective control of outdoor relief.[34]

The period from 1760 to 1776 was thus one of innovation and turbulence for Philadelphia's system of public poor relief. In the face of rising costs, a bold new program was launched in 1766 to deal with the poor. Although the law creating the contributorship instituted a system of divided authority among the officers of the poor, it created a geographically unified system of poor relief. To avoid problems such as costly battles to determine the legal residence of a poor person, the suburban areas of Southwark, Moyamensing, Passyunk, and the Northern Liberties were united with the city for administration of poor relief. In this way a greater Philadelphia agency of poor relief emerged.

Many Philadelphians hoped and believed that the new institution would initiate a glorious, less expensive age of poor relief. But in the years before the Revolution the glories were few, the costs higher. The contributorship's economic plight led to repeated attempts by suburban areas to maintain their own poor. And the economic woes combined with philosophical differences and disputes over power to turn the overseers and managers into pugnacious opponents. The managers, who came from the ranks of the mercantile elite, wanted to save money and reform the idle poor by eliminating outdoor relief and thereby forcing the poor into the house. The overseers, who were drawn principally from the middling section of the mechanic-artisan class, were more concerned with aiding the industrious poor than with reform. And the overseers fought to preserve their long-established right to give outdoor relief.

In 1775 the managers admitted that the house had failed to lower the cost of poor relief. Newspaper essayist "W. R." had said the same thing in 1772, when he asserted that the "pleasing Prospect" of Philadelphia's poor maintaining themselves by labor had proved a chimerical hope.[35] Still, by April 1776 the contributorship—faulty as it was—had carried the day against the overseers and the suburbs. The poor law revisions of 1771 and 1776 sharply curtailed the overseers' ability to dispense outdoor relief. None of the suburban areas had been able to break away from the contributorship. But in 1776 another attempt at overturning the established order, not related to poor relief in Philadelphia, occurred. That action first altered and then helped destroy the contributorship system in a way that seemed to signal that public poor relief would once more focus on aiding rather than reforming the poor.

6

Public Poor Relief, 1776–1800: Change and Continuity

Wars often disrupt and help change social institutions, and the character of the contributorship was certainly affected by the Revolution. Because many Quakers voluntarily withdrew from public affairs or were forced out of office, by the 1780s the management of the contributorship had passed to a much more diverse religious group.[1] But the problems dividing the managers and overseers had not, it appears, been based on religious differences. The decline of Quaker domination did not halt the battles between the public poor relief officials. The new managers, who, like the old ones, represented the elite mercantile segment of society, still maintained that public poor relief should reform the poor. The overseers, who increasingly also came from the mercantile portion of the population, held to the view that relief of the worthy poor was much more important than reform. This old philosophical disagreement, aided by a deepening sense of personal antagonism, kept the managers and overseers embroiled in protracted institutional warfare.

The overseers, using legislation that was a direct result of the effort to win the war, finally managed to gain full control of Philadelphia's system of public poor relief. Given the pronouncements and actions of the overseers, this change seemingly paved the way for the use of public poor relief to aid the worthy poor, rather than as an instrument of reform. And the overseers of the postwar era, like other Philadelphians of the day, helped support the ideal of industrious poverty by stressing that the honest poor deserved special consideration. But the overseers also came to accept the managers' view that, in most cases, the poor who required public assistance brought poverty on themselves through habits that could and should be reformed in the house. Thus, the practice of utilizing poor relief as an instrument of control and reform for the protection of society became yet more deeply entrenched, even as the form of public poor relief in the city was transformed.

As war broke over Philadelphia, its system of public poor relief disintegrated. Despite protests from the managers, by December 1776 the eastern wing of the house was converted into an army hospital. Worse yet, collecting the poor tax, never an easy task, became virtually impossible. The whole system of poor relief fell apart when the British occupied the city in September 1777. In October the British took over the east wing of the house, which the American army had been using. By early December, all of the poor in the house had been moved out and were being quartered in the Free Masons' Lodge, the Friends' major meeting house, and Carpenters' Hall. It thus appears that the British took over the whole house building. Because the overseers stopped functioning when the British occupied the city, no poor tax could be collected during the occupation. The situation of the poor soon became so desperate that the managers were reduced, they said, to borrowing and begging money. In December 1777, when they asked General Howe for help, he and his city officials suggested that a public subscription be taken up to aid the poor. The managers followed this suggestion.[2]

When the British evacuated the city in June of 1778, the American army again took over the almshouse section, but the house of employment section became available for the poor.[3] Having moved them back into the house, the managers lapsed into inactivity; from August 1778 to May 1780 they essentially stopped performing their legal duties.[4] The overseers stepped in and ran the house as best they could. Their chief problem was how to raise money, since by law the managers had to request the levying of poor taxes and, hence, the overseers had no taxing power. Having no choice, the overseers commenced borrowing to fund poor relief. By December 1778 they had obtained £7,100, and in April 1779 they secured another loan of approximately $3,600. In the fall of 1779, when the managers gathered just long enough to authorize a poor tax collection, the already weakened contributorship stood on the brink of financial disaster.[5] Given this fact, the old manager-overseer debate on outdoor relief seemed likely to flair up once more.

In the spring of 1780, as the managers again took up full-time duties, they seemed anxious to avoid manager-overseer squabbles. The managers gave five hundred pounds to the overseers to be distributed as outdoor relief "to such as are real objects of distress." However, just three months later, the managers proclaimed outpensions contrary to law and ordered them stopped. In early April 1781 the managers reversed this policy and allowed the overseers to administer outdoor relief.[6] This game of musical outdoor pensions, which had been going on since 1769, hardly made for orderly and consistent poor relief. Given the divided power of the managers and overseers and the economic woes of the house, it is no exaggeration to conclude that by 1782 Philadelphia's half-public, half-private system of poor relief was one large charitable mess.

The legislature clearly judged that such was the case. In March 1782 it passed a law that allowed for a sweeping restructuring of the whole system of poor relief in Philadelphia. A new comprehensive act was needed, said the lawmakers, for two reasons: the poor in Philadelphia had become very burdensome and expensive, and the cost of maintaining them was likely to increase. Having grossly understated the obvious, the legislators observed that, because many of the contributors had died or were under legal disability, it proved difficult to obtain the requisite number of persons to serve as managers of the house. The "legal disability" resulted from the refusal of a number of the contributors, many of them Quakers, to take the required oath of allegiance to support the revolutionary movement; the legislature, in 1779, had decreed that until the contributors took the oath, they could not participate in contributorship activities.[7]

Given this state of affairs, the Assembly declared that if the contributors did not meet on the second Monday in May to choose twelve managers, or if a majority of those twelve managers failed to meet on the third Monday in May of any year, the contributorship would lose its legal rights. In its place, the overseers of greater Philadelphia would, "for the time being," take over all the powers, duties, and property of the contributorship. The overseers would automatically become an incorporated body called the Guardians of the Poor of the City of Philadelphia. The guardians would be divided into two sections, with one group running the house and the other performing the regular duties of the overseers.[8]

The 1782 law made several important changes that took effect immediately. Passyunk, which twice before had attempted to leave the greater Philadelphia poor relief system, was allowed to secede and maintain its own poor. The legislature had finally realized that Passyunk was not an integral part of the city and that it should not be forced to remain within the greater Philadelphia system.

This act also aided the overseers in two important ways. So that the confusion and inefficiency resulting from replacing the entire set of overseers each March could be avoided, the appointment of overseers was staggered: at all times, one-half of those in office would be experienced. The legislature, surely aware of the differences between the managers and the overseers concerning outdoor relief, allowed the overseers, with the consent of only one justice of the peace, to grant outdoor assistance to any poor person facing "sudden necessity." Although such relief could not exceed three pounds in any three-month period, this provision permitted the overseers to meet their normal outdoor grants easily.[9] The question of outdoor relief had, for the moment, been resolved in favor of the overseers' views.

The Assembly made another change that both the overseers and managers could applaud. It observed that many "disorderly persons, by their own lewdness, drunkenness or other evil practices, have fallen sick and become chargeable" to Philadelphia. Because such people should be obliged to make compensation by servitude, any two overseers, with the approval of two justices of the peace, could bind them out for any sums the overseers saw fit to accept. However, an indenture could only be for the costs incurred in relieving the person, and in no case was the indenture to last more than three years. Further limitations stipulated that no married person and no persons aged forty or older could be bound. Even with these limitations, here was a potentially powerful weapon to keep vagabonds and other undesirables from flocking to Philadelphia.[10]

After the act of 1782 became law, the managers and at least the city overseers worked together with little friction for over a year.[11] Then, in August 1784, the managers took an important, symbolic step by ordering a section of the house partitioned for the use of "some of those who have been obliged thro' Necessity to come into the House and who have been formerly in reputable Circumstances."[12] The overseers, in defending outdoor relief, had long opposed sending the poor of "Honest Sober Character" to the house to be jumbled together with rogues and vagrants. By creating a separate ward for at least some of the honest poor, the managers apparently conceded that not all of the poor entering the house needed reformation. Given this change, the overseers might willingly send more poor people to the house, thereby reducing the cost of outdoor relief and perhaps ending the old debate.

It was not to be. Creating a separate area for some of the poor did not change the prisonlike atmosphere of the house. Indeed, on February 3, 1785, the board of managers visited the house en masse and stood by as the steward read a set of "Orders" to the assembled paupers. The residents were reminded that, when the dinner bell rang, they must "meet at this place, now allotted and appointed for them, to eat together in a decent orderly Manner in their respective Classes or Messes, as they may from Time to Time be ordered and directed by the Steward." The paupers also heard again of their inferiority by the "Order" that they were, at all times, "duly to observe an orderly decent Behaviour and Decorum to each other, as well as to their Supereors in all Cases according to the established *Rules* and *Ordinances*." If a poor person "at any Time became so daringly insolent, in any Instances to transgress and break these our Orders and Regulations upon his her or their being detected in so doing, and the Fact proven, we are fully determined, that all such Transgressors are and shall be deemed unworthy of the Releif of public Charity." Such a person could be thrown out of the house, thrust into the "Black Hole" punishment room, or banished to the workhouse for up to three months. To insure obedience to the rules, the managers ordered that a person be appointed from each class or mess "to see that the present Orders and Regulations are in every Instance duly and strictly observed or faithfully to report every Transgressor, or clamorous and refractory [?] Person who may evince a Disposition to Disobedience and unruly Behaviour opposed to our Intention or this salutary Purpose." These institutional informers would be rewarded for good performance, "but neglecting their appointed Duty and betraying their Trust will surely be doubly Criminal and those Guilty thereof justly Ranked amongst the greatest Offenders." Finally, the steward was to post copies of the rules and ordinances, and he was ordered to remind the paupers frequently of them.[13]

Despite some separation of the different classes of poor, the house obviously remained more a prison than a refuge. In August 1785 the overseers reaffirmed their insistence on the need for outdoor relief by claiming that "the better sort of poor are in general so averse" to entering the house that "they will submit to the greatest suffering & Disstress before they Consent to it, owing to the great number of Rogues Vagrants and disorderly persons" who were maintained there "in idleness." Moreover, the overseers continued, some small families could be supported on outdoor relief for no more than it would cost to maintain one person in the house, because members of the family on outdoor relief could still earn some income. The overseers then caustically oberved that, if the managers alone judged the propriety of aiding the poor out of the house, "we can see no use for overseers of the poor, a few persons appointed to be Collectors, as in the Case of other Taxes, will answer the purpose."[14] The complaints and the essence of the arguments of the overseers and the managers had not changed one iota from their first battle over outdoor relief in 1769. And, as they had been doing since 1769, the overseers continued giving outdoor relief no matter what the managers ordered.[15]

Intermittently from 1785 to 1788, the managers and overseers waged petition warfare and offered public pronouncements blaming the other group for the problems besetting public poor relief. As the managers saw it, their economic woes flowed from the actions of the overseers, and the managers presented a number of claims to prove their case. They bought necessities on credit or at disadvantageous terms only because many of the overseers were dilatory in collecting taxes and giving them to the managers. Equally disturbing, the overseers allegedly spent great and unjustifiable sums on outdoor relief and did so, especially in the suburbs, even though the managers paid weekly pensions to people recommended by the overseers. Clearly, the very high poor taxes could be traced to the failures of the overseers. Indeed, were taxes merely collected on time, the cost of maintaining the poor could be reduced 15-20 percent.[16]

The overseers presented a different view. Collecting the poor taxes proved hard, although the overseers worked diligently to gather the tax. Yes, tax money was spent on outdoor relief, but for obvious reasons, since "the people agree that the House of Employment has been as badly managed as could be." In fact, the city and districts were "run down by the poor of a lazy disposition" wanting entry into the house "to lounge away their time." The overseers expressed confidence that citizens, upon examining the records, "shall see with pleasure how we have laid out our monies for present relief."[17] The overseers, thus, did not deny the managers' charges of failing to provide the house with funds; instead, they openly and defiantly argued for the superiority of outdoor relief for at least the "better" sort of poor.

These petitions and public statements point up the fact that outdoor relief remained, as it had been, the chief issue causing battles between the overseers and the managers. Believing that outdoor relief was, as it historically had been, their province, the overseers fought to be more than tax collectors and clerks. Certainly the arguments they developed over the years are convincing. The house, with its prisonlike atmosphere, evoked the hatred of the poor—whether of "the better sort" or not. Some people or families, especially those unable to labor, probably could be maintained for less by a system of outdoor relief. Finally, since the managers lacked the funds to establish profitable manufacturing, it did not help to send them more people to clothe and feed.

But the managers' position was also logical. The cost of building the house and the difficulties of war forced the house deeply into debt. Unless given special permission, the poor relief officials could levy poor taxes only for the immediate care of the poor. Also, since these taxes were often collected late, the house fell deeper into debt; it was thus difficult to maintain the poor, much less pay debts. With these problems, to say nothing about the inability of most paupers to labor, the establishment of profitable manufacturing was almost impossible. Because of the managers' very real difficulties, the delayed receipt of tax funds made extensive outdoor relief seem grossly unfair. Certainly the overseers appeared more concerned about persons relieved out of doors than about the poor in the house.

Actually, both the managers and the overseers were merely attempting to take care of the poor immediately under their charge. But, with the debts of the house and the nature of the tax structure, it was virtually impossible to do so. The managers' case seems weakened by their admission that the original design of the institution was faulty. If, as they maintained, the poor in the house could not support themselves by working, why keep large numbers in the house? Part of the building could be sold or rented, and costs thus reduced. All that needed to be maintained, in addition to an almshouse, was the hospital section, which performed a needed service for the poor.[18] But, whatever the cost, the contributorship determinedly tried to follow the original faulty design.

No matter how justified each side was, the other refused to acknowledge its own failings. Given this mutual narrowmindedness and given the fact that each group held a different philosophy about dealing with the poor, it is not surprising that the relationship between the managers and overseers remained as strained in the 1780s as it had been in the 1760s and 1770s.

In 1788, possibly with the aid of the weather, the overseers finally managed to do more than talk about the supposed failings of the managers. The contributors, as required by law, met on the second Monday in May and elected managers. On the evening of the eighteenth, the day before the law required the new managers to meet at the house, a heavy rain fell that may have made travel to the house difficult. Whether or not this was the cause, a majority of the newly elected managers did not gather at the house on the nineteenth as the law directed. If the overseers wanted to be technical, the contributorship was dissolved. The overseers wanted to be technical. On May 20 they met and proclaimed that the duties and assets of the contributorship had, for the time being, come to the overseers, who now became the guardians of the poor. Six of the guardians took over management of the house, and the other sixteen continued performing the duties of overseers.[19]

There is no evidence that the overseers actively worked to keep the requisite number of managers from meeting on May 19 as the law directed. Nevertheless, inferences made by the overseers and by a defender of the managers hint at a conspiracy. "Half Earnest," citing the vicious comments made by the overseers about the managers shortly before the contributorship dissolved, claimed that the overseers destroyed the contributorship.[20] The overseers, who called the elimination of the contributorship a "Revolution," said they took an "active & Zealous part" in that revolution. The overseers' statements indicate that they contributed to the idea that the managers lacked the ability to run the house and wantonly neglected it.[21] Thus, even if the overseers did not attempt to stop the managers from meeting, they campaigned against them and helped to ensure that any protest against using a technicality to eliminate the contributorship would not receive a sympathetic hearing.

After assuming the duties of the contributorship, the overseers wrote to the legislature and presented an analysis of the failure of the old system of poor relief. The high cost of building the house, the excessive admittance to it of nonresident poor, the fluctuation of currency during the war, and the vast increase in the numbers of the poor all put the house deeply in debt. These factors were exacerbated by the "continual Dissensions" between the managers and overseers, especially during the late 1780s. The overseers then offered a most revealing statement: the dissensions possibly stemmed from "too great an ostentation of superiority" by the managers and "too great a degree of Jealousy" felt by the overseers. If this analysis is correct, the battle between the managers and the overseers amounted to more than a question of how best to aid the poor. Thus viewed, the battle between them takes on a class tone.[22]

The managers held their power by virtue of being fairly wealthy, for it required a degree of financial power to contribute ten pounds in 1766.[23] The overseers, who held power merely as appointed officials, were probably less likely to have excess time or money to devote to their duties.[24] As one group of overseers noted in 1785, "Every person who hath served as an Overseer knows it to be a troublesome and disagreeable office [in] which much time is lost and monies expended by many who cannot well bear the burden."[25]

The evidence demonstrates that the managers of the contributorship and the overseers did occupy very different socioeconomic stations and that they also differed widely in political philosophy. Including the managers elected in May 1788, a total of twenty-eight different men served between May 1784 and the "Revolution" of 1788. Forty-nine men, all save two serving for a period of one year, functioned as overseers of the poor during the period September 1784 to March 1789.[26] Numbered among the total of twenty-eight managers were at least eight who served as common councillors of Philadelphia; five who served in the Continental Congress; a speaker of the Pennsylvania Assembly; eight who served in the Pennsylvania Assembly; two justices of the peace for the city of Philadelphia; and the president and three directors of the Bank of North America. A consideration of these same positions and of the forty-nine overseers reveals that one overseer may have served in the Pennsylvania Assembly; no overseer held any of the other posts.[27] Given these facts, it is not surprising that the managers enjoyed a greater degree of prestige than did the overseers. Five of the managers (17.9%) were titled "Esquire" either by the managers' minutes or by one of the city directories published in 1785; one of the overseers (2%) was so titled. Four managers (14.3%), none of whom were titled esquire, were listed as "Gentlemen" by at least one of the 1785 city directories; only one of the overseers (2%) was so listed. The difference in prestige is clearly seen in the fact that a city directory, in providing a list of the managers, titled every one of them esquire, even though some were not so titled in the main directory listing.[28] Not only were the managers more socially and politically prominent, they were also, as a group, much more conservative than the overseers. Six of the managers (21.4%) but only two overseers (4%) were founders of the Republican Society.[29]

Public Poor Relief, 1776-1800

Although the managers and overseers of the mid-1780s occupied very different social and political positions, the two groups were much more likely to follow similar occupational pursuits than were managers and overseers of earlier periods.[30] In the early years of the contributorship, over 80% of the overseers came from the mechanic or artisan elements of Philadelphia society; only 28.6% of the overseers who served during the period 1785-89 and whose occupations can be determined came from the mechanic-artisan ranks.[31] By the mid-1780s, 64.3% of the identifiable overseers were engaged in mercantile careers.[32] One of the forty-two overseers whose occupations could be traced ran a boardinghouse and another was a lawyer.[33] Of the managers who served in the same period and whose occupations can be determined, 46.2% came from Philadelphia's mercantile community, and several of the men listed merely as esquire or gentleman in the records (26.9%) also were engaged in mercantile pursuits.[34] Only 19.2% of the managers followed mechanic or artisan occupations.[35] In addition, as with the overseers, one manager ran a boardinghouse and another was a lawyer. Thus, while the overseers were more likely than the managers to be representatives of the mechanic-artisan group, the majority of both groups came from the mercantile segment of society. But, as noted, save for their role in public poor relief, the overseers were far less likely than were the managers to be involved in running the government.

Even though the managers and overseers tended to engage in similar economic pursuits, the two groups occupied different rungs on Philadelphia's economic ladder. The overseers came from what the people of the day would probably have called the solid middling rank. The average tax rating of the forty-two overseers who could be traced in the tax records was just under £700.[36] Excluding Robert Morris, who was personally worth more than all of the overseers who could be located in the tax records, the managers had an average taxable wealth of slightly more than £3,256—more than four times the overseers' average wealth.[37] Moreover, while 21.4% of the overseers were worth £1,000 or more, 86.4% of the managers were so rated; only 7.1% of the overseers were worth even £2,000, but 50% of the managers controlled taxable wealth worth £4,000 or more.

A comparison of the twelve overseers who actually staged the "Revolution" of 1788 and the twelve managers who were ousted from control of the contributorship reinforces and yet refines the general picture. The overseers who destroyed the contributorship were more tied to mercantile endeavors and were wealthier than their fellows. Seven of the ten revolutionary overseers whose occupations can be identified were merchants; one was a shopkeeper and another a grocer. Only one overseer—a tanner and currier—came from the mechanic-artisan segment of Philadelphia society.[38] The average wealth of the ten who could be traced in the tax records was slightly more than £1,089. Five of the ten were worth £1,000 or more, and two of these were worth more than £2,000. A suggestive example of these overseers' solid economic and social standing can be seen in the fact that seven of the ten owned pleasure carriages. The ousted managers followed similar occupations: 66.7% were merchants; 16.7% were listed merely as esquire or gentleman. The managers also included one doctor and one house carpenter. Save for the men denoted by titles of prestige or government service, the occupational breakdown of the two groups is strikingly similar. But the deposed managers were far wealthier than were the victorious overseers. Excluding Robert Morris from the calculation, the managers' average taxable wealth was just less than £4,110. With Morris's taxable wealth of £26,695 added, the managers' average taxable holding jumps to slightly more than £6,014.

As these figures indicate, the public poor relief revolution of 1788 did not represent a conflict between the mechanic-artisan group and the mercantile element. Rather, middling rank members of the mercantile community assaulted other, but much richer and more prominent, members of that community. Yet another crucial difference between the two groups suggests that more than "an ostentation of superiority" among the managers and a feeling of "Jealousy" among the overseers were at issue. Only one of the overseers (8.3%) was a founding member of the conservative Republican Society; six of the twelve managers (50%) were founders of that organization.

The prolonged battles between the managers and the overseers were rooted in divergent views of whether public poor relief should aid or reform the poor. When the contributorship first attacked the principle of outdoor relief, most of the overseers were mechanics or artisans who lived much closer to poverty and who dealt with a wider range of the poor than did the affluent mercantile managers. It seems logical that a concern for the feelings and needs of the poor, as well as a concern over personal power, prompted these early overseers to champion the ideal of outdoor relief, rather than reformation within the prisonlike house. But, although the managers were always richer than the overseers, the difference in occupational pursuits had narrowed considerably by the mid-1780s. The overseers who staged the revolution of 1788 were about as tied to the mercantile world as were the managers they purged. The difference in wealth remained, and the deposed managers were much more conservative, as indicated by their charter membership in the Republican Society. These considerations raise the possibility that different political philosophies may have been as important in 1788 as any philosophical differences. Moreover, the managers' supposed ostentation and the overseers' corresponding jealousy may have been as influential as any difference of attitude on poor relief. Given these considerations, it was quite possible that the long-standing difference of opinion on public poor relief would be almost immaterial to the revolution of 1788. If this was the case, the poor would have found, in the end, that the destruction of the contributorship did not fundamentally alter the emphasis upon reformation, rather than relief, of the poor. Despite the overseers' bold assertions to the contrary, that was precisely what happened.

The destruction of the contributorship, notwithstanding hopes and promises to the contrary, did little to improve the economic woes of Philadelphia's public poor relief system.[39] The continuing economic difficulties led citizens of the Northern Liberties in 1788–89 to ask for separation from the guardianship. The request was denied, but in 1791, Moyamensing persuaded the legislature that it should be separated from the guardianship. The legislature had finally agreed that Moyamensing paid far more than "in justice" it should. This action was fair and long overdue. Moyamensing, like Passyunk, was not a functional part of urban Philadelphia.[40] After 1789, the Northern Liberties and Southwark, which formed integral parts of the city, made no further efforts to secede from the greater Philadelphia system of public poor relief.

Although the destruction of the contributorship did not eliminate the economic problems of Philadelphia's system of public poor relief, the emergence of the guardianship seemed to mark an end to the old battles waged between the managers and overseers. Certainly the guardianship officials, like the overseers before them, voiced commitment to aiding rather than reforming the poor. Unquestionably, the overseers had long been concerned with helping the "good" rather than the "vicious" poor. With the elimination of the contributorship, the stage was set for a return to meeting the needs of the "honest" poor, rather than forcing all poor people into the "bettering" house for reformation.

The guardian managers, once in control, did not totally change the nature of the house. One of their first actions reaffirmed the old rules of the house, ensuring that it would still have a prisonlike atmosphere. But the new managers were determined to see that the "better" poor received better treatment. Shortly after undertaking management of the house, the guardian officials proclaimed that they would "take great care to make proper distinctions between the different Classes in separating with Regard to their several Characters & Conduct." Believing that "there ought to be a difference in the treatment of the Poor," the managers urged the members of the guardianship to "be particular in Characterizing those they send to the House."[41]

The managers' policy of differentiating among the poor can be seen in the allocation of food in the house. As of August 1788, tea was to be given only to "the Aged, reputable and such as are sick." After January 1789, newly arrived paupers afflicted with venereal disease, once cured, faced a diet of bread and water.[42] The new managers also worked to control the "vicious" poor who had found their way into the house. In early October of 1788, they noted the need to erect a fence around the house because the lack of one made it easy to remove house property, and too many of the inmates were disposed to steal whenever they could. Further, easy access to the house allowed rum to be smuggled into the building. This smuggling had to be stopped because, the managers asserted, "the Generality" of the house was "devoted" to rum. The fence went up a year later.[43]

More than a fence seemed necessary to stop the poor from having too much liberty to leave or return to the house. Such freedom of movement proved dangerous; one consequence was intemperance and an "Indulgence in the injurious use of strong Drink," which created disorder. The "good Order" of the house was also being disturbed by "a Door opened for other Irregularities and Abuses." This rather vague comment seems to refer to the fact that men and women paupers managed to get together for "disorderly" behavior. The house steward and matron were ordered to see that such activities stopped.[44]

The guardians' disdain for the "vicious" poor and desire to use public poor relief funds to help the "good" poor were displayed in their views toward orphans. In December 1788 the managers and overseers, meeting as the general board of the guardianship, created a commission to investigate the cost of establishing a foundling hospital for children who had been deserted by their parents. In March 1789, the committee members reported that "humanity" required that the creation of a foundling hospital should be the guardians' top-priority project. Although many in the house got there "by Indolence, Drunkenness and every Vice," they argued, abandoned children "could never have offended Society."[45]

Early in 1789, less than a year after taking control of the house, the guardians carried their desire to aid the honest poor to its logical conclusion. They asked the legislature to extend the vagrant act to the city. This toughly worded law declared that idle and disorderly persons, beggars, and those who refused to work for the usual and common wages given to other laborers in like work would be sent to the county's workhouse for up to one month. This act, the guardians said, should be extended to the city, because the cost of maintaining such people ought to fall on a county rather than on a city and because allowing such disorderly people into the house of employment meant that the "orderly & respectable Poor who go in for Relief & Employment" were improperly mixed with "immoral[,] loose & abandoned people." This structure worked against the original plan of the house.[46]

The guardians, of course, read the 1766 law creating the contributorship incorrectly. The original plan stated that the able-bodied poor, including vagrants and other disorderly people, should be lodged in the house of employment. But by reading the law as they did, they could reserve the house for the "honest" poor. Under this proposal, it would be transformed into a refuge for the "better sort" of poor, while the "vicious" would be kept out and punished, as they should be, in the workhouse.

The legislature accepted the guardians' reading of the 1766 law and went so far as to claim that the house was originally designed "for the accommodation of the poor and infirm and not for the reformation of the idle and profligate." The lawmakers also noted that mixing the proper objects of charity with the disorderly "may be the means of extending the depravity of morals and manners which is ever fatal to the well being of society and the peace and order of government." To remedy this evil, all the people designated as disorderly in greater Philadelphia would be sent to the Philadelphia workhouse, and any disorderly people in the house of employment were to be transferred to the workhouse as soon as possible.[47]

The 1789 revision of the poor law seemed to signal a major change in Philadelphia's system of public poor relief. The experiment of using the house for remolding the "idle," "vicious" poor into the "industrious" poor was to end. The "disorderly" would be controlled and punished by confinement in the workhouse; the house of employment would henceforth be a place of refuge, not a reformatory.

Although the guardians in 1789 rejected the contributorship's view that the house should reform the idle poor, they had to admit that the managers' objection to outdoor relief in the form of pensions was well founded. In late 1793, the overseers, most of whom were members of the mercantile community, adopted the position long supported by the contributorship managers: outdoor pensions would be eliminated.[48] The overseers took this position because such grants were, they said, "an encouragement to Impositions, vice & Immorality, by furnishing the means to procure liquor, &c. which are highly Injurious to the health and morals of the poor of both sexes." Still, the overseers remained committed to the philosophy that some outdoor relief was necessary and proper. Overseers were authorized to spend up to three pounds in any three-month period to aid the poor who faced sudden necessity.[49]

By 1793 the guardian managers began to sound like the old contributorship managers. In March the new managers asserted that, "in many instances," love of rum caused the poverty that made paupers dependent on the guardianship. In line with the view that the house was for the good poor, the managers did not hesitate to toss the most disorderly poor out of the house or to sell such people into servitude. But the new managers also could not resist trying their hand at reforming the idle poor who remained in the house. Paupers, even if they displayed "common decency & decorum," were to have their allowance of meat, sugar, and tea limited if they refused to obey the orders of the steward or matron. The additional amounts of tea and sugar given to women performing more than their assigned tasks could be denied to women guilty of "disorderly behavior." Further, the paupers should be kept hard at labor, since "many" of them "only have fallen into poverty from habits of Idleness, which it is possible with due attention to turn into those of Industry."[50] The managers had changed; the words had not.

In the years that followed, the managers tried various means to ensure that those needing to learn the value of industry did so. Allotments of food became instruments for control and reform. "The Idle, Impudent or disorderly" were to be "entirely stop'd, debarred or restricted" from receiving sugar or other luxury items. In 1799 orders directed that a special list be kept of all men or women able to work, so that "exemplary and suitable" punishments could be inflicted on those "who from idleness or any other cause refuse or neglect to do such Work as they are able and ought to perform."[51]

Rewards, as well as possible punishments, were emphasized in the last years of the century. While the unworthy were denied luxury food items, the "orderly and industrious" got "preference" in the allocation of such items. Also, throughout the period 1795–1800, the managers regularly authorized extra food, clothing, and, in some cases, money to persons judged particularly valuable for their "good Behaviour & Industry." Those people with special skills or those who performed administrative duties were especially singled out for rewards.[52]

The guardianship managers' acceptance of the ideals of the contributorship was clearly demonstrated by the rules they adopted for the house. The old rules remained in force from 1788 to 1796, when they were revised and printed. These rules closely followed the old set, with only two significant changes. Henceforth, persons with infectious diseases were denied admittance; if the doctor determined that anyone in the house had such a disease, that person was to be immediately returned to the care of the overseer who had sent him or her. The other major change was one of tone. The earlier rules demanded that paupers behave "submissively to their superiors & Governors." This wording was slightly softened to say that the poor should behave "respectfully to their superiors and governors."[53] Thus, under the guardianship, the house retained its old atmosphere, and the poor continued, as they had done under the contributorship, to shun it. In 1796, Ann Newton, an old and infirm woman who lacked both funds and companions, refused to enter the house because her deceased husband had requested that she might never go there. Elizabeth Mull, living in what was described as a pitiable situation, similarly could not be convinced to go to the house, although the overseers refused to do anything further for her.[54] Even with the poor law of 1789, the house of employment of 1800 was strikingly like the house of employment of prerevolutionary days.

The American Revolution helped transform the structure of public poor relief in Philadelphia by allowing the overseers the opportunity to overthrow what they saw as the aristocratic contributorship system that emphasized reform rather than relief of the worthy poor. Four years before the 1788 "Revolution," even the managers of the contributorship seemed to have conceded that the poor who had maintained good reputations before entering the house deserved special consideration. The guardians, having wrenched control from the contributors, did, like society at large, seek to distinguish carefully between the worthy and unworthy poor. Nevertheless, the ideal of reform and control did not die once the guardians directed public poor relief. They eliminated outpensions, so long supported by the overseers, lest such aid lead to vice and immorality among the recipients. Additionally, the poor in the house, no matter what their reputation for worthiness, were still expected to behave submissively and deferentially to their superiors. Such was the case because the guardians, like the contributors, came to believe that many people fell into poverty only because of idle ways and love of alcohol and that these evil habits could be reformed by the hard work and deferential behavior required in the bettering house. Indeed, the guardians, most of whom were drawn from the mercantile world the old managers inhabited, came to sound and act like the contributorship officials. Certainly the members of Philadelphia's mercantile community who were involved in public poor relief tended to stress that control of the poor was more important than relief. Unquestionably, the ideal of using public poor relief as an instrument of social control and reform became more deeply entrenched even as the form of relief was transformed. This increased emphasis on distinguishing among different segments of the poor, and the use of relief as a force for social control and reformation of the poor, also characterized Philadelphia's postindependence system of private poor relief.

7

Private Poor Relief: Increasing Emphasis on "A Judicious Choice of Objects"

Important elements of Philadelphia's system of private poor relief held constant in the years 1760–1800. Citizens, perceiving a need for extensive private charity, provided a wide and impressive range of relief for the poor. Throughout the period, some private relief was extended on the basis of what Raymond Mohl, examining New York City of the same period, called "humanitarianism."[1] But in Philadelphia humanitarianism often marched hand in hand with a desire to control or mold the needy in the image of the worthy poor. This was done by limiting private assistance to the industrious poor who could be recommended by respectable or reputable citizens. In such cases, "Christian kindness" was tempered by the effort to make "a judicious choice of objects."[2] The intertwining of relief and control constituted an organic part of private poor relief in the Philadelphia of 1760–1800.

Continuity there was. But Philadelphia's network of private poor relief underwent significant, if at times subtle, change as the colonial city gave way to the revolutionary city. At least three important areas of change can be discerned. First, the postwar era saw a marked expansion of the number of groups, agencies, and proffered plans for assisting the needy. This increased level of activity sprang not just from the growth of population, but also from (1) the greater concern of the potentially poor with directing their own relief and (2) an increased tendency for the nonpoor to use charity as an instrument for anchoring the poor to industrious poverty. Second, in the postindependence era, the granting or withholding of charity reflected the more precise definitions formulated by the dominant society to differentiate between the honest and the vicious poor. Third, the growing emphasis on private charity as an instrument of social control led to the creation of new organizational forms to mold or reform the needy in the image of the submissive, worthy poor.

Throughout the years 1760–1800, Philadelphians asserted that poverty might quickly overtake anyone. Harsh winters or epidemics could plunge part or much of the city into distress. Fire could easily ravage the city, and at least one citizen noted for helping those victimized by fire found himself an object of charity after a fire. Economic failure caused by misfortune might put the most affluent into debtors' prison. Such potential dangers produced outpourings of charity and gave rise to the theme that granting charity constituted a form of insurance. Given the many uncertainties of the day, that insurance certainly seemed necessary. "The cup of misfortune goes round," one Philadelphian forcefully reminded his neighbors, "and it is not in human wisdom to put it by."[3]

Some Philadelphians refused to rely upon the insurance of charity granted by others. Throughout the years 1760–1800, but increasingly after the achievement of independence, groups of Philadelphians banded together in mutual aid societies to fend off potential poverty. Between 1760 and 1785, three occupational groups—carpenters, ship masters, and Episcopal ministers—established societies that assisted members or the widows of members who fell into poverty. A group of Moravians created a similar society in 1770.[4] In the years after 1785, the number of mutual aid societies nearly tripled as, according to a citizen, "the spirit of association" raged in the city. By the end of the century, trade groups, including grocers, pilots, printers, stonecutters, barbers, and bricklayers, had founded groups to aid widows, orphans, and, in some cases, members in need. Ethnic and racial groups including Scots, Germans, and blacks followed the lead of the Moravians and established similar societies. In

1797 members of St. Thomas' African Church joined together against the dangers of poverty.[5]

The creation and dramatic multiplication of mutual aid societies in the years 1785–1800 illustrate that citizens were aware, especially after 1785, that even a skilled trade did not offer sure protection against misfortune and possible poverty. Therefore, Philadelphia workers increasingly embraced the ideal of mutualism, which allowed them to control their own poor relief.[6]

By design, a mutual aid society benefited a limited group of individuals, who voluntarily joined it. The vast majority of Philadelphia's needy had to rely upon public or private charity controlled by others. Private citizens of Philadelphia at times responded to the needs of the poor because of a humanitarian concern for the unfortunate. Of course, some humanitarian endeavors proved fruitless or were only slowly implemented. In 1779 and again in 1791, proposals were made to loan money, at low interest, to the poor; in 1795 "A Plan for Affording Relief to the Indigent Blind" was published. None of these suggestions produced results. Calls for a society to provide meat at a low cost and for a subscription to lower the cost of bread went unanswered, as did a 1796 suggestion for formulating a society for "providing the poor with cheap food during the present Scarcity."[7]

Such efforts probably proved less than total failures. Suggestions about helping the poor, when combined with protests that merchants gouged the poor, may have made Philadelphians more receptive to other calls for relieving the needy.[8] Also, one effort begun in 1800 did lead to success three years later. In December 1800, "Philadelphus" published a series of essays urging citizens to feed the "wretched objects" who thronged the streets of Philadelphia during the winter. His proposal, that public kitchens be opened to provide the poor with good and wholesome food at a very moderate expense, drew favorable comment, and in 1803 private financing enabled the first soup kitchen for the poor to open in Philadelphia.[9] Similarly, after numerous attempts to create a permanent system for providing wood at low rates or for free, a privately financed fund was established in 1793 to supply needy inhabitants of the city with fuel in the winter. This fund still aided the poor as the century ended.[10]

These unsuccessful or only slowly implemented programs merely highlight the many humanitarian efforts undertaken in the Philadelphia of 1760–1800. Some of these programs sprang from the problems caused by natural disasters. When winter closed the port of Philadelphia and, as a result, threw many poor persons out of work, citizens created subscription funds to assist them.[11] If fire reduced people to distress and poverty, charity subscriptions also became the order of the day.[12] When the yellow fever of 1793 broke over the city, the inhabitants quickly saw the need for relief. Cases of yellow fever started appearing in August 1793, and by early September most who could afford to flee the city had gone. Mechanics and artisans, suddenly lacking employment, swelled the ranks of the poor. By the middle of September, a committee of volunteers began distributing relief to the distressed. A month later, upwards of one thousand families a week received support from this committee. When frost ended the epidemic in November, over thirty-six thousand dollars had been spent housing the sick and assisting the needy, with slightly less than ten thousand dollars of that amount going to help the poor subsist.[13]

Organizations designed to carry on their activities over a long period also displayed humanitarian ideals. The German Society was founded in 1764, primarily by people from the mercantile and professional ranks. Called into existence by the pitiable plight of recently arrived German immigrants, many of whom were destined to become indentured servants, the society became as much an immigrant protection as an immigrant aid society. This group vigorously and effectively urged passage of laws to curb abuses in the immigrant transportation system and in the binding of indentured servants. When it appeared that immigrants faced overcharges for their passage, the society went to court to get the fares lowered. The society's fundamental articles specified that relief should be given only to newly arrived Germans, and with few exceptions, the German Society adhered to this rule. The minutes of the society do not reveal the extent of its aid, nor do they suggest that any test was applied to see that only the industrious received assistance.[14]

The philosophy and actions of the Philadelphia Society for Assisting Distressed Prisoners also seems to offer a clear example of a private charity organization formed solely on a humanitarian basis. Organized in February of 1776, this society stated that the sufferings of many languishing in jail called forth "an earnest sympathy for their miseries." Observing that criminals as well as debtors needed assistance, the society proclaimed as its single goal looking after the comfort and support of any needy prisoner. No desire was expressed to superintend the morals of the prisoners, to differentiate among them, or to use charity funds as rewards or punishments for different classes of prisoners. The society observed that its resources would not be used to pay prison fees or to obtain discharges, since the design of the society was "only to alleviate some of the miseries which are the general attendants on jails."[15]

Although this society was clearly a humanitarian endeavor, it was probably called into existence by more than the well-known plight of the normal prison population. By the time the society was formed, people, often of Quaker persuasion, were being tossed into jail on suspicion of opposing the revolutionary movement. Thus, Quakers and others who might not wholeheartedly support the war effort could see this charity work as benefiting their own kind as well as the ordinary prisoners. And this society was, in the main, created by persons who might indeed feel a special affinity with the new breed of prisoner: most of its founders were Quakers. Two of the Quakers who helped establish the organization were free or fighting Quakers who openly joined the American war effort, and another founder, a Lutheran, was also an ardent patriot. Nevertheless, at least six of the thirteen founders stayed in Philadelphia during the British occupation, and five of them faced double taxation in 1779 for failure to take the oath of allegiance to the revolutionary government. Heavily laden as it was with Quakers and a goodly portion of less than ardent patriots, the society may have embarked on its charity effort, at least in part, for special and self-interested reasons.[16]

Philadelphia's humanitarian concern for the plight of the poor can also be seen in the city's response to the danger of smallpox. To help spread knowledge about inoculation against the disease,

Benjamin Franklin distributed free pamphlets. A newspaper essayist who shared the same concern urged anyone who knew of a cure for the disease to offer the information without demanding financial remuneration. In 1774 citizens, mostly Quakers from the mercantile community, banded together in the Society for Inoculating the Poor. The need was obvious: of the 1,344 people who died in the city in the preceding year, about 300 had died of smallpox, and most of these were the children of poor parents who could not afford to pay for inoculation. The society employed eight physicians who inoculated the poor, gave them medicines and advice, and even visited their homes. All these services were provided without charge. Unfortunately, this society apparently fell victim to the war and thus functioned for only a short time.[17]

Obviously, humanitarian concern for the poor existed in the Philadelphia of 1760–1800. But as other efforts to meet the medical needs of the poor demonstrate, humanitarianism often united with a desire to see that only the "worthy" poor gained private relief or that the poor so relieved should serve the needs of the medical profession and society at large. The Pennsylvania Hospital, founded in 1751, aided the sick poor throughout the period. But, the hospital, which was dominated primarily by Quakers, aimed to serve only the worthy, industrious poor. Exceptions were made and especially so if a poor person suffered from a disease the doctors of the hospital wanted to study. Still, by design, few poor save those perceived as being among the worthy found their way into the institution, since a recommendation was required for admittance.[18]

Throughout the period, individual physicians and dentists often offered their services to the poor without charge, but some demanded that the poor be "well recommended."[19] Some physicians even expected their aid to produce tangible rewards for themselves. In 1794 a Dr. Price established a lying-in hospital for indigent Philadelphia women. This service would benefit the poor and also, as Dr. Price openly said, improve his course on midwifery. Benjamin Rush, who advocated assisting the poor without charge, told students they would learn more in one year working with the poor than in seven years of hospital practice.[20]

The educational benefit gained by the medical profession from the poor did not end with this symbiotic relationship. The poor could also serve once dead. In 1765, Dr. William Shippen, publicly explaining how he obtained cadavers, denied taking bodies from church or private burial places. He stated that only the bodies of people who committed suicide or those publicly executed were used for study, "except now and then one [was obtained] from the Potters Field, whose death was owing to some particular disease." The Potters Field was the burial place of many of the city's poor, especially blacks, and of friendless strangers who died in the city.[21]

The actions of dentists and physicians who limited aid to the well-recommended poor illustrate the dual nature of Philadelphia private poor relief in the period 1760–1800. It often sprang from more than abstract humanitarianism; aid and control were often interlocking goals.

The dual nature of the city's private poor relief system is clearly demonstrated by the philosophy and functioning of church philanthropy. Throughout the period in question, religious organizations undertook extensive and impressive projects to aid the needy of their faith. Such efforts were anchored in Christian kindness, but they also reflected the ideal that benevolence should benefit the worthy poor or lead the poor onto the path of worthy poverty. The Society of Friends, which firmly believed that it should superintend the morals of its members, maintained a structure of poor relief that closely paralleled the public system. In 1713, almost two decades before the first city almshouse was built, the Friends opened an almshouse that functioned throughout the rest of the century.[22] Before anyone gained entrance to it, a careful check was made to insure that he or she was not only a Quaker but also of good moral character.[23] A visiting committee established rules for the almshouse and saw that "disorderly" people were removed.[24]

The Episcopal Christ Church and its daughter institution, St. Peter's Church, also operated an extensive program of poor relief. In the 1760–1800 period, regular charity sermons raised money for the congregation's poor and for people in prison. The succor given to prisoners went primarily, or solely, to debtors.[25] The church officers distributing such aid were ordered "to use great Care" so that only "the most deserving & necessitous re-

Private Poor Relief

ceived assistance."[26] After 1773, the congregation ran its own almshouse. However, only "poor and distressed" women of the Episcopalian faith could gain admission, and the widows of clergymen were given preference. Outdoor pensions, including provisions to pay for rent, went to men and women who could not be accommodated in the almshouse.[27] To enter that institution, or to receive any aid, one needed recommendations from "respectable" members of the congregation. And, of course, those receiving assistance were expected to maintain a reputable deportment.[28]

Other religious denominations also engaged in charitable endeavors that required the members to display a moral, worthy life-style. The poor of the First Baptist Church received money for rent, medical costs, and basic living expenses. When a member of the congregation met with a loss because of fire, a collection was made for him. Because people receiving such assistance were expected, as were all members, to avoid sinful acts, it must have been with a feeling of anger that the recorder wrote in 1763: "John Williams after receiving charity of the church, suspended for drunkenness—"[29] The Catholic congregation of St. Mary's also helped "well recommended" poor members.[30]

The ethnically based St. Andrews Society and Society of the Sons of St. George, each founded by leading Philadelphians, also followed the dual pattern that united concern for the poor with a desire to support industrious poverty for the protection of society at large.[31] The St. Andrews Society, founded by Scots in 1749, was designed as a social and a relief society. The Society of the Sons of St. George, created by Englishmen in 1772 as a social organization, quickly became a charity-granting agency as well. These societies, both of which ceased meeting during the war and did not begin again until the late 1780s, functioned in similar ways.[32] Each group restricted its activites to helping fellow countrymen, including city residents as well as immigrants. A wide range of assistance was undertaken. Money went for immediate relief, to prevent seizure of goods for debt, to help people suffering losses from fires, and to pay for funerals and for medical costs. Grants were also given to persons moving to other parts of America or returning to their native land. Occasionally money was loaned or given to those establishing businesses. Referrals and recommendations for employment were granted.[33] Before dispensing assistance, these societies examined the applicant's moral character, and anyone not considered industrious and sober did not receive aid.[34]

The assistance offered by the Philadelphia Society for Alleviating the Miseries of Public Prisons (founded in 1787) also emphasized the dual goal of private poor relief. This prison society modeled itself on the 1776 Philadelphia Society for Assisting Distressed Prisoners. The new organization, unlike its predecessor, was not predominantly a Quaker creation. The first president of the 1787 society was an Episcopalian; one vice-president was a Lutheran and the other a Quaker. But the founders of the society were, as was typical with such organizations, primarily drawn from the city's mercantile and professional ranks.[35]

The 1787 society, like its predecessor, was reportedly called into existence by a sensitivity to the miseries of Philadelphia prisons. But, unlike its predecessor, the 1787 society believed that it must watch over the morals of prisoners. This organization also departed from its 1776 counterpart by pledging to secure the release of persons incarcerated for owing small sums. However, before paying a prisoner's fees or small debts, the society followed the dual goal by investigating the prisoner's reputation and character to insure that he or she was a "proper object."[36]

The response to the yellow fever outbreaks of 1797 and 1798 reveals the same trend toward greater emphasis on the dual goal of aid and control. During the yellow fever scourge of 1793, relief was apparently given without any differentiation between the industrious and the idle poor; nor was there a clear effort to control the poor. But after 1793, Philadelphia's response to yellow fever embodied the dual pattern of poor relief.

In mid-August 1797, the dreaded fever again visited Philadelphia.[37] On August 19 an essayist urged those who could to flee the city. But he recognized that flight was impossible for "the poor, who have neither places to remove to, or funds for their support, as they depend on their daily labour, for daily supplies." Tents should be erected on the bank of the Schuylkill, the writer said, so the poor could move there and be supported with little expense. It is not clear if this essay influenced the newly created board of health, but on August 21 it reported that 180 tents were ready for use.[38] People had to apply for orders from designated officials if they wanted to move to the tents.[39] On August 29 the legislature voted ten thousand dollars to help relieve the sick and indigent in Philadelphia. By September 6, as a committee began distributing these and other donated monies, a significant new policy was implemented: to receive aid, the poor had to produce recommendations signed by "one or more reputable inhabitants."[40] This requirement graphically demonstrates how deeply the recommendation system had become entrenched in the private poor relief system.

When yellow fever reappeared in 1798, the utilization of relief as an instrument of social control became even more pronounced. Citizens who could not move to the tents and who needed aid again had to produce "certificates from one or more respectable inhabitants." Poor people wanting to enter the encampments provided for the destitute had to do more than apply for admission; this time they had to obtain recommendations from respectable citizens.[41] Those housed in the newly created encampment on Master's Field in the Northern Liberties were also expected to follow published rules designed to keep the camp well regulated. Liquor was, of course, forbidden. Slight offenses were punished by the temporary withdrawal of food grants. Persons committing more serious offenses were to be thrown out of the camp. The regulations were not taken lightly. Armed guards patrolled the area "to preserve order and prevent any individuals from transgressing the rules." As "A Friend to Merit" contended, the encampment was valuable because it preserved the morals as well as the lives of the poor.[42] In 1798 aiding the poor recommended by the respectable citizens, protecting the morals of the poor, and insuring that the poor were orderly seemed as important as relief itself.

Philadelphians pursued goals of private poor relief that wedded aid to social control in the prerevolutionary era. But the use of private poor relief as an instrument of social control became even more pronounced in the postwar period. The humanitarianism of the 1776 prison society gave way by 1787 to the ideal of giving special consideration to the worthy poor and to controlling the morals of prisoners. The first great yellow fever disaster of 1793 caught Philadelphians off guard, and they responded with relief unfettered by an effort to distinguish among and to control the poor. But when yellow fever struck in 1797 and 1798, the dual goal replaced the simple humanitarianism of 1793. These are not isolated examples. In postwar Philadelphia, the dispensing of private charity increasingly and more stridently emphasized the dual goal of matching Christian kindness with a judicious choice of worthy recipients.

The more vigorous pursuit of the dual goal is illustrated by the increasingly sophisticated way in which private charity groups of the revolutionary city joined in the effort to distinguish between the worthy and the vicious poor. When creating the Philadelphia Dispensary for the Medical Relief of the Poor in 1786, the founders proved especially sensitive to the needs and feelings of the industrious poor. All large cities contained many sick poor "whose former circumstances and habits of independence will not permit them to expose themselves as patients in a public hospital," and these people deserved aid given with a due regard for their laudable deportment. By treating the poor as outpatients, the dispensary attempted to allow the breadwinner to continue working while it granted the sick relief "in a manner perfectly consistent with those noble feelings of the human heart, which are inseparable from virtuous poverty."[43]

Although many of the founders of the dispensary were Quakers, the agency was brought into existence by people who represented a cross section of Philadelphia's religious spectrum. To a man, however, the founders were physicians, merchants, or ministers. They established the dispensary as a contributorship, and for every guinea donated each year, a member had the right to have two poor people helped at any one time. The individual contributors determined if the former circumstances and habits of independence made a person worthy of relief. Poor persons unable to convince a contributor of their virtuous poverty need not apply. The inability to gain a recommendation weighed heavily on the poor, since the dispensary was designed to meet all medical needs, including obstetrical care. Its staff consisted of the six attending and four consulting physicians, as well as an apothecary. People unable to go to the dispensary were visited in their homes. Special efforts were made to inoculate the poor against smallpox, and when the poor needed medicine, that too was provided. But to receive any aid, a person had to produce a contributor's written recommendation.[44]

The dispensary touched the lives of many poor Philadelphians. The institution's minutes indicate that, from 1786 to December 1800, a total of 16,855 people procured assistance; in 1800–1801 an additional 2,335 patients were helped.[45] Although some of the needy surely went to it more than once, probably no medical institution in Philadelphia helped more poor people than did the dispensary. But it followed the dual goal of aid and control by utilizing a carefully refined definition of worthy poverty.

The increasing effort to use privately funded philanthropy as an instrument for social engineering in the revolutionary city also called forth two significant new organizational forms: the reclamation society and the uplift society. Reclamation societies tried to lure the idle or vicious poor back onto the path of industry and virtue. Uplift organizations aimed to keep the potentially poor from falling into poverty or to lift those in poverty by teaching the glories of industrious poverty. These new forms of private charity were designed to aid the poor and also to benefit society at large. With the emergence of reclamation and uplift societies, the postwar use of private poor relief as an instrument of social control reached new, more sophisticated heights.

Privately based reclamation societies did not make their appearance until late in the period. Founded in 1795, the Female Society for Assisting the Distressed, which limited membership to Quaker women, aided people without regard to race, religion, or national origin. Although assistance went to both the worthy and the unworthy poor, the Female Society gave special attention to reclamation. Thus, the founders of the society recommended to the membership, "when humanity degraded by vice is cast in their way, to compare the situation of the melancholy objects with their own—to reflect on their unguarded Education and the exposure to trials and temptations which in the Bosom of affluence and under the shelter of a Parental Wing they have never known—this will incline them [the society members] to cast over the failings of an unhappy fellow Creature the Veil of Charity and by a benevolent attention to their wants and sufferings endeavor to allure them into the path of virtue."[46]

The impressive efforts of these Quaker women to aid and reform typically took them to dingy cellars and garrets where people lived "in extreme wretchedness," sometimes without furniture save for an old door thinly covered with shavings, which served as a bed. Persons like Susannah Weiss, who was recommended as an honest industrious woman, got help from the Female Society when she had had to sell her clothes to buy firewood.[47] The society engaged in a wide variety of relief activities: members distributed food, clothing, fuel, furniture, and money and obtained medical assistance for the sick. Poor women who ran small shops had their stock replenished, and women who could not do strenuous labor received items to spin so that they could support themselves. These Quaker women worked to see that persons they deemed entitled to public outdoor relief obtained it, and those who might be sheltered in the city's house of employment were urged to go there. When it seemed appropriate that other private relief groups help a poor person, the society informed those associations of the individual's plight.[48]

In 1798 the society opened a house of employment, or house of industry, as it was later called. The house was, again, designed to aid and also, where necessary, reform the poor. Women could go to the house and receive wages for spinning while a nurse cared for their children. In addition, both women and children received three sound meals a day. The society believed that contact with the house would lead, or keep, the women and their children on a virtuous path. Persons seeking employment were told to see that they and their children arrived on time and to "come clean and decent." The rules stipulated that the women should work diligently and without interruption. At the evening meal, the paupers listened to a chapter of the Bible or a short passage from some other book adapted to the "situations and capacities" of the poor. It was also "requested" that the women and children "observe a quiet orderly conduct on leaving the house." In sum, the poor were told to adopt and exemplify the life-style of the industrious, deferential poor. This institution, which stressed relief, control, and reformation of the poor, functioned well into the nineteenth century.[49]

Despite the great breadth of activities undertaken by the Female Society, it assisted only a few poor people. Rarely did more than fifty people at any given time receive aid in their homes; as late as 1800, the average number of women and children accommodated by the house of industry was no greater. However, when the organization received donations during yellow fever or winter periods, it was able to help many more of the needy. One donation of £132 provided relief for 106 people.[50] Even operating on this limited scale, the society offered real and continuing support to Philadelphia's most destitute poor, and in so doing it sincerely hoped to "allure" those "degraded by vice . . . into the path of virtue."

A more specialized reclamation society for women came into existence in 1800. The Magdalen Society, as its name indicated, sought "to aid in the restoring to the paths of virtue" women who had become prostitutes. This society, unlike most other private charity organizations, was founded by people who were not drawn primarily from the mercantile or professional ranks of the city. In offering advice to the fallen women, the society stressed that "good Behaviour is the surest way to obtain friends and reputation." In seeking "to return to the World," the women should, of course, "be diligent and industrious" while at work, and they should also "be neat and cleanly" in their dress while avoiding "Finery or Fashion." Lest the women receive help and then slip back toward "Destruction," the society warned that "the Hand, which hath now relieved you, can never be extended to you again."[51] This organization thus combined aid for the poor with a desire to protect moral virtue in the city. While functioning only for a brief period at the end of the century, this institution signaled the movement toward the extensive system of reformation associations that flourished in the nineteenth-century city.[52]

Whereas reclamation societies sought to protect society by reforming those who supposedly had fallen away from virtuous poverty or who had never been numbered among the worthy, uplift societies, also a product of the postwar era, joined in the effort to protect society by trying to keep people from falling into poverty or by showing the potentially dangerous poor the glories of honest poverty. The ethnic aid societies, which often focused attention on the needs of immigrants, typically mixed socializing with efforts to relieve the worthy poor. Such organizations were not uplift societies. But in 1794 a group of inhabitants primarily from the mercantile and professional ranks, many of whom may have been themselves recent immigrants, founded an innovative immigrant assistance society.[53] This organization, the Philadelphia Society for the Information and Assistance of Persons Emigrating from Foreign Countries, blended humanitarianism with a conscious desire to benefit the city as well as to provide uplift. Pledging itself to give financial assistance to immigrants from any country, the society did not specify that aid would be limited solely to the industrious but rather noted: "Considering all men as brothers, it will be our pleasure to hold succour to a fellow creature, because he is a man, evidently in want of it." This stated emphasis on relief without concern for a poor person's worthiness, if implemented, shows that not all private relief efforts of the late eighteenth century sought to distinguish between the worthy and the idle poor.

As this society's name suggests, it attempted to do more than give immediate relief to the needy immigrant. A principal object was "by advice to render the necessitous independent upon others, to enable him to direct his talents to their proper ends, and to restore him at once to the community and himself." To keep newly arrived immigrants from falling into distress, the society attempted to discover the names and addresses of persons who ran boardinghouses and to ascertain the cost of such accommodations. Having this information would obviously benefit immigrants, but, for the long term, the vital issue was finding regular employment for them. To accomplish this goal, the society tried to gather and disseminate information on job opportunities anywhere in the United States.[54] These were surely difficult tasks which may explain why the organization stopped functioning shortly after 1800.[55]

This society's limited success does not detract from its innovative character. Its founders perceived that immigrants faced

Private Poor Relief

problems that could not be handled just by ethnic organizations; the needs of the city and the nation demanded that all immigrants be helped. By going beyond mere immediate relief to focus on finding employment, the society attempted to prevent distress. Keeping immigrants out of poverty obviously benefited society at large as well as the new arrivals. As Philadelphians of the postwar era stressed, immigrants might resort to a life of vice and crime because work was often hard to find. By laboring to break this cycle, the Information and Assistance Society attempted to keep immigrants from being a "dangerous acquisition." Indeed, the society believed that immigrants should not be allowed to form a pool of unemployed or underemployed workers that could be tapped as needed to benefit the business community of the city: the danger to the social fabric was too great. Jobs had to be obtained for immigrants even if that meant finding them work elsewhere in America. The Information and Assistance Society thus displayed more concern for maintaining order in the city than for fostering its economic growth.

Newly arrived immigrants were not the only potentially poor group that Philadelphians perceived as a possibly dangerous acquisition. It was argued that free blacks, most of whom were poor, also needed to be uplifted. This issue became all the more pressing when Pennsylvania, as a direct result of revolutionary ideology, passed a law in 1780 providing for the gradual abolition of slavery. Free blacks, it was thought, required assistance and also needed to be shown the benefits of honest poverty. An uplift society would help them and, not incidentally, society at large. To meet this perceived need, the Committee for Improving the Condition of the Free Blacks, a daughter institution of the Quaker-dominated Pennsylvania Abolition Society, came into being in late 1789. The committee, consisting of twenty-four persons elected annually, worked through four subcommittees. A committee of inspection was to "superintend the morals, general conduct, and ordinary situation of the free negroes; and afford them instruction and advice, occasional charities, protection from wrongs, &c." A committee of guardians placed children in apprenticeships with "suitable" persons. The guardians also worked to insure that the Abolition Society obtained the right of guardianship over people so bound. The committee on education was to see that black children received schooling. Such children were, it was specifically noted, to "receive a deep impression of the most important, and generally acknowledged, moral and religious principles." A committee of employ tried to procure constant employment for free blacks able to work, "as the want of this would occasion poverty, idleness and many vicious habits."[56]

This program of action reveals that the founders of the committee were as concerned with maintaining social order as with helping blacks. It is an open question which goal was more important, or if they were coequal. Certainly the committee poured great effort into what it called superintending the social actions of blacks. The committee of guardians, as well as the committee of inspectors, frequently visited blacks in Southwark to give them "friendly admonitions against . . . improprieties in their conduct." In the summer of 1797, a number of committee members stated their belief that "much good would result from proper endeavours to discourage the practice which sometimes prevails amongst the black People, of assembling in large numbers to dance and frolic." To eliminate these "irregularities and disorders," three groups of committeemen marched into the southern parts of the city and suburbs. In two houses where "indecent and licentious" actions were occurring, "much expostulation was used and discouragement given to such practices."[57]

This procedure seemed so valuable and necessary that a resolution was passed providing that various of the committees of the organization were to work together "to carry the Business into further effect as they may judge expedient." In consequence, a special committee "for suppressing of irregularities amongst the Black People" was formed, which, with other similar committees, functioned with various degrees of intensity through 1798.[58]

While pouring great energy into supervising the morals of free blacks, the committee performed a variety of good works that materially benefited them.[59] The committee usually could place those blacks who applied for help in finding work. Whenever possible, black children were apprenticed into trades offering good prospects for future economic security. The committee also expanded the educational opportunities available to black youths. Financial and other assistance flowed to large numbers of blacks not entitled to public poor relief, and, at least once, this agency advanced a loan to help establish a manufacturing enterprise run by blacks. Further, when masters abused their apprentices, the committee of guardians intervened; when laws on vagrants and runaways seemingly discriminated against blacks, the committee worked to change these laws.[60] The committee, then, provided valuable assistance for free blacks, but it never forgot that one of its main goals was to ensure that they fit the mold of the industrious. Certainly blacks, most of whom were numbered among the poor, should, as the committee saw it, realize their proper station and act accordingly. Thus the committee expected the blacks it aided to display "a becoming deference" and was pleased when they did so.[61]

The Female Association of Philadelphia, which began functioning in 1800, maintained that even the "worthy" poor needed to be uplifted. The association, which offered aid to women "of good characters" and their children, worked through local managers who visited the home of each applicant "to examine particularly into her moral character, her situation, her habits and mode of life, her wants, and the best means of affording relief, so that assistance may not be extended to the vicious, and idle, when it is due only to the honest and industrious suffering under sickness and misfortune." Emphasizing that "a permanent improvement in the condition of such poor has been aimed at, rather than their temporary relief," the association delineated its view of the importance of uplift by proclaiming that "it endeavors by advice, by direction and encouragement, wishing thereby, to rouse them from that state of apathy and indolence, into which their situation tends to throw them, and to make them useful to the community."[62]

Philadelphians thus maintained a complex structure of private poor relief in the years 1760–1800. Although that system was not totally transformed during the revolutionary era, it underwent significant modification, especially in the last decade and a half of the century. One important suggestive measure of change comes from the development of mutual aid societies, which increased dramatically in number in the years after the war. Whatever else it shows, this increase illustrates an effort to avoid being dependent upon the largess of others. The quest for such independence may merely reflect a natural desire to be secure in the knowledge that, if needed, aid will be forthcoming. But the quest may also reflect the fact that potentially poor Philadelphians did not want to be forced to exhibit the becoming deference that private poor relief groups usually expected. Deference was not a minor issue. It implied that the poor person met the standards of life-style set by those controlling poor relief, and, in the same years when the number of mutual aid societies rose sharply, private poor relief agencies increasingly acted upon the ideal that relief could and should be used as an instrument of social control.

Throughout the period under study, one can find examples of efforts to aid the poor that seem rooted simply in a basic humanitarian concern. This is especially true of the responses when natural disasters, such as severe winters, fires, and the yellow fever of 1793, reduced people to great distress. Yet by the end of the period even the assistance called forth by natural disasters often became an instrument for social control. A minor but illustrative example occurred in 1791. After an extensive fire burned through eighteen to twenty buildings, most of which were wooden structures, the normal practice of raising money by subscription was implemented. But those gathering aid to help fire victims refused to assist owners of frame houses because such buildings were "considered dangerous to the community, and ought rather to be discountenanced."[63] This action clearly suggested that those who did not conform to the needs of the society at large would be punished. One was obliged to accept the views of those who controlled private charity, or one would have to do without private poor relief. The shifting response to natural disasters and the increasing use of private benevolence as a tool for social control are also demonstrated by the different responses to yellow fever outbreaks: the humanitarianism of 1793 gave way, in 1797 and 1798, to the pursuit of the dual goal.

The shift in Philadelphia's response to natural disasters underlines the fact that private charity in the Philadelphia of 1760–1800 was rooted, and after the achievement of independence more firmly so, in the dual interlocking ideal that (1) private poor relief should aid the worthy poor, but (2) such relief should also control the poor and, where necessary, force them to follow the path of deferential industrious poverty. In the postwar years, private charities worked toward this dual goal in more sophisticated and innovative ways, as the efforts of the dispensary, reclamation societies, and uplift agencies reveal.

The groups and organizations that pursued the dual goal often had a strong Quaker influence, but representatives from Philadelphia's wide spectrum of religious denominations joined in the effort. The same cannot be said of the city's economic groupings. The private relief organizations that embraced this dual goal were almost invariably founded by people from the mercantile ranks and, to a lesser extent, people in the professions. Only rarely was a mechanic or artisan either a founder or early director of a relief society of this sort. Thus, in private charity as in public poor relief, it was the economically secure mercantile element, often supported by established members of the professions, who most emphasized that poor relief should control and reform as well as aid the needy. In this way, those who had gotten the most from the established socioeconomic system worked to keep control in their hands.

Social control was, thus, an increasingly organic part of Philadelphia's private aid to the poor in the period of the mid-1780s and following. Perhaps the clearest example of this intensified desire to direct and control the poor can be seen by examining yet another effort to "uplift" the poor. Indeed, nowhere is the postindependence quest for social control of the poor more pellucidly demonstrated than in the efforts to provide education for the city's poor.

8

*Educating the Poor: The Postwar Quest
for Teaching Industrious Poverty*

Philadelphians evidenced little zeal for educating the poor in the years between 1760 and 1785. But beginning in 1785 and throughout the rest of the century, an explosion of interest in educating the poor occurred. Some Philadelphians who sought increasing educational opportunities for the poor voiced a democratic credo: educating the poor would offer them the chance to rise if they had talent, and it would afford them greater opportunity to be partners in the political process. These citizens can reasonably be described as the "Optimists" for they voiced faith in the inherent worthiness of the poor. But few working to provide educational opportunities for the poor were Optimists, and their quest for a free, secular educational system failed. The great majority of those who proclaimed the need for educating the poor in the period 1785–1800 emphasized the threat posed by the uneducated poor. These "Pessimists" did not see the poor as essentially worthy, nor did they hold that education might allow the poor to improve their social or political position. The Pessimists felt that education should train the poor to accept peacefully and deferentially an inferior station in life. A desire to control the poor, rather than a desire for their advancement, motivated the Pessimists' actions, and the educational structure instituted in the last fifteen years of the century embodied their views.

In the quarter century following 1760, Philadelphians displayed a limited interest in increasing educational opportunities for the poor. People in charge of binding out poor children attempted to see that they received some educational training. Boys were normally to receive instruction in reading, writing, and arithmetic; girls were to be taught to read and write. Yet it proved very difficult to know if such stipulated instruction was actually given.[1]

Even before 1760, the College of Philadelphia maintained a charity school for both boys and girls. The existence of this charity school did not, however, reflect a deep commitment to educating the poor. The proposal to establish this school to provide the poor with free instruction "in useful Literature and the Knowledge of the Christian Religion" originated in 1740 and was probably inspired by the visitations of the Reverend George Whitefield. Trustees erected a building to house the charity school and to serve as a meeting hall, but the school never began operation. When this building was sold to the group, headed by Benjamin Franklin, that wanted to create an institution of higher education in the city, the original trustees insisted that the new institution operate a charity school. The new directors unenthusiastically concurred. Franklin and the other founders of the college were interested in higher education, rather than education for the poor.[2] This lack of interest was reflected in the directors' *Proposals*, written by Franklin in 1749, which nowhere argued that education for the poor was important, and in the 1749 constitution of the new institution, which stipulated that "when the Fund is sufficient to bear the Charge, which it is hoped, thro' the Bounty and Charity of well-disposed Persons, will soon come to pass, poor Children shall be admitted and taught gratis, what shall be thought suitable to their Capacities and Circumstances."[3] By 1765 it was said that several hundred "destitute" youths had received some training at the school and thus been "rendered useful to the Community." Still, between its opening in 1751 and 1790, only about twelve hundred students—an average of less than thirty-one pupils a year—received instruction at the charity school.[4]

Efforts to provide educational opportunities for the children of the poor were not limited to public institutions. In 1773 an anonymous benefactor or benefactors raised three hundred pounds to found a charity school in the southern part of Philadelphia. The goal was to educate thirty poor children for a period of five years, and it was hoped that, once established, the school would receive the funds necessary to perpetuate it. A school did open on Lombard Street, but, as records do not mention its operation after 1773, quite possibly it became one of the educational casualties of the war.[5]

Religious and ethnic groups also provided educational opportunities for segments of Philadelphia's poorer element.[6] Quakers provided education for both poor boys and girls throughout the late colonial period. In 1770, Quakers established a school for blacks, and in 1784 a second school to accomplish the same goal opened. In 1774 a bequest of the Reverend Thomas Bray financed another school for blacks. Germans provided charity education in the 1750s, but by 1763 their charity school movement had fallen apart. In 1781 the German Society requested and received legislative permission to establish a school or schools in Philadelphia to instruct the children of poor Germans. But in 1788, "Philanthropos" noted that German inhabitants still lacked a system of schooling that would be *"free* to the poor and *cheap* to all."[7]

The nature of Philadelphians' efforts to provide education for the poor prior to 1785 is perhaps most clearly seen in the lack of theoretical statements. An examination of works published in Philadelphia before 1785 uncovered few statements arguing that the poor must be educated.[8] In 1773, "Amor Virtutis" did decry the "Profanity and vicious Conduct" among the city's youth, calling for the children's "Tutors" to somehow stop the practice. But he was speaking not just—if at all—about poor youths. In 1780 a contributor to the *Pennsylvania Packet* argued that if blacks were granted their freedom, they should receive one year's free education to keep them from becoming "a burden, or a nuisance to the public."[9]

There are a number of possible reasons why only limited efforts to educate the poor occurred during the years before 1785. The crisis of empire and the subsequent fighting of the Revolution probably diverted energies, money, and interest from the concerns of education.[10] Still, even considering the disruptive influence of the Revolution, this fact is clear: in the period 1760–84, Philadelphians simply did not seem very concerned with providing education for the poor or with analyzing the effect education might have on them.

As Philadelphians showed increasing concern about the poor during the postwar era, the indifference toward educating them faded away. In the last fifteen years of the century, Philadelphians dramatically expanded educational opportunities for the poor. Significantly, in virtually every case, the actions taken to offer education put great emphasis on teaching religion and moral values. This stress upon a moral education stemmed from a desire to mold and control the poor by making them accept the model of industrious, deferential poverty.

In 1786 the school for free blacks run by the associates of the Reverend Mr. Bray, which had stopped functioning during the war, reopened as the Negro Charity School. Although students could attend free of charge, the school taught only reading for boys and sewing and knitting for girls.[11] A year later a group of gentlewomen established a school for poor boys in the Northern Liberties. The school accommodated thirty youths and offered free instruction in the principles of general religion as well as in reading, writing, and arithmetic. This was envisioned as the first of a number of such schools to be supported by the Institution of Charity-Schools.[12] In 1788, when the Episcopal churches established a free school for poor children of both sexes, the press applauded their action and called upon other religious groups to join in this good work.[13]

While these piecemeal attempts at providing education for some poor children were being mounted, an ever-increasing number of people urged the establishment of Sunday schools. The campaign began in 1785 and drew increased support until, in December 1790, a number of gentlemen met together and established the Society for the Institution of First-Day or Sunday Schools in the City of Philadelphia, and the Districts of Southwark and the Northern-Liberties. These schools operated each Sunday in the forenoon so that they would not interfere with attendance at church, and children attending the schools were expected to partake in religious services. Even if the children did not attend church services, they still received a rudimentary introduction to religion, for the schools taught reading and writing, using the Bible as a text. The schools, maintained by subscriptions given by members of the Sunday School Society, provided this education free of charge.[14]

The society opened its first school in March 1791, and within three weeks, upwards of 120 poor children and apprentices "who would otherwise be barred from the plainest education" were receiving instruction. Soon, since large numbers of children wished to attend, the society ran schools Sunday evening as well as Sunday morning. This favorable response prompted a call for new members to provide additional funds. In 1795, when about one hundred males and eighty females attended the schools, the society reported that it had provided schooling for 954 children since the first school opened; by 1800 a total of 2,127 young people had received instruction.[15]

In the same year the Sunday School Society was founded, the Committee for Improving the Condition of the Free Blacks began functioning. As noted, one of its goals was to expand the educational opportunities for blacks. This organization appointed a committee of education, which in 1790 began a free evening school for blacks that operated six nights a week and offered instruction in reading, writing, and arithmetic. Students who could not pay for books and paper received them free of charge. In 1793 the committee obtained a frame house on Cherry Street, located in the northwest section of the city, to serve as a permanent school accommodating one hundred students; it functioned until the eve of the nineteenth century.[16]

Within two years of the founding of the Cherry Street school, this education committee began a study of the feasibility of establishing a school in the Northern Liberties and discussed the possibility of having the legislature give blacks greater opportunity to obtain instruction. In November of 1795 the committee agreed that the convention of the Pennsylvania Abolition Society should petition the legislature "to set on foot Free Schools without Discrimination of Color, and in populous Towns to promote particular Institutions for the Education of Blacks." When it appeared that the legislature would not enact the needed laws, a special committee was created to solicit funds from the parent society or from interested individuals so that the education committee could establish schools in both the Northern Liberties and Southwark.[17]

The committee soon began negotiations with a group of Northern Liberties blacks to establish, jointly, a school in that area. When these efforts ended in failure, the committee used its own resources to open a school there but decided to close it, after less than a year of operation, because it was "very inadequate to the cost."[18] Although its own suburban school failed, the education committee did not abandon the goal of providing instruction for the poor blacks who lived in Philadelphia's environs. A new program to provide financial assistance for privately run black schools was initiated. At first the committee expressed satisfaction with the work of Amous White and Absalom Jones, the two black teachers who ran these schools. However, in December 1799, the committee concluded that neither man was properly qualified to teach by saying that White, while "well meaning," had a "deficiency" in school learning and that Jones, while careful "to do his duty," was "too easy." Further, in part because the committee considered Ann Williams, the black who taught at the Cherry Street school, qualified to teach only reading, it was decided to close that school. Although the committee had had nothing but praise for Eleanor Harris, the black who taught at Cherry Street from 1793 until her death in 1798, it decided in late 1799 that, however "desirable" it might be to have black teachers, "it is not practicable at present, to have black Children properly taught by a black person." It was impossible, said the committee, because of "the present stage of their improvement," to find any "person of color" to teach black children.[19] Given Harris's fine performance, it seems odd that the committee came to the conclusion that it could not find a single black competent to teach. Possibly the members were most concerned with instilling their values in the children. For whatever reason, they wanted a school located in the center of the city "which might be very frequently visited" and which, taught by a white instructor, "would better answer . . . the proper & effectual education of the Black Children." To implement this policy, they hired Tiberius Bryen, a white man, to teach blacks in a school established near Sixth and Walnut streets. This school opened in September 1800, and the committee quickly expressed pleasure with its "order" and "progress."[20]

In the postwar era, black Philadelphians did not leave the education of their children solely to others. The African Methodist Episcopal Church, located on Sixth between Pine and Lombard streets, operated a free school on Sundays. By mid-1796, upwards of 150 blacks were being taught, and, because the building housing the school could not accommodate all who wanted instruction, the church issued a public request for assistance to carry on the work.[21]

In the years 1785–1800, large committees and churches were joined by other private groups attempting to provide educational opportunities for the poor. Three young women established a school for poor and neglected children in 1796, and by 1800 they taught about fifty students a year. In 1798 a group of young men, mostly apprentices and clerks, opened a similar school for indigent boys; it provided instruction to between twenty and thirty boys in a night school during the period 1799 to 1801. In the latter year, the number of men joining the society increased markedly and the group opened a day school. When the Female Association of Philadelphia was created in 1800, it too reflected the increasing interest in educating children "in Reduced Circumstances." The association passed a resolution proclaiming the education of poor children "a favorite Object" whenever the group's funds would allow. The desire to educate disadvantaged Philadelphians even reached into the prison, where a school opened in 1798 to teach "the necessary parts of [a] Common English education."[22]

Although many charity schools were established in the latter part of the eighteenth century, no general system of public education emerged in Philadelphia during this period. The failure to establish a general system was not the result of an absence of concern or action. In 1787, Benjamin Rush published an essay offering the inhabitants of greater Philadelphia a plan for educating their children. He proposed that the legislature let the city levy a tax totaling a thousand pounds upon all estates in the city and suburbs. This equal tax, "so light as scarcely to be felt by any body," would allow the creation of free schools, which were needed because the funding of charity schools tended to be precarious. Because Rush felt that careful instruction in the

Christian religion was as important as the teaching of reading and writing, he proposed that the children of similar religious denominations be educated together. Indeed, the individual schools should be operated by the various denominations themselves. The city would function only as a treasurer allocating tax support according to the number of children each group instructed.

Rush's proposed system emphasized education for the poor. "If any religious society should decline accepting of the bounty of the city, from having provided for the education of their poor by private contribution, let their proportion of it be thrown into the poor tax of the city, if it should not be required for the poor children of the less wealthy societies."[23] Although this proposal gained applause in the public press, it was not implemented, quite possibly because the plan for Sunday schools supported by subscription undercut any chances Rush's plan had for success. In fact, Rush himself abandoned this program and worked for the establishment of Sunday schools.[24]

Two years later, "H" urged that the city government enact an ordinance establishing a town school to teach reading, writing, and arithmetic, as well as "the first principles of Religion," to the children of the poor not already being educated by religious societies. The cost of maintaining this school, which the author estimated at not more than £150 a year, would be borne by the city. This suggestion also gained support in the press when "K" claimed that "all classes of people" approved the plan, but it produced no action, again possibly because of the Sunday schools: the Sunday School Society came into existence six months after "H" made his plea.[25]

Once the Sunday schools began operation, efforts to establish a system of free schools shifted to the state level. In January 1795 a writer in the *Federal Gazette* chided the state legislature for not giving systematic attention to establishing a system of general instruction. Hinting that possibly 90,000 of the 135,000 children in the state who were too young to work received no education, he offered a plan for educating Pennsylvania's boys and girls. The state should be divided into school districts of six square miles and into school divisions one-fourth that size. Once a school building was erected in the center of each school division, no child would have to travel over one and one-half miles to school. Because the district would hire only one teacher, each divisional school would operate only three months in the year. This system would be financed by the government, either by general and county taxes or by giving the schools land to use or sell.[26]

Although it is not clear just how influential this plan was, by early 1796 the state legislature considered a bill to establish publicly supported schools. It evoked strong opposition, as well as enthusiastic support. On February 6 the press printed a Quaker memorial that protested the bill, arguing that Quakers should not be taxed for a general system of education since they maintained their own system and also a school for blacks. Most observers did agree that, as a group, the Quakers opposed tax-supported schools, but it was also asserted that the great majority of Pennsylvanians supported the call for a system of general education.[27]

Save for the Quaker memorial, the press contained only essays in support of the principle of a tax-supported educational system. The day before the Quaker memorial appeared, "Philanthropos" published a long defense of the bill in the *Aurora*. Reminding opponents of the bill that "in the opinion of every liberal and well organized mind nothing could vie in importance with that of public education," he noted that the state constitution directed that schools *"shall"* be established, so as "not to confine education to the wealthy, but to extend it to the poor." Obviously the answer to these needs was, he maintained, not subscription schools, but rather tax-supported schools. The editor of the *Aurora* voiced approval of this argument by urging that the state's printers, who were "friends to a general education," reprint the essay.[28]

Four days later, "Icacopina" echoed similar thoughts by maintaining that, "agreeable to our constitution," the state of Pennsylvania "is considered as one great family, having one common interest, hence there should be one general system of education, where every child of the great family will have an equal right to be taught, the expense of which should be paid out of the public treasury." When the legislature failed to act on the edu-

Educating the Poor

cation bill, "E" published a series of essays presenting the case for publicly funded schools.[29]

These pleas did not move the majority of the legislators, and the bill failed. Despite this loss, some Philadelphians continued to call for free schools and also persisted in their search for the best ways to provide education for the state's citizens. In 1799, Dr. George Logan, a representative from the city and a Quaker, introduced another education bill into the legislature, calling for a statewide system of public township schools. The teachers, chosen by the overseers of the poor, who would supervise the schools, would give instruction in reading, writing, and arithmetic to every person in the township who wanted it. Thus, the system could educate adults as well as children. The schools should be maintained by public funds of the county where the school was located. The *Aurora*, which printed a copy of the proposed act, added its endorsement by expressing the hope that this plan would serve as a basis for a publicly supported free school system.[30] It did not. Pennsylvania entered the nineteenth century without a system of free elementary schools.

This failure to convince either the city or state government to create a public education system does not detract from the concern Philadelphians evidenced for education. They had often tried to establish free schools; their record in founding charity schools during the last fifteen years of the century was very impressive; and when this ferment of educational activity is compared to the absence of effort before 1785, the increased concern with education is all the more dramatic.[31]

Granting that there was this dramatic increase, the question becomes, Why did it happen? Part of the answer lies in the fact that Philadelphians realized that it was the poor who were not receiving a full chance to obtain even a plain English education. No matter what type of institution writers on education supported—Sunday schools, free public schools, or church charity schools—their comments stressed that the people who lacked education were the city's poorer elements. The *Gazette of the United States* put the problem in simple, sharp contrast: "The rich can buy learning—it is a luxury. But to the poor it is a necessity and to them, O Americans, it is denied." The *Gazette* hinted at the extent of the problem when it added, "Shall we not blush at the degraded state of great numbers of the laboring poor!" The Sunday School Society agreed that "numbers of children, the offspring of indigent parents, have not proper opportunities of instruction, previous to their being apprenticed to trades."[32] Benjamin Rush, in urging the creation of a system of religious education for the poor, reminded his readers that the children of the poor formed "a great proportion of all communities," especially in the densely populated parts of the state. "E," in arguing for an extensive system of public education in 1796, was more specific. "Is it not true then," he asked rhetorically, "that more than one half of the children who reside in those of our large cities, where no public schools exist, are not instructed in reading, writing, and arithmetic?"[33]

Given this argument, the question yet remains, Why did the increased concern for educating the poor exist in the last decade and a half of the century? As might be expected, numerous reasons were advanced. One major argument for improving the education of the general citizenry, including the poor, was the new political power of the people after the Revolution. Certainly in Philadelphia the franchise had been greatly expanded during and after the revolutionary war, and reformers believed that education was needed to prepare the mass of the citizenry for their new political role. Education of the citizens, and especially of the poor, was also viewed by most Philadelphians as a way to a better society. However, despite the acceptance of these points, two groups, moving from different philosophical bases, supported efforts to educate the poor.

One group of educational reformers, the "Optimists" discussed at the beginning of this chapter, emphasized ideals and goals normally associated with the Enlightenment in America. Believing that people possessed inherent worth and dignity, the Optimists embraced the natural-rights philosophy and called for an educational environment that would produce a more egalitarian society.[34] Thus, they held that education for the poor constituted an essential first step toward giving all citizens a chance to rise in society. "Give to all the means of knowledge," the argument went, "and leave it to nature to make out the differences between their children." "E" echoed this view as he maintained that even the poorest of Pennsylvania's youths should find education within reach, so that they would have "a reasonably equal chance to participate in the advantages of a free society."[35] As one Optimist reminded his readers, "In a republican government we are told that the supreme power derives from the people. But what sort of power will that be, which flows from an ignorant people. The fact is, the power does not flow from such ignorant people, the enlightened and wealthy few alone possess the power." Another writer argued that education for the poor was essential, for if the mass of the people had knowledge, they would be removed "from the influence of the aristocratic few." Thus, "instead of being the tools, they become partners, perhaps the rivals, of the men of wealth and education." Other such reformers maintained that only an educated populace could "judge for themselves," "guide," and even "awe" their rulers.[36]

The Optimists, in stressing that education should lead to a greater opportunity for social and political equality, vehemently opposed charity schools. Charity schools did not foster equality; they perpetuated a servile attitude and insulted the people. The Optimists constantly reminded the public of the section in the Pennsylvania Constitution that ordered the legislature to support education, and they maintained that "learning, like liberty, should be the natural inheritance of our children, whether rich or poor."[37] If the Optimists had their way, education for the poor would be a significant step toward achieving the progressive and egalitarian goals of the Enlightenment. But, because the Optimists spoke for only a minority of Philadelphia's educational reformers, that is not what happened.

The second and far larger group of reformers, the "Pessimists," agreed with the Optimists that the poor should be educated, and the Pessimists also held that environment was critical in the development of the poor. Here the philosophical agreement stopped. The Pessimists did not share the Optimists' faith in the inherent worth of the poor, nor did they want education to produce a more egalitarian society. Their desire to see the poor educated was rooted in fear, and they did not express the hope that education might give the poor a chance to rise or to share in the government. The Pessimists emphasized the evil the poor were doing and would continue to do unless educated; they stressed that education would help keep the poor deferential and in their proper place. It was this view of the road educational reform should travel that dominated the expansion of education for the poor in the years after the Revolution.

It is extremely difficult to determine which Philadelphians supported the Optimist view, since most espousing this philosophy wrote under pen names. The *Aurora*, which considered itself a voice for democratic ideals and for the mechanic and artisan groups of the city, did argue for a free system of general education.[38] This isolated example can give us no more than a clue to the supporters of the Optimist position. But the clue is rather suggestive, once one discovers the identity of some of the leading Pessimists. The Sunday School Society, the most extensive and successful private educational endeavor of the period 1785–1800, firmly embraced and acted upon the Pessimist view of the poor.[39] Therefore, an analysis of the founders of this society provides an indication of the types of Philadelphians who were most likely to be Pessimists. The thirteen founding members of the society represented a diversity of religious groups that matched well with the idea, expressed by one founder, that the Sunday schools should be operated by all denominations.[40] The same diversity was not reflected in the occupational grouping of the founders: with only one possible exception, they were members of the mercantile community or of the professions.[41] Save for Samuel Powell, who was one of the richest men in Philadelphia, they were not among the top economic elite of the city. But, with the exception of Mathew Carey, all were men of some wealth. For example, 85.7 percent of the founders who can be identified in the tax records owned a dwelling and plate, and 57.1 percent owned some kind of pleasure carriage. Carey was also atypical in that he was the only founding member who strongly supported the Constitution of 1776. Four of the other twelve organizers of the society appear to have avoided involvement in politics; but four of the remaining eight were charter members of the Republican Society, and another was associated with the Republican Society's effort to have the College of Philadelphia returned to the original trustees.[42] As a group, then, the creators of the Sunday School Society represented (1) the diverse religious groupings in the city; (2) the mercantile and professional segments of Philadelphia's population; (3) the economically secure elements of society; and (4) the politically neutral or politically conservative Philadelphians. Once again it was the established and reasonably affluent members of society, and especially those who came from the mercantile or professional ranks and who rejected the Constitution of 1776, who spoke and acted for control of the supposedly dangerous poor.

Pessimists, such as the founders of the Sunday School Society, offered an extensive set of arguments in support of their view that poor children needed education based on correct moral principles. A favorite theme held that the environment in which poor children lived worked to make them a threat to society. In urging the creation of Sunday schools to educate the children of the poor, the argument went: "What good can be reasonably expected, from that part of the community, whose infancy and youth are consumed in one uninterrupted scene of idleness, villainy, and all kinds of low craft and theft (in which they are but too often countenanced and encouraged by their parents) untinctured by the very elements of cultivation and knowledge; and who, of course, can hardly, when arrived at maturity, be supposed of a relish but for debauchery?" Hence, education, especially a religious education, was absolutely essential, so that "we might, entertain a well founded hope that the rising generation (of the above [poorer] classes) would prove very different from their fathers." Speaking of "the inferiors, the labouring part of the public," "Lutius" noted that "we find . . . many rooms filled with children of both sexes, the innocence of whose minds is early lost by the brutality of their parents, and [who have] confidence alone in their wretched inheritance."[43] Thus, as the Pessimists saw it, the poor needed education to "break the entail of ignorance and vice in some, or continue the descent of virtue and knowledge in other families." Education would aid those "who, although perhaps tainted by the example of their parents, were not too hardened to be recalled."[44]

The Pessimists, and often the Optimists, constantly spoke of education overcoming the evils of vice, idleness, and disorder among the poor and argued that educating the poor would develop a society of "virtue, order, and happiness."[45] The case for educating the poor was not left in these vague generalities: reformers specifically denoted the evils that education could eradicate. Both Optimists and Pessimists stressed above all else that, since "ignorance is the true cause of all mischief," education of the poor would stop political tumults. For if one gave knowledge to the children of the poor, "they will never be the instruments of injuring mankind." Indeed, "teach a people their moral relations, illumine their understandings, tear away the veil of error and delusion, and you render them the warm and affectionate advocate of virtue and good government." The failure to educate the masses was foolhardy, for "an ignorant and ferocious people . . . will often be induced to rouse from a stupid apathy under the power of despotism." Whether Optimist or Pessimist, the reformers could agree that "a school-house will turn out in the end a better security of the public peace, than a regiment of the horse guards."[46]

While both reform groups supported education as the way to political stability, the Pessimists were more concerned with teaching the poor their responsibilities than with making them partners in the governmental process. Education would "beget in our poor people a love of their rulers, and an attachment to good government." Stressing the value of a religious education, one Pessimist noted the happiness he had in seeing a person who had had his mind "prepared" to respond properly to the people he had been trained "to treat with honour, due submission and proper respect."[47]

Although both reform groups sought to maintain a tranquil political society, the Pessimists were equally concerned about preventing social disorder and crime. At the simplest level, educating the poor seemed essential to improving their conduct. "The profane and indecent language which assaults our ears in every street, can only be restrained by extending education to the children of poor people."[48] Sunday schools would stop "the cursing and swearing . . . which this young and rising generation are too much indulged in." The children of the poor who engaged in such profanity "associate with, and contaminate the children of persons in the higher ranks of society."[49] The Pessimists readily agreed that poverty, "when accompanied with ignorance, always leads to vice."[50]

Crime was the ultimate vice, and Pessimists emphasized that educating the poor would reduce criminality in the city, since seven-eighths "of the wretches who suffer punishment for crimes, are destitute of learning." Of those who were sent to the gallows, there were "very few, especially of the natives of America, . . . whose fate could not justly be ascribed to the neglect of their youth."[51] "H" went so far as to claim that crimes "can be prevented only, by means of *good education*." When the indigent received education, "then our streets will be no more crouded with the votaries of ignorance or vice, nor our persons endangered by the midnight robbers or assassins."[52]

As the Pessimists viewed it, educating the poor was also the means of obtaining better servants. Education would not only teach the poor to hate idleness; it would teach them to accept "the stern habits of industrious labour." Benjamin Rush, one of the founders of the Sunday School Society, in arguing for a plain but useful religious education for poor children, noted that such an education would make them "dutiful children—teachable scholars—and, afterwards, good apprentices—good husbands—good wives—honest mechanics—industrious farmers—peaceable sailors—and, in every thing that relates to this country good citizens." "Lutius," claiming that education would improve the morals of the poor, exclaimed, "How many valuable servants of every denomination should we have in store for the rising generation." The Pessimists thus agreed that the education the poor should receive had to be "suitable to their . . . station in life," which did not include the countinghouses, the professions, or the councils of state.[53]

All reformers stressed the financial wisdom of educating the poor. Benjamin Rush proclaimed that "by lessening the quantity of vice, we shall . . . lessen the expences of jails, and of the usual forms of law which conduct people to them." Indeed, the expense of apprehending and jailing criminals amounted to more than it would cost to educate the poor.[54] Nor was that the only sound financial reason for educating the poor. Education would, as it reformed the poor, reduce their number, because "poverty is often the defect of education."[55] The poor, if educated, and especially if educated in the mechanical arts, would have the ability to provide for themselves. Equally important, a properly conducted education would instill in the poor an abhorrence of idleness. Clearly, such education pointed the way to lower taxes as well as to a lower crime rate.[56]

Not all Philadelphians supported these efforts. Those who opposed educating the poor argued that giving them schooling would make them "idle, vicious and proud." Once educated, the poor "become discontented with their lot, and even if they could change it to their own advantage, the case would not be mended, for others must be found to take their places. The drudgery of the world must be done."[57] Some opposed schools far more subtly. One writer in the *Packet* began his comments on education by saying that public schools deserved government assistance, yet ended by maintaining that children should be forced to labor so that they could pay for their education. It was essential that poor children work at an early age, since it would make them "better apprentices, better servants, and every way more useful members of society." Undoubtedly, this writer could not agree with the essayist who maintained that "learning ought to be free as air."[58]

By 1800, Philadelphians had not made education as free as air. But many had come to emphasize that "the lower class of mankind are generally injured by being deprived of the means of education, and then insulted for not being intelligent and orderly." Philadelphians had managed, especially in the last fifteen years of the century, to establish a number of charity schools. Almost all these schools offered a plain religious education. Whatever else they taught, they stressed the evils of vice and the glories of industry and godly order. This was the kind of education that the people from the mercantile and professional ranks who founded the Sunday School Society wanted the poor to have. This was the kind of education the Pessimists, as a group, wanted offered. And it was the Pessimists, with their emphasis on the reduction of social disorder, vice, and crime, who most influenced the new educational activity. Indeed, examining the public comments on educating the poor, it is obvious that the majority of reformers were more concerned with keeping the poor deferentially submissive than with helping them possibly improve their lot. For those who believed in the inculcation of deference, education for the poor became a form of insurance. The paramount concern was the needs of the society, not the needs of the poor. Dr. Benjamin Rush presented this view in its simplest, most brutal form: Philadelphians should not exhaust the city's benevolent funds on medical aid for the poor, because "their morals are of more consequence to society than their health or lives." If few educational reformers were willing to go that far, the majority surely could agree with Rush's quotation of the lines: "Blessed is he that considereth the poor, the Lord will deliver him in time of trouble."[59] What bothered most educational reformers in the years 1785–1800, as well as those who opposed educating the poor, was that the time of trouble was already upon them. Thus, the expanded efforts to educate the poor, like the moral crusade discussed in Chapter Three, stemmed from a hope that they could be trained to accept their place in society deferentially. And, once again, those who most actively worked to achieve this goal were Philadelphians who followed mercantile or professional pursuits and who were among the affluent of the city.

Conclusion

*The Revolution, Change, and the
Quest for Deference among the Poor*

This examination of the life of the poor and the responses to poverty in the Philadelphia of 1760–1800 reveals that significant social change did accompany the Revolution. And some Philadelphians, often embracing Enlightenment ideals, did work to achieve reforms that would make independent Philadelphia a more open, more egalitarian society. But many articulate citizens, as evidenced by their words and deeds, did not want to see their society transformed in this way. Rather, they wanted to check what they perceived as the increasingly dangerous poor by training or forcing them to accept their station in life deferentially. Members of the mercantile and professional classes, who were among the affluent of the city, were especially prone to join in efforts to stem what they perceived as the danger from below. And they worked hard to try to check the effects of the Revolution when those effects seemed to produce greater equality and freedom of action for the poor.

Although important social changes did occur in revolutionary Philadelphia, the Revolution did not signal a general improvement in the material position of the poor. In the decade and a half before the war, the great bulk of Philadelphia's wealth was concentrated in the hands of a few citizens. The same situation prevailed in 1800. Some of the poor may have improved the

Conclusion

quality of their dress in the revolutionary era, but throughout the last four decades of the eighteenth century the poor were readily distinguishable by the inferior quality of their clothing. Certainly their housing pattern did not improve. In 1800, as in 1760, they were typically segregated in the least desirable sections of the city, where they lived in poor housing. Nor did the Revolution alter general attitudes toward the poor. Throughout the period 1760–1800 the poor were told that they must be industrious, must be deferential. In these and other ways, the Revolution failed to move Philadelphia toward a more egalitarian society by 1800.

An analysis of reforms that might have significantly affected the poor also suggests that the Revolution did not exert a strong democratizing influence on Philadelphia society. Some changes did improve the life of the poor, but, as an instrument for improvement, the transforming hand of revolution fell rather lightly on the poor of Philadelphia. The criminal justice system underwent reform, but a prime reason for change was the hope that crime could be controlled, at a time when Philadelphians increasingly feared criminality in their midst. The Constitution of 1776 observed that punishments more proportionate to the crimes should replace the extensive use of the death penalty. To implement this policy, and to deter crime, the Constitution urged the legislature to institute punishment by hard labor for noncapital crimes. Despite these pronouncements, the Assembly did not move quickly to reform the criminal punishments system. Until 1786, a number of crimes still carried the death penalty, and not until that year did the Assembly move to correct and reform criminals by putting them at hard labor. A reform spirit, therefore, produced important alterations in the criminal code only when assisted by the growing desire to mold and control the poor. In addition, significant reforms in both criminal and debtor laws were enacted in the same bill in 1791. In that year the legislature decreed that persons found innocent of criminal charges would not have to pay court costs, and poor persons held only for court costs could use the laws for insolvent debtors to obtain their freedom. In these ways, reforms suggested by the Constitution of 1776 and backed by Enlightenment reformers were enacted, albeit slowly, by the end of the century.

Thus, while the hand of revolution moved slowly, it did, under press of a desire to control criminality, bring about substantial reform in the justice system.

The Revolution also helped produce reforms in Pennsylvania's, and consequently in Philadelphia's, system of imprisonment for debt, and these improvements benefited the poor. One basis for them was the Constitution of 1776, which said that debtors who openly and honestly gave up their estates should not be imprisoned. But this reform depended upon the legislature's taking action, and, as late as 1789, the lawmakers had to concede that persons suffered long confinements for debts or for fines or forfeitures not exceeding a value of five pounds in each category. Not until 1798 was an act passed that offered debtors willing to surrender their possessions an opportunity to avoid being imprisoned during the court process required to settle their accounts. Moreover, until 1792, imprisoned debtors were expected to pay for their own maintenance. Thus, the Constitution's directive on debtors was not implemented until the last decade of the century, when Philadelphians became deeply concerned with the idleness that imprisonment for debt seemed to help foster. Still, when the reforms did come, they were important.

Two further reforms of the revolutionary era, on first examination, seemingly show that the poor of Philadelphia benefited from the Revolution. One is Pennsylvania's reexamination of the institution of slavery. In 1780 the legislature, mindful of the state's deliverance from the "tyranny" of England and believing that "all are the work of an Almighty Hand," attacked slavery in Pennsylvania. "We are enabled this day to add one more step to universal civilization," the legislators boldly declared, "by removing as much as possible the sorrows of those who have lived in undeserved bondage." This rhetoric was hyperbolic. The law declared that henceforth persons born into slavery would be treated as indentured servants and gain their freedom and freedom dues at age twenty-eight, while those already slaves would remain slaves for life.[1] Had this law freed all slaves, it still would not have brought an extensive change, since the number of slaves in Philadelphia and even in the state was quite small. Moreover, the transformation in law, limited as it was, was not matched by a transformation in attitudes. Free blacks still were "despised" by many; they still faced contempt.[2] Even the Committee for Improving the Condition of the Free Blacks, which attempted to superintend their morals, was pleased when it found a becoming deference among them. In 1799, after having applauded the ability of a black teacher from 1793 until her death in 1798, the committee argued that it could find *no* black qualified to teach black children. Perhaps unaware of the incriminating irony of its comment, in 1800 the committee said of blacks: "The prejudices of many of their well wishers are not yet surmounted."[3] Again, the touch of a transforming hand, pointing toward a more egalitarian society, fell lightly.

The one sweeping change wrought by the Revolution that affected the mass of the poor and that points to an important equalizing social change in Philadelphia occurred in the political sphere. Unquestionably, the Revolution brought about a great extension of the franchise by giving even the poor an established role in electoral politics. Some hoped that this change, instituted by the 1776 Constitution, would profoundly alter the nature of society: "*Now all men will* be put on a level with respect to THIS GRAND RIGHT OF VOTING AT ELECTIONS, and that may in time bring them to a level *in every other respect.*" It was not to be. Having the vote did not equal political or social power. Even when the mass of adult males could vote for members of the Assembly, they could not be sure that the legislature would effectively work for the interests of the many. At least until 1796, the expanded franchise did not mean that adult male Philadelphians would be able to determine who would run the reincorporated city government. Nor did having the power of the franchise, for either the poor or those who proclaimed themselves friends of the poor, necessarily equal having the ability to run for office or to be elected. Clearly, the vote was not a sure instrument for social leveling.

Save for the extension of the franchise, for the poor of Philadelphia the Revolution produced rather limited changes leading toward a more egalitarian society. But the extension of the franchise was a critical social change that combined with other changes in the roles and actions of the poor to produce a world that many abhorred. These Philadelphians, who often came from the economically secure mercantile and professional ranks of the city, preferred that the poor act as they were believed to have acted in colonial days. And, despite the turmoil caused by the movement toward Revolution, affluent citizens often perceived the late colonial period as an era with a properly ordered social system. Alexander Graydon proclaimed the prewar years a tranquil and happy golden age. "Peter Easy" approved the fact that the prewar vote rested in the hands of those worth at least fifty pounds, because he considered that this requirement kept government orderly, dignified, and safe from unscrupulous agitators. It seemed that, for the most part, the poor in colonial days submissively, deferentially accepted rule by those noted, as Rush put it, for "their wealth, virtue, learning, and liberality of manners."[4] But the maintenance of such deference was not left solely to chance. A number of institutions and practices worked to insure that the poor remained orderly and deferential. The extensive bound labor system of slavery, apprenticeship, and indentured servitude gave masters authority to regulate the actions of many of the city's workers. The extensive use of the recommendation system helped insure that the poor would behave in the proper way. Still, it seemed that only minimal efforts were required to remind the mass of the colonial poor that they should follow the path of industrious, deferential poverty. Indeed, as a group, Philadelphia's colonial poor supposedly knew their place and generally kept to it, even in such simple but symbolically important matters as dress.

This image of the poor willingly embracing deference in a happy and tranquil colonial Philadelphia was a caricature of reality. Denied the vote, the poor had little opportunity to challenge the selection of public officials. Nor did those who lived above poverty and who had the vote necessarily willingly defer to persons called their betters. As "A Brother Chip" observed, skillful political maneuvering rather than freely given deference was a key to keeping political power in the hands of the men of wealth, learning, and liberality of manners. Further, the deference proclaimed as a hallmark of the poor in their general social intercourse was not necessarily freely given. The recommendation system worked to force the poor, and the near poor,

Conclusion

to accept the actions and decisions of the more "respectable" citizens. Nor were the poor always quietly deferential and happy, at least outwardly, with the world that was colonial Philadelphia. "Tom Trudge" denounced the way the needs of the poor were neglected in the paving and cleaning of streets. Poor persons lodged complaints against the prisonlike atmosphere of the house of employment. The militia, in the mid-1770s, railed against the exclusion of the poor from the normal electoral process. The image of a golden colonial age, happy and tranquil, in which the poor as a group were deferential and orderly *was* a caricature, but it had a powerful appeal for many established, respectable Philadelphians. It was the world they wanted to preserve even after independence. Unfortunately, that world appeared to be crumbling under the pressure of the revolutionary era.

It seemed painfully clear to these well-to-do citizens that the Revolution weakened important institutions which helped control the actions of the poor and that the Revolution dangerously undermined the ideal of deference. During the war, few persons were indentured as servants, and most who had been indentured became free wage earners by the war's end. The war did not destroy indentured servitude, but it eliminated at least a full generation of indentured servants and helped accelerate the movement toward an ever-expanding population of free wage earners. The labor strife of the 1790s illustrated the decline in the bound labor system. Worse yet, large numbers of servants and apprentices, as well as other poor persons, served in the militia and there gained a taste for independent action and power. Rather than avoiding politics and deferring to gentlemen officers, the rank and file of militiamen demanded the vote in state politics and exercised the right to elect many of their officers. Militia service for the poor thus helped subvert the ideal of deference. Nor was the militia satisfied merely with the expanded franchise. The events surrounding the Fort Wilson incident revealed not only that militiamen would challenge the established government, but that they would not even defer to their own supposed radical leaders. Many Philadelphians perceived with horror the possibility that deference among the poor and the lower orders in general would be a casualty of the war.

It could be seen in the matter of dress. With the coming of the Revolution, it appeared that, increasingly, the poor tried to dress above their station. They were not very successful in the effort, but this departure from the situation that supposedly existed in colonial Philadelphia illustrated a dangerous shift. The very language of the poor drew more attention from established Philadelphians in the revolutionary era: allegedly, they filled the air with profane and indecent language, which contaminated the children of higher ranks. And tippling houses, those breeders of vice and crime among the poor, multiplied at an alarming rate in the revolutionary city.

Many established Philadelphians refused to stand idly by while the pillars of their cherished temple of order and deference came crashing down. In the revolutionary era, they mounted a vigorous campaign to reestablish, as much as possible, deference and industry among the poor; and they worked to dilute the potential political power of the poor, as the case of Israel Israel illustrates. If these Philadelphians could have their way, the stream of social revolution would be confined within narrow banks and the flow toward a more egalitarian society would be stopped.

In postindependence Philadelphia, close analysis was undertaken to determine the causes of nonindustrious poverty and to attack those causes. Love of alcohol was judged a prime reason for much idle poverty, and so energy was poured into reducing the number of taverns. The nonindustrious poor supposedly wanted to be idlers and would steal to avoid honest work; therefore, the wheelbarrow criminal law was instituted, on the theory that manual work struck more fear into the hearts of idlers than did corporal punishment. Public statements on the causes of idleness stressed the misery and ruination awaiting those who trod the path of idleness. Idlers endangered themselves, their families, and society. The terms "vicious" and "vulgar" were used more and more to depict these undesirable types.

The case of the industrious was far different. More flattering terms—"honest," "good," "deserving"—were increasingly used to describe the industrious poor. Industrious poverty was held up as a badge of moral purity of which one could be proud and was depicted as offering much more than a sense of moral pride.

Conclusion

A constant and virtually unchallenged theme voiced in revolutionary Philadelphia was that riches brought cares and often misery, but that honest poverty led to happiness on earth and probably to a place in heaven. Surely the intelligent poor person would quietly accept his lower station in life. If large numbers of the poor accepted such arguments, Philadelphia would again enjoy the support for order and tranquility that came from the well-behaved poor.

The more sophisticated analysis of poverty that emerged in revolutionary Philadelphia served as a basis for intensified efforts to utilize charity as an instrument of keeping the poor on the path of industrious poverty. On one level, the moral worth of the laboring poor was stressed. In late 1784, for example, a special apartment was opened in the almshouse for some of the poor who had fomerly been in "reputable Circumstances." The Philadelphia Dispensary, founded in 1786, served the "virtuous" poor who could not bring themselves to enter a public hospital. The message was unmistakable: the industrious poor *were* the deserving poor, and they merited extra consideration in their time of need.

The corollary of this point was that the vulgar, idle poor did not deserve help. They were to pay the price for vicious poverty, and part of the price included denial of relief. This philosophy existed in colonial days, but in postindependence Philadelphia it came to permeate most private poor relief. The key was increased utilization of the recommendation system that required a poor person to obtain a reference from a "respectable" citizen in order to gain assistance. This system, which embodied the fullest ideal of deference, worked to deny aid to those viewed as idlers: because of the system, a poor person seeking aid needed to know, at a minimum, how to display a becoming deference. The increasing use of the recommendation structure as an instrument of social control is sharply illustrated by the different responses to the outbreaks of yellow fever in the 1790s. No recommendations were required to obtain aid when the fever made its first calamitous visit in 1793; but in 1797 and 1798, when yellow fever again struck the city, persons needing aid had to get recommendations. As an added measure in 1798, the poor who moved to the tent encampment for safety and relief had to obey strict rules designed to protect their morals, and armed guards attempted to ensure that the rules were not transgressed. Established citizens of the revolutionary city had become keenly aware that, even amid the chaos of yellow fever, Christian kindness needed to be tempered by a judicious choice of objects, so that only the worthy poor received aid.

The postwar movement toward greater use of relief as a prod to support industrious poverty and to reform the vicious poor exerted a commanding influence and led to other innovations. In the days of the contributorship, the overseers of the poor had rejected the ideal of using public relief primarily as an instrument of reform. But the overseers turned guardians also embraced the view that public poor relief could and should reform the idle. Revolutionary Philadelphia produced the city's first private reclamation societies designed to reform the vulgar poor and return them to the path of virtue, and uplift societies made their first appearance in the same period. These agencies strove to insure that the poor did not fall into vicious poverty and that they learned to behave properly.

The most extensive uplift effort designed to support industry and deference came in the efforts to provide education for the poor. Postindependence efforts to analyze the value of educating the poor and to expand the education available to them were most impressive. Some Philadelphians who supported expanding educational opportunities voiced the Enlightenment ideal that education should further the movement toward a more egalitarian society. But those who rejoiced in seeing the minds of the poor "prepared" to treat their superiors "with honour, due submission and proper respect" carried the day.

Support for this vigorous and extensive campaign to lead, train, or force the poor to accept their lot submissively came from Philadelphians who rejected the ideal that society should become more egalitarian. These citizens were most likely to be economically secure members of the mercantile or professional ranks; they had gotten a great deal from the established social order, and they agreed with the essayist who in 1799 observed: "The malignancy of a cancer is not more rapid or deadly in its progression, than the spirit of modern levellers—It is a fire that readily finds fuel in the hearts and feelings of the lowest part of creation, and unless it is checked in its first glimmerings, may involve the whole social fabric in a general and irrevocable conflagration."[5] Fearful lest they be consumed, many respectable, established Philadelphians manned a fire line during and after the Revolution. With increasing forcefulness, they sought to extinguish what they felt was the raging fire caused by the levelers. They worked hard, and they appeared to have contained the eighteenth-century fire. But people of the stripe of "Peter Easy" realized that such fires have a way of smoldering, and as they faced the nineteenth century, these Philadelphians knew that their days on the fire line were not over.

The desire to squelch the spirit of these modern levelers was a vital part of the social change that occurred in revolutionary Philadelphia. And those who rejected the ideals of an egalitarian society were able effectively, even with the significant expansion of the franchise, to limit democratizing reforms in Philadelphia. For Philadelphia's poor the flood of an egalitarian revolution was confined within rather narrow banks.

Philadelphia and Interpretations of Colonial and Revolutionary America: A Brief Analysis

The foregoing study of poverty and the response to poverty in Philadelphia covers but a small part of the history of late colonial and revolutionary America. And it must be emphasized that the conclusions offered hold only for Philadelphia from 1760 to 1800. Still, it seems appropriate to assess how the study either supports or challenges major interpretations of Philadelphia history and of the American revolutionary era.

Historians have long disagreed about the nature of America's colonial and revolutionary society. An earlier view, formulated by historians who have been dubbed the "progressives," saw colonial and revolutionary society as filled with class division and class antagonism. Some in this group even claimed that the desire to remake society was a fundamental cause of the Revolution.[6] This view was, in turn, challenged by historians who claimed that early society was close to being a middle-class democracy, at least for whites.[7]

Today these older views have been modified; yet the essence of each position remains. What can be called the new middle-class view offers a picture of Philadelphia and of society that, in broad outline, depicts the following image. Prosperity was, at least in Philadelphia, a "commonplace" thing.[8] The people of colonial and revolutionary Philadelphia, and of society as a whole, had an excellent opportunity to improve their socio-economic position.[9] Given such a world, the people of Philadelphia, like those of other areas, had a marvelous sense of community. The citizens lived so close together, at least in the city, that they were able to know one another and to work together to achieve harmony in society.[10] Thus, although people disagreed over issues, few if any of the lower orders wanted to overturn the existing social, economic, and political world. Mechanics and artisans wanted to join with others in running the government and society, but the existence of this desire does not show class division.[11] This sense of community and lack of class division can be seen, it is maintained, in the fact that all colonial Philadelphians, and colonial Americans generally, embraced the ideal of deference. Indeed, it was simply assumed and accepted as a fact of life that the wealthy should direct the affairs of state.[12] The new middle-class view maintains that this sense of community, supported by easy mobility and opportunity, lasted through the American Revolution because Americans found a great unifier in the republican philosophy. Once directing their own destiny, Americans, it is said, became less willing to endure domestic violence; instead, they worked together to achieve political progress.[13]

Reflecting its more sophisticated analysis, the new middle-class view does not claim that colonial society was so good that changes were unnecessary. Rather, it argues that the American Revolution did transform society by making that society even more open, even more egalitarian, as slavery came under attack and the liberating force of republicanism exerted its influence. Of course, say the new middle-class historians, these transformations were not the product of conflict among classes.[14] Following this line, the new middle-class interpretation has turned the old "progressive" argument on its head. Transformation did not occur because the forces of democratic thought battled an en-

Conclusion

trenched and antidemocratic aristocracy. Rather, the people, working in harmony most of the time, improved what little needed to be improved in the social fabric.

The claims of the new middle-class view are themselves being questioned by historians who, although they have modified the older view, accept major tenets of the argument presented by the so-called progressive historians. And this study of poverty and the responses to poverty in the Philadelphia of 1760–1800 supports the thrust of what can be called the class-division interpretation. Certainly the conclusions of this study agree with those of other works which have shown that, even if one ignores the problem of slavery, colonial and revolutionary America was hardly a middle-class democracy.[15] Too many Philadelphians lived in poverty or near poverty to justify the claim that the citizens enjoyed a general prosperity. And the image of easy mobility for Philadelphians, which is strikingly reminiscent of the booster literature produced in the eighteenth century, simply will not stand close scrutiny. Philadelphia did not, as Jackson Turner Main argued on the basis of very little and questionable evidence, offer the poor a good chance to improve their lot.[16] Nor can one support the idea of easy mobility by claiming that the West always offered opportunity. One obvious problem is that, even if the West did provide a chance for mobility, mobility within the city is not thereby demonstrated. Equally important, it was not so easy to move up by moving West, as Philadelphians cogently noted.[17] Philadelphians of that day, including some who promoted the city as a place that offered a chance for improved social standing, believed that they lived in a world where opportunities for those at the bottom of the society were severely limited. And the evidence suggests that this view matched reality.

The claim that Philadelphia enjoyed a real sense of community and agreement on fundamental issues is also open to serious challenge. People were not jumbled together in one rather happy and homogeneous community. The poor were detectable by the way they dressed. The rich and the poor were not likely to live in the same immediate area, nor were they likely to frequent the same taverns. Nevertheless, the class-division view which suggests that the poorer elements of society had their own basically unified culture remains more of a hypothesis than a proven fact.[18] And the historians who stress class division must offer far more detailed evidence before we can accept the claim that Americans of the lower orders had a well-developed sense of what E. P. Thompson has called "the moral economy," in which the commonalty voiced opinions and exerted a right to regulate economic matters.[19] Still, as the present study demonstrates, many Philadelphians did display, at least at times, what can be called a sense of "moral economy."

This work also shows that the commonalty did not necessarily accept the ideal of deference. Unquestionably, many affluent Philadelphians believed that the lower ranks were, as the period progressed, showing disturbing signs of independent political activity. The Constitution of 1776 played a vital role in helping to foster such feelings. By allowing virtually every adult male into the normal electoral process, it fundamentally transformed the political structure and atmosphere of the city. Those who rejected democratic ideals worked to destroy the Constitution and to keep political control in the hands of the affluent few, as the battles over reincorporation illustrate. Of course, one might expect such class antagonism in Pennsylvania, which supposedly had the most democratic constitution of any of the states. But other states also moved toward a more democratic structure in their constitutions.[20] And Massachusetts adopted a very conservative constitution in 1780 amid bitter political fighting, which featured division based on differing attitudes toward the ideal of democratizing the political system.[21] Therefore, it does not appear possible to dismiss the class division and antagonism in revolutionary Pensylvania as the product of a "radical" constitution. Philadelphians did unite on some political issues, such as the adoption of the United States Constitution.[22] But a commitment to republicanism did not stop class antagonism from infecting much of the politics of the day.

The new middle-class interpretation also misses the mark when it postulates that the Revolution produced a rather harmonious effort to correct the few ills of society. Recent studies of Indians and women suggest that, for them, the Revolution did not signal a new and more egalitarian world.[23] The Revolution did, however, produce an attack upon the institution of slavery.

Conclusion

Indeed, one can with fair accuracy speak of an abolition movement, or at least a gradualist abolition movement, in the North in the period under study.[24] And Ira Berlin has shown that, as a group, blacks did improve their position because of the Revolution.[25] But in Pennsylvania the improvement in the status of blacks was much less than thoroughgoing. Despite its small black population, the state passed only a gradual, rather than a full, emancipation law. Equally important, the Revolution apparently had surprisingly little influence on attitudes toward blacks. Even those who considered themselves friends of abolition and of free blacks often displayed as much interest in controlling them by forcing them to conform to the white ideals as they did in accepting them into society as potential equals. Perhaps Philadelphia was unique. But until the issue has been studied far more extensively than it has, we must reserve judgment on the degree to which the Revolution did truly transform the status of blacks.[26] Considering the less powerful as a group, it appears that the Revolution did not transform their world and provide full partnership in society. Of course, it would be ahistorical to judge the revolutionary period by modern standards. Still, measured against the rhetoric of that day, it seems that the Revolution produced far less social reform for the less powerful than the stated ideals would lead us to believe should have occurred.[27]

This analysis of poverty also challenges what is, in fact, a major supporting argument for the new middle-class interpretation, the argument that charity was not used in the eighteenth century as an instrument of social control; that, rather, simple humanitarianism reigned.[28] If this interpretation is correct, it suggests (1) that if there was fear of those at the bottom of society, it was very limited, and (2) that society did have a sense of community. But this study reinforces the caution Raymond Mohl displayed when he gingerly suggested that the major seaport cities of the era probably developed in similar ways. Mohl's study of poverty in New York City during the period found that eighteenth-century humanitarianism in that city was unencumbered by a desire to control or to reform the poor.[29] The situation was obviously quite different in Philadelphia. It is impossible at this time to know whether Philadelphia or New York was the more typical of major cities in the revolutionary era.

Indeed, only when we have far more studies of the cities and of the small towns will we be able to comment meaningfully on even the urban poor of the era. Nevertheless, the Philadelphia case demonstrates that David Rothman's sweeping claim that poor relief was not used for control or reform in eighteenth-century America is simply wrong.[30]

This work, then, offers little support for the new middle-class interpretation. In its general thrust, it joins those studies which emphasize that class division was a vital force in the revolutionary era. It supports the view that the American Revolution did produce a battle over who should rule at home, as well as a battle for home rule.[31] Certainly few Philadelphians of the revolutionary era doubted that they were living through such a struggle. Once we do study, on a wide scale, the nature and meaning of poverty in late colonial and revolutionary America, we may discover that what happened in Philadelphia happened elsewhere as well.

Appendix A
Methodology of Biographical Tracing

In all but a few instances, the lists of founders or members of the various organizations analyzed did not identify the people involved other than by name. Because of this fact, some people with common names simply could not be positively identified. However, most persons on the lists could be tracked down by using the following rule: if only one person with the name I was tracing appeared on the tax list for the period being examined, or if only one such name appeared in the appropriate city directory or directories, I assumed that the person on the list in question was the person on the tax list or in the city directory. And, if another primary or secondary source referred to a person by this name, I also assumed that the person involved was the person I was attempting to trace. Given this procedure, a few errors may have crept into some of the identifications offered. Still, it seems very unlikely that the possible errors would significantly modify the general descriptions.

Three tax lists were used to determine wealth-holding patterns. Two of them, which appear in volume 14 of the third series of the *Pennsylvania Archives*, record the provincial tax assessment for 1769 and 1774. These records give the number of acres owned, the number of horses and cattle owned, the number of servants, and the total tax to be paid. The tax records for the years between 1779 and 1783, contained in volumes 14–16 of the same source, usually give less information than the earlier lists and were used to determine a person's occupation only when no other listing could be found. The county tax lists for 1785 and 1787, which are housed in the Philadelphia City Archives, also were not used to trace wealth, because three city wards are missing from the 1785 records and two city wards are missing from the 1787 list. These missing wards are crucial, because one must have a full set of tax listings to be able to get a reasonably accurate picture of a person's taxable wealth. This is the case because main tax entries merely listed the property located or associated with places of residence. If a person owned taxable property elsewhere in the city, that fact is not indicated in the main entry. Hence, one must examine the citywide tax listings, entry by entry, to discover items marked as belonging to a particular estate, and then the value of the estate holdings must be added to the total given in the main entry. Because of these considerations, the tax list of 1791, also housed in the Philadelphia City Archives, was used to determine the taxable wealth of those who belonged to organizations functioning from the mid-1780s on. Using the 1791 list has another advantage. The first two city directories, neither of which is as complete as one would wish, were published in 1785. The next directory was not published until 1791, but it is a rather full one. The 1791 directory allows a double check on the names and occupational listings given in the 1791 tax list. And having the addresses given in the directory also allows for positive identification in a few cases.

The county tax list of 1791 is itself not complete. All of the lists for the city wards have survived, as has the list for the eastern section of Southwark. A 1791 tax list for the western portion of the Northern Liberties is also available; but for the eastern section of the Northern Liberties, the 1792 list had to be used, since there is no surviving 1791 tax list for that area. Thus, any property held in western Southwark or in the rest of Philadelphia County or elsewhere is not included in the wealth holdings here analyzed. And such holdings, in the case of the very rich, might be considerable, as indicated in note 34 to Chapter One, below.

The 1791 county tax list records the tax value of an individual's land, buildings, plate, horses, cows, servants, slaves, ground rents, and wagons or pleasure carriages; in addition, a person was rated either for an occupation or per head. It does not appear that the occupational tax, which was called a personal tax in some cases, was determined by a set formula. It seems rather to have represented the assessor's educated guess of the value of a given individual's occupation. Because of the way ground rents were evaluated and assessed, I have used the total value of buildings rather than the final tax assessment on those buildings. If a person had to pay a ground rent for the land on which his buildings stood, the cost of the ground rent was multiplied by 10 and then subtracted from the tax value of the building. This procedure, which was designed to reflect the tax value of ground rents, could, if followed here, produce a final tax figure that would significantly misrepresent individual holdings. For example, George Bringhurst owned a dwelling worth seven hundred pounds. But, because he paid a ground rent of sixty pounds per annum, the taxable value of the house was dropped to one hundred pounds. Using the latter figure would grossly understate Bringhurst's economic position. Indeed, the fact that he could afford to pay such a high ground rent suggests that he had a solid income. Retaining the original dwelling value, accordingly, gives a better indication of his total wealth. On the other hand, I have counted the ground rent value as given when it was part of someone's estate, because the way ground rents were assessed does reflect their value as income producers over time.

Three further points about how total wealth was determined need to be made. If both a father and a son appeared in the tax records, I counted only the estate holdings that could positively be identified as belonging to the one I was tracing. And in the very few cases where one of the people on my lists held property in conjunction with someone else, I have added one-half of the value of the jointly held property to the holdings of the person on my list. Finally, although I twice went through the 1791 tax list, entry by entry, I probably missed some items belonging to persons on my lists of founders and officials. It still seems most unlikely that such omissions would materially alter the general comments offered in the text.

Another problem concerning all of the tax lists must be emphasized. The tax listing for members of the mercantile class and for the very rich is quite likely to understate their actual wealth. This happens in the case of the merchants because many items associated with commerce and finance, such as ships and loans, were not taxed. In the case of the very rich, part of the problem stems from the fact that they may well have held property outside the city and suburbs (see the sources cited in note 14 to the Introduction).

Information concerning religious and political activity was collected from a wide variety of sources, cited below in the notes. Such information was also obtained from the *Dictionary of American Biography*; from James G. Wilson and John Fiske, eds., *Appleton's Cyclopaedia of American Biography*, 6 vols. (New York, 1887-89); and from Arther L. Jensen, *The Maritime Commerce of Colonial Philadelphia* (Ann Arbor, Mich., 1963). The most useful of the many works consulted were J. Thomas Scharf and Thompson Westcott, *History of Philadelphia, 1609–1884*, 3 vols. (Philadelphia, 1884); Richard A. Ryerson, *The Revolution Is Now Begun: The Radical Committees of Philadelphia, 1765–1776* (Philadelphia, 1978); Stephen J. Brobeck, "Changes in the Composition and Structure of Philadelphia Elite Groups, 1756–1790" (Ph.D. diss., University of Pennsylvania, 1973); Robert L. Brunhouse, *The Counter-Revolution in Pennsylvania, 1776–1790* (Harrisburg, Pa., 1940); and John H. Powell, *Bring Out Your Dead: The Great Plague of Yellow Fever in Philadelphia in 1793* (Philadelphia, 1949).

Appendix B
Criminals in Philadelphia, 1794–1800

The statistics in tables 1–4 are derived from the Philadelphia City Archives, Philadelphia County Prison Sentence Docket, 2 December 1794–February 1804. The source normally lists name, age, race, place of birth, crime, court where tried, prosecutor's name, sentence, when discharged, by whom and how discharged, or if died or escaped. Less frequently, there is a notation of occupation upon conviction or a reference to a particularly distinctive characteristic. All people listed in the tables were convicted at the Philadelphia mayor's court.

In computing the various percentages, allowance had to be made for the fact that not all convicts had full disposition records. Since the background data was taken when a convict left prison, if he escaped or died the normal information would not be listed; also, the clerk of the prison was occasionally absent when prisoners were released, which again meant no disposition. And when a convict was a repeat offender, one is sometimes referred to nonexistent records for the disposition. Because of these problems, the following percentages have been figured on the following basis: (1) when figuring the percentage of convicts born in any given geographical area, only those with dispositions were put into the computation; (2) since, even if no general disposition was made, it was usually noted if a prisoner was black, the percentage of black criminals was determined by figuring the percentage of black criminals to all others with or without dispositions. Repeat offenders were counted only once.

Table 1
Yearly Percentages of Criminals Convicted at Philadelphia's Mayor's Court from December 1794 to 1800

Year	Total Number	Repeaters	Blacks with No Disposition[b]	Nonblacks with No Disposition	Men	Women	Born in Ireland	Born in Other Foreign Countries	Born in the United States[c]	Born in Pennsylvania	Born in Philadelphia	Total Blacks	Pardoned[d]
1794[a]	16	0	0	0	56.3	43.8	25.0	43.8	31.3	0	12.5	50.0	62.5
1795	56	3.6	7.1	16.1	76.8	23.2	27.9	34.9	37.2	9.3	2.3	32.1	37.5
1796	71	2.8	5.6	18.3	69.0	31.0	38.9	31.5	29.6	7.4	5.6	28.2	21.1
1797	45	15.6	4.4	22.2	71.1	28.9	39.4	21.2	39.4	3.0	6.1	24.4	22.2
1798	56	5.4	3.6	8.9	78.6	21.6	36.7	16.3	47.0	6.1	8.2	25.0	3.6
1799	68	14.7	5.9	17.7	67.6	32.4	28.8	26.9	44.2	7.7	3.9	33.8	2.9
1800	37	10.8	10.8	24.3	70.3	29.7	25.0	25.0	50.0	8.3	8.3	37.8	10.8

Note: All percentages are rounded off to the nearest tenth.

a. Includes only the December session.
b. Includes three persons born in Guinea and one person described as a "yellowish man," who were not specifically listed as blacks or mulattoes.
c. Includes those persons born in Philadelphia and Pennsylvania.
d. The normal requirement was to leave the state and never to return. This was occasionally modified to specify either that the person was to stay out of the state for a number of years or that he was to leave the United States forever.

Table 2
Percentage of Criminals Convicted
in Philadelphia's Mayor's Court,
1794–1800, by Place of Birth

Place of birth	Percentage of total
Ireland	31.7
Other foreign countries	28.2
United States[a]	40.1
Pennsylvania[b]	12.0
Philadelphia	6.0

Note: All percentages are rounded off to the nearest tenth.
a. Includes those born in Philadelphia and Pennsylvania.
b. Includes those born in Philadelphia.

Table 3
Percentage of Criminals Convicted
in Philadelphia's Mayor's Court,
1794–1800, by Race

Race	Percentage of total
Whites	67.6
Blacks[a]	31.8
"Indians"[b]	0.6

Note: All percentages are rounded off to the nearest tenth.
a. Includes three persons born in Guinea and one person described as a "yellowish man," who were not specifically listed as blacks or mulattoes.
b. Presumably American Indians.

Table 4
Occupations of Criminals Convicted at Philadelphia's Mayor's Court, 1794–1800

Occupation	Total number	Percentage of total	Occupation	Total number	Percentage of total
Laborer	17	26.98	Millwright	1	1.59
Mariner	5	7.94	Musician	1	1.59
Blacksmith	4	6.35	Plasterer	1	1.59
Carpenter	4	6.35	Printer	1	1.59
Shoemaker	3	4.76	Saddler	1	1.59
Silk weaver	2	3.17	Silver carver	1	1.59
Silversmith	2	3.17	Seamstress	1	1.59
Baker	1	1.59	Tailor	1	1.59
Barber	1	1.59	Tobacconist	1	1.59
Butcher	1	1.59	Waiter	1	1.59
Cabinetmaker	1	1.59	Weaver	1	1.59
Cook	1	1.59	Wood sawyer	1	1.59
Engraver	1	1.59	Baker or shoemaker	1	1.59
Farmer	1	1.59			
Flax dresser	1	1.59	Miller and copper	1	1.59
Gardener	1	1.59			
Glassmaker	1	1.59	Weaver or brick mason	1	1.59
Highchair maker	1	1.59			

Note: All people whose occupations could be determined have been included; four people listed as servants have been counted as having no occupations because it is not clear if these were domestic or bound servants, the latter of whom might have had a variety of trades. Because only 63 out of 321 convictions (with repeat criminals subtracted from each total) had occupations listed, the percentages must be viewed with caution. All percentages are rounded off to the nearest hundredth.

Abbreviations

Archives

APS	American Philosophical Society
CCA	Christ Church Archives, Philadelphia
HCA	Haverford College Archives
HSP	Historical Society of Pennsylvania
PCA	Philadelphia City Archives
PFMMA	Philadelphia Friends Monthly Meeting Archives

Newspapers Published in Philadelphia

Am. Daily Adv.	*Dunlap's American Daily Advertiser*, 1791–93; *Dunlap and Claypoole's American Daily Advertiser*, 1793–95; *Claypoole's American Daily Advertiser*, 1796–1800; *Poulson's American Daily Advertiser*, 1800
Aurora	*General Advertiser*, 1790–94; *Aurora. General Advertiser*, 1794–1800
Daily Adv.	*The Daily Advertiser*, 1797
Fed. Gaz.	*The Federal Gazette, and Philadelphia Evening Post*, 1788–93
Freeman's Journal	*The Freeman's Journal: or, the North-American Intelligencer*, 1781–92
Gale's Indep. Gaz.	*Gale's Independent Gazetteer*, 1796–97
Gaz. of U.S.	*Gazette of the United States*, 1790–1800

Indep. Gaz.	*The Independent Gazetteer; or, the Chronicle of Freedom,* 1782–96
The Mail	*The Mail; or Claypoole's Daily Advertiser,* 1791–93
Mer. Daily Adv.	*The Merchant's Daily Advertiser,* 1797–98
Nat. Gaz.	*The National Gazette, A Periodical Miscellany of News, Politics, History, and Polite Literature,* 1791–93
New World	*The New World; or, the Morning and Evening Gazette,* 1796–97
Penn. Chron.	*The Pennsylvania Chronicle, and Universal Advertiser,* 1767–74
Penn. Eve. Her.	*Carey's Pennsylvania Evening Herald,* 1785–88
Penn. Eve. Post	*The Pennsylvania Evening Post,* 1775–84
Penn. Gaz.	*The Pennsylvania Gazette,* 1760–1800
Penn. Journal	*The Pennsylvania Journal, and Weekly Advertiser,* 1766–93
Penn. Mer.	*The Pennsylvania Mercury and Universal Advertiser,* 1784–92
Penn. Packet	*The Pennsylvania Packet; and General Advertiser,* 1771–90
Penny Post	*The Penny Post,* 1769
Phila. Gaz.	*The Philadelphia Gazette and Universal Daily Advertiser,* 1794–1800
Phila. Min.	*The Philadelphia Minerva,* 1795–97
Porcupine's Gaz.	*Porcupine's Gazette and United States Daily Advertiser,* 1797–99
True Am.	*The True American and Commercial Advertiser,* 1798–1800
U.S. Recorder	*Carey's United States Recorder,* 1798

Philadelphia City Archives, Unpublished Governmental Records

MMHE: 1766	Minutes of the Managers of the House of Employment for 1766
MMHE: 1769–78	Minutes of the Managers of the House of Employment for 1769–78
MAHM: 1780–88	Managers of the Alms House Minutes for 1780–88
MAHM: 1788–96	Managers of the Alms House Minutes for 1788–96

Abbreviations

MAHM: 1796–1803 — Minutes of the Managers of the Almshouse for 1796–1803
MGOP: 1768–74 — Minutes of the Guardians of the Poor of the City of Philadelphia and Districts Annexed, 1768–74
MOPCP: 1774–82 — Minutes of the Overseers of the Poor of the City of Philadelphia for 1774–82
MOPCP: 1782–87 — Minutes of the Overseers of the Poor of the City of Philadelphia for 1782–87
MGBGP: 1788–95 — Minutes of the General Board of the Guardians of the Poor for 1788–95
MGPCP: 1795–1801 — Minutes of the Guardians of the Poor in the City of Philadelphia for 1795–1801
RMCBOP: 1787–96 — Rough Minutes of the City Board of the Overseers of the Poor and Guardians of the Poor for 1787–96

Published Governmental Records

Penn. Archives — Pennsylvania Archives
Penn. Statutes — Pennsylvania Statutes at Large for 1682–1801

Historical Journals

PMHB — *Pennsylvania Magazine of History and Biography*
WMQ — *William and Mary Quarterly*, 3d ser.

Notes

Introduction

1. *The American Revolution Considered as a Social Movement* (Princeton, N.J., 1926), p. 11.
2. E. James Ferguson, *The American Revolution: A General History, 1763–1790*, rev. ed. (Homewood, Ill., 1979), p. 227.
3. "The American Revolution Considered as a Social Movement: A Re-Evaluation," *American Historical Review* 60 (October 1954): 1–12.
4. For typical studies see, e.g., Charles Lawrence, *History of the Philadelphia Almshouses and Hospitals* (Philadelphia, 1905); and William C. Heffner, *History of Poor Relief Legislation in Pennsylvania, 1682–1913* (Cleona, Pa., 1913). Valuable exceptions that are sensitive to attitudes toward poverty include Raymond A. Mohl, *Poverty in New York, 1783–1825* (New York, 1971); William H. Williams, *America's First Hospital: The Pennsylvania Hospital, 1751–1841* (Wayne, Pa., 1976); Gary B. Nash, "Poverty and Poor Relief in Pre-Revolutionary Philadelphia," *WMQ* 33 (January 1976): 3–30; and Gary B. Nash, "The Transformation of Urban Politics 1700–1765," *Journal of American History* 60 (December 1973): 605–32.
5. Often following the lead of Jesse Lemisch, historians have recently devoted greater energy to examination of the lower classes. See Lemisch's "The American Revolution Seen from the Bottom Up," in *Towards A New Past: Dissenting Essays in American History*, ed. Barton J. Bernstein (New York, 1968),

pp. 3-45, and "Jack Tar in the Streets: Merchant Seamen in the Politics of Revolutionary America," *WMQ* 25 (July 1968): 371-407. On Philadelphia, see especially Gary B. Nash, "Social Change and the Growth of Prerevolutionary Urban Radicalism," in *The American Revolution: Explorations in the History of American Radicalism*, ed. Alfred F. Young (DeKalb, Ill., 1976), pp. 3-36.

6. Quoted in "The Memorial," *Aurora*, 28 July 1796. Here and elsewhere, eighteenth-century quotations are given as printed; corrections or emendations are added in brackets only to avoid confusion or misreading. Titles or captions to items that appeared in newspapers have been shortened and, where necessary, rendered in normal type.

7. On the general influence of Enlightenment ideals, see Merle Curti, *The Growth of American Thought*, 3d ed. (New York, 1964), pp. 98-201, and especially pp. 115, 123, 147-50, 161, 178.

8. *Memoirs of a Life, Chiefly Passed in Pennsylvania, within the Last Sixty Years* . . . (Harrisburg, Pa., 1811), p. 102.

9. 22 Aug. 1787.

10. "To the Citizens," *Indep. Gaz.*, 28 Mar. 1787.

11. The case for unity is given in Sam Bass Warner, Jr., *The Private City: Philadelphia in Three Periods of Its Growth* (Philadelphia, 1968), pp. 3-45 (quotations from pp. 8, 11).

12. David J. Rothman presents the opposite view in his *The Discovery of the Asylum: Social Order and Disorder in the New Republic* (Boston, 1971), p. xix. See also pp. xii, xvi, xviii, 3, 5, 14, 20, 28; and cf. Mohl, *Poverty*, p. 262.

13. For claims that republicanism exerted a unifying influence, see especially Gordon S. Wood, *The Creation of the American Republic, 1776-1787* (Chapel Hill, N.C., 1969), pp. 42-45 and passim; and Pauline Maier, "Popular Uprisings and Civil Authority in Eighteenth-Century America," *WMQ* 27 (January 1970): 33-34.

14. Richard G. Miller, *Philadelphia–The Federalist City: A Study of Urban Politics, 1789-1801* (Port Washington, N.Y., 1976), p. 151; Hannah B. Roach, "Taxables in the City of Philadelphia, 1756," *Pennsylvania Genealogical Magazine* 22, no. 1 (1961): 9; Gary B. Nash, "Urban Wealth and Poverty in Pre-Revolutionary America," *Journal of Interdisciplinary History* 4 (Spring 1976): 548 n; John K. Alexander, "The Philadelphia Numbers Game: An Analysis of Philadelphia's Eighteenth-Century Population," *PMHB* 98 (July 1974): 314-24. See also n. 25 to Chapter One, below.

15. HSP, "Plan for a Society to lend Money to the Poor on Interest," ca. 1790–91, in Miers Fisher Papers.
16. Thomas F. Pettigrew, Robert T. Riley, and Reeve D. Venneman, "George Wallace's Constituents," *Psychology Today* 5 (February 1972): 47–49, 92.
17. *A Complete Dictionary of the English Language, . . . By Thomas Sheridan, a. m.*, 4th ed. (Philadelphia, 1789).
18. "A Useful Hint," *Mer. Daily Adv.*, 19 Aug. 1797; "Miletius," *Aurora*, 30 Aug. 1792; "Human Mind," *Penn. Packet*, 25 May 1772.
19. Tench Coxe, *A View of the United States of America . . .* (Philadelphia, 1794), p. 442; "Address," *Penn. Mer.*, 14 Sept. 1790; Johann D. Schoepf, *Travels in the Confederation*, trans. and ed. Alfred J. Morrison, 2 vols. (Philadelphia, 1911), 1: 99. Cf. Jackson T. Main, *The Social Structure of Revolutionary America* (Princeton, N.J., 1965), pp. 72–73, 113 n, 271–72. Here and later, the citations are representative selections taken from the many available examples.
20. *Gale's Indep. Gaz.*, 3 Jan. 1797; "To the Printer," *Penn. Packet*, 13 June 1774; Benjamin Rush to Charles Nisbet, 27 Aug. 1784, in Benjamin Rush, *Letters of Benjamin Rush*, ed. L. H. Butterfield, 2 vols. (Princeton, N.J., 1951), 1: 336.
21. "Address," *Phila. Gaz.*, 22 May 1800; Duke De La Rochefoucault Liancourt, *Travels through the United States . . .*, trans. H. Neuman, 2 vols. (London, 1799), 2: 382; "Phileleutherous," *Penn. Gaz.*, 2 Feb. 1780; HSP, "Penn. Abolition Society. Committee For Improving Condition of Free Blacks, Minutes, 1790–1803," 10 Apr. 1790, 30 Nov. 1795, and passim (hereinafter HSP, Penn. Abolition Soc.: 1790–1803).
22. "A few days," *Gale's Indep. Gaz.*, 11 Nov. 1796; HSP, "Rough Sketch of address . . . 1 Mon. 1766," in Dreer Collection; MAHM: 1780–88, 8 Dec. 1784. Cf. Main, *Social Structure*, pp. 73–74.
23. See Chapters One and Seven, above. Mechanics and artisans ran the gamut from being little, if any, above poverty to being extremely wealthy. Hence, the mechanic–artisan group cannot rightly be depicted as either poor or affluent: one must examine the individual and the individual occupation. See Charles S. Olton, "Philadelphia Artisans and the American Revolution" (Ph.D. diss., University of California, Berkeley, 1967), pp. 7–16, and *Artisans for Independence: Philadelphia Mechanics and the American Revolution* (Syracuse, N.Y., 1975), pp. 7–11; and Jesse Lemisch and John K. Alexander, "The White Oaks, Jack

Tar, and the Concept of the 'Inarticulate,'" *WMQ* 29 (January 1972): 109–27.
24. Rush to Ebenezer Hazard, 8 Nov. 1765, in Rush, *Letters*, 1: 18. On disturbances see J. Thomas Scharf and Thompson Westcott, *History of Philadelphia, 1609–1884*, 3 vols. (Philadelphia, 1884), 1: 403; *Indep. Gaz.*, 16 Apr. 1794; and *Gale's Indep. Gaz.*, 3 Jan. 1797.
25. "Poverty," p. 13.
26. On the city's population see Alexander, "Numbers Game," p. 324.
27. "To the Public," *Penn. Packet*, 11 Mar. 1784.
28. The number aided by public charity alone makes the total one in six. See MAHM: 1780–88, 3 Mar. 1784.
29. Cf. Gary B. Nash, *Red, White, and Black: The Peoples of Early America* (Englewood Cliffs, N.J., 1974), p. 232.

Chapter 1: "The Punishment of Dependence"

1. It must be remembered that the following analysis of distribution of wealth is based on records that underestimate the concentration of wealth. See n. 14 to the Introduction, above.
2. Gary B. Nash and Billy G. Smith, "The Population of Eighteenth-Century Philadelphia," *PMHB* 99 (July 1975): 366, 368 n.
3. The statistics were computed from the tax lists in Hannah B. Roach, "Philadelphia's Colonial Poor Laws," *Pennsylvania Genealogical Magazine* 22, no. 3 (1962): 171–85. A similar concentration of wealth in the urban areas of 1767 and 1774 is revealed in Nash, "Urban Wealth," pp. 549–51.
4. *Philadelphia*, pp. 5, 6, and Table 1 (p. 6), from which the first two sets of statistics were computed.
5. *Penn. Journal*, 27 Sept. 1786.
6. "For the Pennsylvania Packet," *Supplement* to *Penn. Packet*, 23 Nov. 1772; *Fed. Gaz.*, 27 June 1789.
7. *Penn. Chron.*, 13 Aug. 1770; but cf. Benjamin Rush to Humane Society of Massachusetts, 9 Mar. 1793, in Rush, *Letters*, 2: 629.
8. *Aurora*, 28 Aug. 1793.
9. *Penn. Gaz.*, 2 Feb. 1780.
10. "An American," *Penn. Gaz.*, 29 Oct. 1788; Schoepf, *Travels*, 1: 117–18; Coxe, *A View*, pp. 38, 95–97, 438.
11. Foreign travelers often held that the lower classes lived better in the New World than in the Old. See Schoepf, *Travels*, 1: 55,

79, 86, 99–100; and J. P. Brissot DeWarville, *New Travels in the United States of America 1788*, ed. Durand Echeverria (Cambridge, Mass., 1964), p. 205.

12. To many Philadelphians, prices were not as low, wages not as high, and life not as good as they should have been. See *Penn. Gaz.*, 7 Jan. 1762; "A Poor Tradesman," *Penn. Mer.*, 21 Dec. 1787; and "A Friend," *Fed. Gaz.*, 27 Apr. 1793.
13. *Whereas the Number of Poor* . . . (Philadelphia, 1764); HSP, "Rough Sketch of address . . . 1 Mon. 1766," in Dreer Collection.
14. "A Friend," *Penn. Gaz.*, 15 Mar. 1775; "Harrington," ibid., 30 May 1787; *The Pennsylvania Magazine: or, American Monthly Museum* 1 (October 1775): 483; "A Manufacturer," *Penn. Packet*, 20 Dec. 1788; *Penn. Mer.* 7 July 1789; "A Friend," *Indep. Gaz.*, 21 June 1783.
15. "At the anniversary," *Indep. Gaz.*, 21 May 1791.
16. "Thoughts on Good Times," *Freeman's Journal*, 9 July 1788.
17. "A Friend," *Fed. Gaz.*, 7 Apr. 1790.
18. Ibid., 21 Dec. 1790; HSP, "St. George's Society Minutes . . . April 23, 1772 to December 17, 1812," 24 Jan. 1774, petition of John Parker (hereinafter HSP, SGSM: 1772–1812).
19. *Penn. Packet*, 31 Dec. 1787; *Aurora*, 19 Nov. 1791; MAHM: 1780–88, p. 48.
20. *Indep. Gaz.*, 31 Dec. 1785; *Penn. Gaz.*, 12 Jan. 1791. During mild winters, they could, in the view of some Philadelphians, live fairly well. See *Freeman's Journal*, 6 Jan. 1790; and *Penn. Journal*, 17 Mar. 1790.
21. *Phil. Gaz.*, 2 May 1794; "A plain . . . Friend," *Penn. Packet*, 26 Aug. 1785; HSP, SGSM: 1772–1812, Rules and Constitution and 23 Apr. 1773; Karl F. Geiser, "Redemptioners and Indentured Servants in the Colony and Commonwealth of Pennsylvania," *Yale Review* 10, supplement no. 2 (August 1901): 39.
22. *Penn. Eve. Her.*, 1 Aug. 1785; *Aurora*, 30 Sept. 1794.
23. James Mease, *The Picture of Philadelphia* . . . (Philadelphia, 1811), pp. 280–86.
24. "Dennis K——y," *Indep. Gaz.*, 10 July 1787; *Penn. Eve. Her.*, 18 Sept. 1787.
25. Mr. Smith kindly allowed me to examine a manuscript copy of his " 'The Best Poor Man's Country': Living Standards of the 'Lower Sort' in Late Eighteenth-Century Philadelphia," *Working Papers* 2, no. 4 (1979): 1–70, which is a publication from the Regional Economic History Research Center of the Eleutherian Mills–Hagley Foundation, Greenville and Wilmington,

Delaware. Although the analysis Smith offers is as firmly rooted in solid data as possible, this valuable essay illustrates the difficulties of constructing an accurate standard-of-living scale. Firm data on employment are nonexistent; retail prices must be estimated; information on wages is too often spotty. Mr. Smith analyzes the economic reality of life for the lower classes of Philadelphia in this period in his forthcoming dissertation, tentatively titled "The Working Classes of Philadelphia during the Revolutionary Era" (University of California, Los Angeles).
26. Jackson T. Main's claim that "in Philadelphia the chance to rise was indeed a good one" (*Social Structure*, p. 194) is contradicted by his own evidence, as Jesse Lemisch ("American Revolution," p. 33 n) notes. Cf. also James Henretta, "Economic Development and Social Structure in Colonial Boston," *WMQ* 22 (January 1965): 77.
27. *Penn. Statutes*, 3: 224–25; 8: 95. I do not know how rigidly the law was enforced in the city.
28. John F. Watson, *Annals of Philadelphia, and Pennsylvania, in the Olden Time* . . . , enlarged by Willias P. Hazard, 3 vols. (Philadelphia, 1884), 1: 176, 186, 187, 189, 191. See also "A Matrimonial," *Phila. Min.*, 11 Apr. 1795; and Ian M. G. Quimby, "Apprenticeship in Colonial Philadelphia" (M. A. thesis, University of Delaware, 1962), p. 62.
29. *Penn. Journal*, 15 May 1760. Some groups, such as common seamen and vagrant beggars, were also viewed as recognizable by their dress. See "Effects," *Penn. Gaz.*, 12 Feb. 1767; and *Indep. Gaz.*, 15 May 1784, 18 Sept. 1788.
30. "Simplicius Honestus," *Penn. Packet*, 9 Nov. 1772; "Monitor," ibid., 1 Jan. 1776; "A Merchant," *Penn. Journal*, 19 Jan. 1774.
31. "Luxury," *Aurora*, 15 Feb. 1796.
32. *New World*, 6 Jan. 1797. See also *Phila. Min.*, 11 Apr. 1795; "Philanthropos," *True Am.*, 6 Nov. 1798; and *Philadelphia Monthly Magazine* . . . 1 (April 1798): 228–29.
33. La Rochefoucault, *Travels*, 2: 386; Issac Weld, *Travels Through the States of North America* . . . (London, 1799), p. 15.
34. La Rochefoucault, *Travels*, 2: 382; Benjamin Davies, *Some Account of the City of Philadelphia* . . . (Philadelphia, 1794), p. 89; MAHM: 1788–96, 23 Feb. 1789. One exception to this pattern was that the very wealthy often maintained country estates that might be used on a regular or only semiregular basis. See Carl Bridenbaugh and Jessica Bridenbaugh, *Rebels and Gentlemen: Philadelphia in the Age of Franklin* (New York, 1942), p. 12;

and Jacob Hiltzheimer, *Extracts from the Diary of Jacob Hiltzheimer, of Philadelphia, 1765–1798*, ed. Jacob C. Parsons (Philadelphia, 1893), passim.
35. Computed from the tax lists in Roach, "Philadelphia's Colonial Poor Laws."
36. Computed from PCA, Constables' Tax Returns to Assessors for 1780; and PCA, county tax for Southwark, 1781.
37. PCA, Constables' Tax Returns to Assessors for 1780, p. 120; cf. pp. 116–22 passim.
38. Compiled from Bureau of the Census, *A Century of Population Growth* (Washington, D.C., 1909), pp. 142–43.
39. *Philadelphia*, p. 8; see also pp. 6–12 passim with statistics computed from Table 2 (p. 8).
40. Number of laborers and percentages derived from HSP, "Enumeration of the Taxable Inhabitants within the County of Philadelphia 1800"; cf. Norman J. Johnston, "Caste and Class of the Urban Form of Historic Philadelphia," *Journal of the American Institute of Planners* 32 (November 1966): 334–50.
41. "Casca," *Indep. Gaz.*, 28 Apr. 1789; "A Citizen," *Fed. Gaz.*, 14 Oct. 1793; *Penn. Journal*, 8 Aug. 1787; *Penn. Eve. Her.*, 4 Aug. 1787; HSP, Penn. Abolition Soc.: 1790–1803, 10 Aug. 1797.
42. Watson, *Annals*, 1: 483; *Penn. Packet*, 26 Oct. 1772; *Porcupine's Gaz.*, 13 Oct. 1798.
43. Quotations from *Phila. Gaz.*, 5 June 1799; and "An Inspector," *Am. Daily Adv.*, 5 and 12 Feb. 1796. See also Graydon, *Memoirs*, p. 34; Watson, *Annals*, 1: 101; "Housekeeper," *Penn. Eve. Her.*, 28 Mar. 1787; *Penn. Packet*, 24 May 1787; *Gale's Indep. Gaz.*, 25 July 1797; and "Mayor," *The Mail*, 29 Feb. 1792.
44. Rush to John Swanwick, n. d., in *Indep. Gaz.*, 21 Dec. 1793.
45. Benjamin Rush, *The Autobiography of Benjamin Rush* . . . , ed. George Corner, Memoirs of the American Philosophical Society, vol. 25 (Princeton, N.J., 1948), pp. 83–84; "Clergyman," *Phila. Gaz.*, 8 Apr. 1795; W. E. B. DuBois, *The Philadelphia Negro: A Social Study* (Philadelphia, 1899), pp. 299–301; HSP, Samuel Duffield to Alexander J. Dalles, 27 July 1794, in Gratz Collection; "The Yellow Fever," *Porcupine's Gaz.*, 9 Aug. 1798.
46. "Tom Trudge," *Penn. Chron.*, 27 Mar. 1769; *Penn. Gaz.*, 11 Apr. 1765; "By the Mayor, Recorder, and Aldermen, and the Commissioners for paving and cleansing the Streets, &c" (broadside; Philadelphia, 1765); Charles S. Olton, "Philadelphia's First Environmental Crisis," *PMHB* 98 (January 1974): 90–100.
47. *True Am.*, 9 Aug. 1798; *Daily Adv.*, 24 Aug. 1797.

48. PCA, Minutes of the Board of Health for 1798–99, 11 Aug. 1798; "Citizens," *Gaz. of U.S.*, 23 Mar. 1796.
49. Rush, *Autobiography*, p. 84; Watson, *Annals*, 1: 405, 483, 486, 559; "Observer," *Aurora*, 17 Feb. 1796; *Nat. Gaz.*, 2 Oct. 1793.
50. Rush, *Autobiography*, p. 84; *Phila. Gaz.*, 8 Apr. 1795; "Citizens," *Gaz. of U.S.*, 23 Mar. 1796.
51. At times, and especially during yellow fever periods, persons who would not normally be considered poor had to be able to obtain recommendations. See "Z," *Am. Daily Adv.*, 25 July 1799; "A Great Many," *Porcupine's Gaz.*, 7 Sept. 1797; *Indep. Gaz.*, 15 Mar. 1794; and Thomas Condie and Robert Folwell, *History of the Pestilence, commonly called yellow fever, . . . 1798* (Philadelphia, 1799), pp. 9, 62, 63.
52. "To the Spinners," *Penn. Journal*, 16 July 1775; *Penn. Gaz.*, 29 Sept. 1768; "Mess.," *Penn. Packet*, 25 Sept. 1786; HSP, SGSM: 1772–1812, 23 July 1779; HSP, petition of 11 Oct. 1790, in Gratz Collection, under Hucksters' Petitions; HSP, petition of Evan Lloyd, ca. January 1801, in Society Miscellaneous Collection, Box 3-B; HSP, petition of Samuel Walton, ca. October 1800, in ibid., Box 4-A (hereinafter HSP, Soc. Misc. Coll.).
53. HSP, SGSM: 1772–1812, 23 Jan. 1797 and passim; *Penn. Chron.*, 22 Jan. 1770. See also Chapter Seven, below.
54. MGOP: 1768–74, 16 Dec. 1771; MOPCP: 1774–82, 26 Dec. 1775, 10 and 16 Sept. and 30 Dec. 1779, 17 Feb. 1780; HSP, Samuel Rhoads, Jr., et al. to Philadelphia Overseers of the Poor, 27 Nov. 1771(?), in Gratz Collection, under Overseers of the Poor; see also subsequent discussion in Chapter Six.
55. Advertisement by Dr. Day, *Penn. Journal*, 10 Nov. 1773. Most doctors who gave free assistance to the poor did not say that they required recommendations.
56. "Tents," *Porcupine's Gaz.*, 25 Sept. 1798; HSP, Philadelphia Society for Alleviating the Miseries of Public Prisons, passim, and especially George Duffield to John Connely, 26 Jan. 1789, and "John W. Crum's Address 14 May 1788," filed under Case 42, 2d Floor (hereinafter HSP, Soc. for Alleviating Miseries: files); PCA, "Minutes of Board of Inspectors [of the Philadelphia Jail] from May 1794 to August 1801," 23 Jan. 1798.
57. 30 July 1798; "Of Sufficiency," *Penn. Mer.*, 1 Oct. 1784.
58. *Penn. Eve. Her.*, 23 Apr. 1785. Cf. *Pennsylvania Magazine . . .* 1 (May 1775): 199; *Philadelphia Monthly Magazine . . .* 1 (May 1798): 280–81.
59. HSP, Penn. Abolition Soc.: 1790–1803, 18 Sept. 1791, 22 Mar.

1793; "Health-Office," *Phila. Gaz.*, 1 Nov. 1798; HSP, "Thomas," broadside dated January 1769; HSP, "Prisoners in New Jail" to Benjamin Rush, 16 Sept. 1800, in Papers of Benjamin Rush, 21: 7.
60. "A Merchant," *Penn. Journal*, 19 Jan. 1774; "Strictures," *Penn. Eve. Her.*, 25 Aug. 1787. See also "Monitor," *Penn. Packet*, 1 Jan. 1776.
61. "To the Free Africans," *Am. Daily Adv.*, 16 Jan. 1796.
62. Weld, *Travels*, p. 13 and passim.

Chapter 2: The Context

1. Graydon, *Memoirs*, p. 102; for a suggestive comparison on the importance of such change, see Walter H. Houghton, *The Victorian Frame of Mind, 1830–1870* (New Haven, Conn., 1957), pp. 1–23 and passim.
2. Alexander, "Numbers Game," p. 324; *Return of the whole number of persons . . . for the second census . . .* (Washington, D.C., 1802), p. 49.
3. "No. I," *Aurora*, 23 Sept. 1797; Coxe, *A View*, pp. 61, 94–95; "Emigration," *Penn. Packet*, 10 Sept. 1789.
4. Benjamin Franklin's famous denunciation of the "Palatine Boors," published in a 1755 work, was expunged from later editions (see Leonard W. Labaree and William B. Willcox, eds., *The Papers of Benjamin Franklin*, 23 vols. to date [New Haven, Conn., 1959–   ], 4: 225–35). Such negative comments on immigrants were only rarely offered in colonial days.
5. 7 July 1787.
6. Coxe, *A View*, p. 74; *Penn. Journal*, 4 Feb. 1789.
7. *Penn. Mer.*, 3 June 1790.
8. *Penn. Packet*, 1 Mar. 1786.
9. "Charlotte," *Penn. Eve. Her.*, 10 Aug. 1785; *Gaz. of U.S.*, 8 Nov. and 17 Dec. 1798; "Irish Rebels," *Porcupine's Gaz.*, 28 Nov. 1798. See also the sources cited in n. 48 and n. 49 to this chapter.
10. Gary B. Nash, "Slaves and Slaveowners in Colonial Philadelphia," *WMQ* 30 (April 1973): 246; Edgar J. McManus, *Black Bondage in the North* (Syracuse, N.Y., 1973), p. 207.
11. Richard B. Morris, *Government and Labor in Early America* (New York, 1946), pp. 35, 500; Chessman A. Herrick, *White Servitude in Pennsylvania* (Philadelphia, 1926), pp. 97–98, 254.
12. Sharon V. Salinger (in "Colonial Labor in Transition: The Decline of Indentured Servitude in Late Eighteenth-Century Philadelphia," presented at the 1978 meeting of the Organization of

American Historians) documents the decline of bound labor, although she overstates the totality of the move toward free labor by 1800.
13. John R. Commons et al., *History of Labour in the United States*, 4 vols. (New York, 1918–35), 1: 37, 58–60, 61–65, 69–71, 108–9, 121–22, 126; Philip S. Foner, *History of the Labor Movement in the United States*, 6 vols. to date (New York, 1947–   ), 1: 71, 76 n; Morris, *Government and Labor*, pp. 201, 203.
14. Commons, *History of Labor*, 1: 5, 7–8, 11–12, 15, 19–20, 25, 72, 75, 87, 104, 105, 111, 132–33.
15. John K. Alexander, " 'A Year . . . Famed in the Annals of History': Philadelphia in 1776," in *Philadelphia: 1776–2076—A Three Hundred Year View*, ed. Dennis Clark (Port Washington, N.Y., 1975), pp. 25–26; Chilton Williamson, *American Suffrage from Property to Democracy, 1760–1800* (Princeton, N.J., 1960), pp. 33–37; Edward P. Allinson and Boies Penrose, *Philadelphia, 1681–1887: A History of Municipal Development* (Philadelphia, 1887), pp. 3, 8–9, 52–59; John K. Alexander, "Deference in Colonial Pennsylvania and That Man from New Jersey," *PMHB* 102 (October 1978): 422–36.
16. *Penn. Gaz.*, 27 Sept. 1770.
17. "The Young Owl," *Penn. Packet*, 17 Feb. 1772. Cf. Chapter Three below.
18. Alexander, "Deference," pp. 431–36; Nash, "Transformation," passim; Merrill Jensen, "The American People and the American Revolution," *Journal of American History* 57 (June 1970): 28–30; Eric Foner, *Tom Paine and Revolutionary America* (New York, 1976), pp. 63–69.
19. In addition to the material in the text, see "Civis" and "To the Electors," *Penn. Gaz.*, 1 May 1776; J. Paul Selsam, *The Pennsylvania Constitution of 1776: A Study in Revolutionary Democracy* (Harrisburg, Pa., 1936), pp. 190, 206, 208–12; and John N. Shaeffer, "Public Consideration of the 1776 Pennsylvania Constitution," *PMHB* 98 (October 1974): 415–37.
20. "A Dialogue," *Penn. Eve. Post*, 24 Oct. 1776.
21. Theodore Thayer, in *Pennsylvania Politics and the Growth of Democracy, 1740–1776* (Harrisburg, Pa., 1953), pp. 211–27, gives the most accurate copy of the document from which the quotations are taken (pp. 212, 213, with emphasis added).
22. Rush to Anthony Wayne, 19 May and 5 and 18 June 1777, and Rush to John Adams, 8 Aug. 1777, in Rush *Letters*, 1: 148, 149–52.
23. After protracted political warfare, a more conservative constitu-

tion was enacted in 1790, but it did not significantly alter the voting requirements. See Robert L. Brunhouse, *The Counter-Revolution in Pennsylvania, 1776–1790* (Harrisburg, Pa., 1940).
24. "Address," *Penn. Gaz.*, 21 Oct. 1772; "Publicus," ibid., 13 and 20 Jan. 1773.
25. "Examiner," *Penn. Eve. Post*, 15 Oct. 1776; "Mechanic," *Indep. Gaz.*, 8 Jan. 1785; "Citizen," ibid., 28 May 1789; "One of the People," *Penn. Mer.*, 7 Oct. 1790; "School Boy," *Aurora*, 11 Feb. 1795; "Squib," *Fed. Gaz.*, 18 Jan. 1790. Innumerable further examples can be given, and some appear in the text of this chapter.
26. "Valerius," *Freeman's Journal*, 31 Dec. 1783; "Friend," *Penn. Gaz.*, 8 Mar. 1786; "Freeman," *Fed. Gaz.*, 7 Nov. 1792.
27. "Anti Protexus," *Gaz. of U.S.*, 26 May 1794; "Whitlock," *Penn. Eve. Post*, 27 May 1777; "Farmer," *Indep. Gaz.*, 22 May 1790; "Correspondent," *Aurora*, 21 Aug. 1794; "Remarks," *Penn. Gaz.*, 16 May 1787.
28. *Penn. Packet*, 20 Oct. 1784; *Aurora*, 23 Apr. 1799. Freneau was, in fact, in a very insecure economic position. See Jacob Axelrad, *Philip Freneau: Champion of Democracy* (Austin, Tex., 1967), pp. 332, 352–53.
29. A more detailed narrative and documentation are available in my article "The Fort Wilson Incident of 1779: A Case Study of the Revolutionary Crowd," *WMQ* 31 (October 1974): 589–612.
30. *Penn. Packet*, 19 Jan. 1779; Morris, *Government and Labor*, p. 199.
31. *Penn. Archives*, 1st ser., 7: 392–94 (quotation from p. 394).
32. *Penn. Eve. Post*, 29 May 1779.
33. *Penn. Packet*, 1 July 1779.
34. William B. Reed, ed., *Life and Correspondence of Joseph Reed . . .*, 2 vols. (Philadelphia, 1847), 2: 151.
35. Samuel Shaw to Winthrop Sargent, 10 Oct. 1779, in "Captain Samuel Shaw's Revolutionary War Letters to Captain Winthrop Sargent," ed. Nicholas B. Wainwright, *PMHB* 70 (July 1946): 300; Henry Laurens to John Adams, 4 Oct. 1779, in *The Works of John Adams*, ed. Charles F. Adams, 10 vols. (Boston, 1850–56), 9: 499; Samuel Patterson to Caesar Rodney, 6 Oct. 1779, in *Letters to and from Caesar Rodney*, ed. George H. Ryden (Philadelphia, 1933), pp. 323–24. See also E. A. Benians, ed., *A Journal by Thos: Hughes . . .* (Cambridge, Eng., 1947), p. 72.
36. *To the merchants and traders of Philadelphia . . .* (Philadelphia, 1779), passim; *Penn. Archives*, 1st ser., 7: 738, 740, 741, 745,

Notes to Chapter Two

747–49; *Penn. Eve. Post*, 12 Oct. 1779; see also *Penn. Journal*, 20 Oct. 1779, on the possibility of added violence.
37. "Valerius," *Freeman's Journal*, 7 Apr. 1784; Watson, *Annals*, 1: 425; "Jack Tar," *Indep. Gaz.*, 26 Jan. 1788.
38. Brunhouse, *Counter-Revolution*, pp. 135–40 (quotation from p. 136); Scharf and Westcott, *History*, 1: 428–31.
39. Benjamin Rush to Charles Lee, 24 Oct. 1779, and Rush to John Montgomery, 27 June 1783, in Rush, *Letters*, 1: 244, 302.
40. John H. Powell, *Bring Out Your Dead: The Great Plague of Yellow Fever in Philadelphia in 1793* (Philadelphia, 1949), pp. 69, 177–92 passim; *Fed. Gaz.*, 19 Dec. 1793; *Penn. Gaz.*, 7 May 1794; *Aurora*, 13 Oct. 1795, 6 Sept. 1797; *Porcupine's Gaz.*, 29 Aug., 6 Sept., and 28 Oct. 1797; "Friend," *Phila. Gaz.*, 25 Aug. 1797; "Philanthropos," ibid., 10 Oct. 1797.
41. James Hardie, *The Philadelphia Directory and Register . . .* (Philadelphia, 1793), p. 101; "Electors," *Phila. Gaz.*, 9 Oct. 1797.
42. *Gaz. of U.S.*, 9 Oct. 1797; "Amity," *Am. Daily Adv.*, 10 Oct. 1797.
43. Percentages computed from returns given in *Porcupine's Gaz.*, 13 Oct. 1797, and *Aurora*, 24 Feb. 1798. See also "Philadelphian," *Gaz. of U.S.*, 21 Feb. 1798.
44. *Porcupine's Gaz.*, 13 and 16 Oct. 1797.
45. "Election," *Phila. Gaz.*, 7 Feb. 1798; "Republican," *U.S. Recorder*, 17 Feb. 1798; "Democrat," ibid., 20 Feb. 1798; "Truth," *Gaz. of U.S.*, 20 Feb. 1798; *Am. Daily Adv.*, 22 Feb. 1798.
46. *U.S. Recorder*, 17 Feb. 1798; "Friend," *Phila. Gaz.*, 13 Feb. 1798; "Fair Play," *Aurora*, 18 Jan. 1798.
47. In addition to the citations already given, see endorsement statements in *Am. Daily Adv.*, 12, 14, 15, 16, 19, 20, and 21 Feb. 1798.
48. "Communications" and report of endorsement meeting at James Cameron's house, *Penn. Gaz.*, 21 Feb. 1798; "Common Sense," *Phila. Gaz.*, 17 Feb. 1798; "Manlius," *Gaz. of U.S.*, 12 Jan. 1798; "Fact," ibid., 15 Feb. 1798; "Citizen," ibid., 19 Feb. 1798; *To the Friends of Israel Israel* (broadside; Philadelphia, 1798), which also appeared as *An die Freunde des Israel Israel* (broadside; Philadelphia, 1798).
49. "Communications," *Penn. Gaz.*, 21 Feb. 1798; "Foresight," *Gaz. of U.S.*, 21 Feb. 1798.
50. Percentages computed from the returns given in *U.S. Recorder*, 24 Feb. 1798, and *Aurora*, 26 Feb. 1798.
51. "Election," *Porcupine's Gaz.*, 24 Feb. 1798.
52. Ibid., 24 and 26 Feb. 1798. A special plea had been made for

Quakers to support "peace and order" by voting for Morgan. See "Friend," *Gaz. of U.S.*, 20 Feb. 1798.
53. "Returns," *Aurora*, 24 Feb. 1798; "Complete Statement," ibid., 26 and 28 Feb. 1798.
54. "Triumph," *Gaz. of U.S.*, 24 Feb. 1798; cf. "Election," *Porcupine's Gaz.*, 24 Feb. 1798.
55. The examples that follow are developed in far greater detail in my "Philadelphia's 'Other Half': Attitudes toward Poverty and the Meaning of Poverty in Philadelphia, 1760–1800" (Ph.D. diss., University of Chicago, 1973), pp. 71–103.
56. Allison and Penrose, *Philadelphia*, pp. 3, 8–9, 52–59; Scharf and Westcott, *History*, 3: 1736–37 n; Brunhouse, *Counter-Revolution*, pp. 152–53.
57. Brunhouse, *Counter-Revolution*, pp. 152–53, 184–85.
58. "The Memorial," *Indep. Gaz.*, 12 Nov. 1785; for similar arguments in favor of reincorporation, see "A native," *Penn. Packet*, 17 Nov. 1785; "Debate," ibid., 25 Sept. 1786; "Conclusion," ibid., 26 Sept. 1786; "A.B.," *Freeman's Journal*, 23 Sept. 1786.
59. List of members from "The Memorial," *Indep. Gaz.*, 12 Nov. 1785. On how these men were traced, see Appendix A. For reasons explained in that appendix, the wealth given is as of 1791. Use of the 1791 statistics may overstate the men's wealth in 1785, but the general picture is still clear.
60. Petition published in *Freeman's Journal*, 23 Sept. 1786.
61. *Penn. Eve. Her.*, 30 Nov. 1785.
62. *Penn. Statutes*, 13: 193–214; Brunhouse, *Counter-Revolution*, pp. 184–85. The strong majority in the legislature held by the conservative Republican group that had long favored incorporation may have accounted for the lack of opposition. The opposition may also have been quieted by the claim that the city had to be reincorporated if the state was to have any chance of having the federal capital located at Philadelphia. See *Penn. Gaz.*, 5 Nov. 1788; cf. ibid., 3, 10, and 24 Sept. 1788.
63. *Indep. Gaz.*, 26 Mar. 1789.
64. *Fed. Gaz.*, 28 Mar. 1789.
65. Brunhouse, *Counter-Revolution*, p. 221.
66. "Spectator," *Penn. Gaz.*, 24 Feb. 1790; "A Drayman," *Indep. Gaz.*, 9 Apr. 1791; "Correspondent," *Aurora*, 26 Mar. 1794; "Town Meeting," *Phila. Gaz.*, 7 May 1795; "Memorial," ibid., 26 May 1795.
67. *The Mail*, 28 Nov. 1792; *Indep. Gaz.*, 1 Dec. 1792.
68. *Aurora*, 13 June and 8 July 1794.
69. *Penn. Statutes*, 15: 462–63.

Chapter 3: Perceptions of "The Other Half"

1. "Effects," *Penn. Gaz.*, 12 Feb. 1767.
2. "Human Mind," *Penn. Packet*, 25 May 1772.
3. "Milabos," *Penny Post*, 23 Jan. 1769.
4. "Human Mind," *Penn. Packet*, 25 May 1772; "From the Universal Magazine," *Penn. Gaz.*, 18 Nov. 1772; "Useful Hints," *Penny Post*, 18 Jan. 1769.
5. "Thoughts," *Penn. Packet*, 13 Jan. 1772; "Young Owl," ibid., 17 Feb. 1772.
6. But she also said of poverty: "There must be something more dreadful in it than I can see." See Eva Eve Jones, ed., "Extracts from the Journal of Miss Sarah Eve . . . of Philadelphia in 1772–73," *PMHB* 5, nos. 1 and 2 (1881): 192.
7. *Supplement* to *Penn. Packet*, 17 Feb. 1772.
8. "Effects," *Penn. Gaz.*, 12 Feb. 1767.
9. *Penn. Archives*, 8th. ser., 7: 5830; "Thoughts," *Supplement* to *Penn. Packet*, 24 Aug. 1772; "Elector," *Penn. Journal*, 3 Oct. 1781.
10. *Pennsylvania Magazine* . . . 1 (March 1775): 140; *Penn. Gaz.*, 5 Sept. 1771.
11. *The Mail*, 29 July 1791; "Idleness," *Penn. Gaz.*, 15 May 1790; "Industry," ibid., 25 Aug. 1785.
12. "Ministers," *Penn. Mer.*, 21 June 1788; "The Dram-Shop," *The Mail*, 20 Sept. 1792; *Penn. Packet*, 9 Nov. 1786.
13. *Fed. Gaz.*, 29 Mar. 1790; Thomas Scott, *A Sermon, preached at St. Peter's church . . . 1792* (Philadelphia, 1792), pp. 6, 9; Society for Alleviating the Miseries of Public Prisons, *Extracts and remarks on the subject of punishment* . . . (Philadelphia, 1790), p. 3; PCA, Guardians of the Poor, "Daily Occurrences at the Almshouse, March 26, 1792, to June 7, 1793," 26 Mar. 1792, 7 June 1793.
14. MAHM: 1788–96, pp. 422–23. Cf. Coxe, *A View*, pp. 438, 441–42; and *Indep. Gaz.*, 30 Jan. 1788.
15. "Industry," *The Dessert to the True American*, 29 Dec. 1798; *The Mail*, 17 Aug. 1791; "Industry," *Daily Adv.*, 28 Apr. 1797; *Penn. Journal*, 13 Aug. 1788.
16. "Flower Girl," *Phila. Min.*, 7 May 1796 (emphasis added); *Aurora*, 3 Mar. 1795.
17. "Felicity," *Phila. Min.*, 7 Oct. 1797; "Prosperity," ibid., 15 Apr. 1797; poem by Robert Ferguson, *Penn. Mer.*, 13 Jan. 1786; "Lines," *The Mail*, 17 June 1793; "Riches," ibid., 1 Apr. 1793;

"Riches," *U.S. Recorder*, 13 Mar. 1798; "Poverty," *Penn. Eve. Her.*, 16 May 1787.
18. "Be Merry," *Penn. Eve. Her.*, 25 Jan. 1785; "Medium," ibid., 29 Jan. 1785; "Riches," ibid., 19 May 1787; "To live," *Phila. Min.*, 7 Mar. 1795.
19. "Riches," *Penn. Eve. Her.*, 19 May 1787; "Be Merry," ibid., 25 Jan. 1785.
20. "Miletius," *Aurora*, 30 Aug. 1792; "Medium," *Penn. Eve. Her.*, 29 Jan. 1785; "Riches," ibid., 19 May 1787; "Monitor," *Penn. Packet*, 23 July 1789.
21. "Advantages," *Phila. Min.*, 20 Feb. 1796; "Riches," ibid., 12 Nov. 1796; "Virtue," ibid., 5 Aug. 1797; "Happiness," *Penn. Packet*, 4 Sept. 1790; "Disinterestedness," ibid., 9 June 1796; "Contentment," *Penn. Mer.*, 20 Jan. 1786.
22. "Curse," *Penn. Packet*, 4 July, 1788; "Ode," ibid., 17 July 1790; "On the Times," *Phila. Min.*, 9 July 1796; "Eastern Maxiums," ibid., 30 July 1796; "Sonnet," ibid., 17 Feb. 1798; "Poverty," *Penn. Eve. Her.*, 16 May 1787; "Riches," *U.S. Recorder*, 13 Mar. 1798.
23. "True Happiness," *Daily Adv.*, 23 June 1797; "On the employment," *Freeman's Journal*, 7 Mar. 1787.
24. "Contentment," *Penn. Mer.*, 27 Aug. 1785; "Reflections," ibid., 17 Sept. 1784; "Soliloquy," *Penn. Packet*, 25 May 1790.
25. "Moralist," *Fed. Gaz.*, 14 Nov. 1793; "Friendless Orphan," *Indep. Gaz.*, 4 Aug. 1784; "Elegy," *The Mail*, 14 Jan. 1793; "On Content," *Penn. Packet*, 13 Oct. 1789.
26. "Moralist," *Fed. Gaz.*, 14 Nov. 1793; "The Poor Man's Address," ibid., 8 Dec. 1796; "Equality," *Aurora*, 28 Feb. 1794.
27. "On Content," *Penn. Packet*, 13 Aug. 1789; "The Poor Man's Address," *Phila. Gaz.*, 8 Dec. 1796; "Happy Cottager," *Gaz. of U.S.*, 14 June 1800; "Moralist," *Phila. Min.*, 7 May 1796; "Fragment," ibid., 10 Sept. 1796; "Epitaph," ibid., 12 May 1798.
28. *Aurora*, 1 Aug. 1794; "EPITAPH," *Penn. Packet*, 5 July 1798; "An Essay," ibid., 28 Dec. 1787.
29. "Affliction," *Penn. Packet*, 29 Aug. 1785; "Advice," ibid., 21 June 1787; "Contented," ibid., 13 Apr. 1790; "Soliloquy," ibid., 20 May 1790; "Lottery," ibid., 28 Aug. 1790; "Happiness," *Penn. Mer.*, 26 Aug. 1785; "Avarice," *Freeman's Journal*, 26 Oct. 1785.
30. "Essay," *Penn. Packet*, 28 Dec. 1787; "Moralist," ibid., 16 Jan. 1790; "Ode," *Penn. Mer.*, 11 Oct. 1791; "Idea," *Phila. Min.*, 9 May 1795.
31. "Moralist," *The Mail*, 25 Feb. 1792.

Notes to Chapter Four

32. In the course of research, I may have missed other publicly printed attacks on the crusade. But even if several more such comments exist, they would be dwarfed by the great mass of items that formed the crusade.
33. "Of Sufficiency," *Penn. Mer.*, 1 Oct. 1784.
34. *Freeman's Journal*, 8 Feb. 1786.
35. "On Charity," *Am. Daily Adv.*, 7 Oct. 1797; see Chapter Seven below for the fuller development of this point.

Chapter 4: Social Disorder, Crime, and Punishment

1. Curti, *Growth*, pp. 163–65.
2. Labaree and Willcox, *Papers of Benjamin Franklin*, 3: 10, 11; *Penn. Archives*, 8th ser., 7: 5592; HSP, "Mayor's Court Docquets From October Sessions 1766 to January 1771 Inclusive," passim; "A Citizen," *Penn. Packet*, 26 Oct. 1772.
3. *Penn. Statutes*, 8: 99; Scharf and Westcott, *History*, 1: 265; Carl Bridenbaugh, *Cities in Revolt*, rev. ed. (New York, 1971), pp. 108–10, 297.
4. *Penn. Archives*, 8th ser., 6: 5266. The listing of criminals is in *Penn. Journal*, 18 Dec. 1766; on the economic position of the occupations, see Main, *Social Structure*, pp. 72–81.
5. The basic law, passed in 1718, is in *Penn. Statutes*, 3: 199–214; see also Harry E. Barnes, *The Evolution of Penology in Pennsylvania: A Study in American Social History* (1927; reprint ed., Montclair, N.J., 1968), pp. 28, 37, 52–53.
6. Barnes, *Evolution of Penology*, p. 71.
7. *Penn. Statutes*, 4: 171–83 passim.
8. Ibid., 7: 347; 13: 257.
9. See ibid., 4: 211–15, for law and quotations; cf. 2: 249–51. A 1765 law may have repealed the earlier limitation, but the law was not unquestionably repealed until 1798. See ibid., 16: 98–99; cf. 6: 459–60.
10. Ibid., 6: 392–93; 7: 347.
11. *Penn. Chron.*, 25 Dec. 1769, 29 Jan. 1770; *Penn. Gaz.*, 10 Mar. 1763; "P. B.," ibid., 21 Dec. 1774.
12. *Penn. Eve. Post*, 3 Feb. and 12 Mar. 1776; HSP, Philadelphia Society for Alleviating the Miseries of Public Prisons: Minutes, 1787–93, 13 July 1789 (hereinafter HSP, Soc. for Alleviating Miseries, 1787–93). For an analysis of the membership of this organization, see Chapter Seven below.
13. Thayer, *Pennsylvania Politics*, p. 222; "Charitable," *Penn. Mer.*,

4 Feb. 1785, 22 Jan. 1787. *Penn. Statutes*, 4: 183, gives a guide to the various acts passed after 1776.
14. *Fed. Gaz.*, 8 Oct. 1790. These are the only general returns of the total number of prisoners I have found.
15. *Penn. Eve. Her.*, 23 Apr. 1785; "Honestus," ibid., 3 May 1786.
16. "A Citizen," *Penn. Packet*, 30 Aug. 1787; "Justice in Mercy," *Penn. Gaz.*, 7 Dec. 1785. Cf. "Citizens," *Indep. Gaz.*, 29 Nov. 1783; ibid., 16 Nov. 1786.
17. "Constitution" and "Observations," *Indep. Gaz.*, 19 Mar. 1787; HSP, Soc. for Alleviating Miseries: files, "Report of the Acting Committee . . . ," 4 Aug. 1788. On the founders of this society, see Chapter Seven below.
18. *Penn. Journal*, 24 Nov. 1787; HSP, Soc. for Alleviating Miseries: files, committee meetings of 16 Jan., 6 and 26 Feb. and 3 and 13 Mar. 1789; HSP, Soc. for Alleviating Miseries, 1787–93, 18 Oct. and 21 Dec. 1790; HSP, "Minutes of the Corporation [of Philadelphia, 1789–93]," 1 Dec. 1789.
19. *Penn. Statutes*, 14: 267–69 (quotation from p. 267).
20. *Penn. Eve. Post*, 24 Feb. 1776; "An old Man," *Indep. Gaz.*, 2 Nov. 1782; "Jail fees," *Penn. Eve. Her.*, 4 Nov. 1786; *Penn. Packet*, 25 Sept. 1786; HSP, petition of Thomas Wise dated 13 Nov. 1784, filed under Soc. Misc. Coll., Box 3A-B.
21. "Observations," *Indep. Gaz.*, 19 May 1787; HSP, Soc. for Alleviating Miseries; files, petitions of Eliz Donnovan (13 Feb. 1788) and William Leslie (14 Aug. 1787). Cf. ibid., George Duffield to John Olden, 8 May 1788, and associated petitions.
22. *Penn. Packet*, 25 Sept. 1786.
23. On checking reputations see HSP, Soc. for Alleviating Miseries, 1787–93, 13(?) Jan. and 6 and 20 Feb. 1789; HSP, Soc. for Alleviating Miseries: files, George Duffield to John Olden, 8 May 1788, Thomas Cutubert(?) to George Duffield, 3 May 1788, Thomas Welch to President and Supreme Executive Council, 2 May 1788. On the general action see ibid., "Fees assumed for the Following Prisoners" and "The Prison Society—To John Reynolds [ca. July 1788]"; and *Penn. Statutes*, 13: 257–58. Cf. *Penn. Gaz.*, 16 Nov. 1785.
24. HSP, Soc. for Alleviating Miseries, 1787–93, 21 Dec. 1790; *Penn. Statutes*, 14: 136–37, 268.
25. HSP, Soc. for Alleviating Miseries, 1787–93, 9 July 1792.
26. *Phila. Gaz.*, 13 Jan. 1794; *Am. Daily Adv.*, 22 Mar. 1796.
27. Quotations from *New World*, 2 Nov. 1796. See also issues of 16 Nov. and 10 Dec. 1796; and *Penn. Statutes*, 15: 501.
28. "Beccaria," *New World*, 16 Nov. 1796; letter of Daniel Thomas,

Aurora, 3 Mar. 1794; PCA, "Minutes of Board of Inspectors [of Philadelphia Jail] from May 1794 to August 1801," 19 May 1795, 19 Dec. 1797; "Prison," *Gaz. of U.S.*, 1 Feb. 1800; Barnes, *Evolution of Penology*, pp. 114–15.
29. *Penn. Gaz.*, 5 Feb. 1767; *Penn. Archives*, 8th ser., 7: 5968.
30. *Penn. Mer.*, 11 Mar. 1788; cf. "Amicus," ibid., 10 June 1788.
31. Of items dealing with trading justice activity, those cited in n. 29 to this chapter are the only ones I discovered dated before 1785; over fifty such items appeared in the years 1785–89.
32. *Freeman's Journal*, 2 Nov. 1785.
33. Quotations from *Indep. Gaz.*, 6 May 1786. See also "Astrea," ibid., 21 May 1787; "Casca. No. IV," ibid., 28 Apr. 1789; "Monus," ibid., 1 May 1789; and "Zenophon," *Penn. Mer.*, 26 June 1788.
34. Some of the people who supported reincorporation argued that that action would do away with trading justices. But such comments did not, it appears, form a major part of the effort to attain reincorporation. See "Civis," *Fed. Gaz.*, 3 Mar. 1789; "Philo-Roscius," *Indep. Gaz.*, 16 Jan. 1789; and *Penn. Gaz.*, 4 Feb. 1789.
35. "Volucius," *Penn. Mer.*, 1 July 1788; "A Citizen," ibid., 3 July 1788; "Aristides," *Indep. Gaz.*, 17 Sept. 1785; *Penn. Eve. Her.*, 27 July 1785; "A. B.," *Penn. Packet*, 9 Sept. 1785.
36. "A Citizen" and " A Friend," *Indep. Gaz.*, 14 June 1787; "A Hint," ibid., 22 Aug. 1787; "A Young Lawyer," ibid., 23 Aug. 1787; *Penn. Eve. Her.*, 10 Mar. 1787. It appears that neither the subscription fund nor the lawyers' association came into being.
37. "Civis," *Fed. Gaz.*, 3 Mar. 1789; "A Friend," *Indep. Gaz.*, 14 June 1787.
38. *Penn. Statutes*, 13: 201; 14: 329; "A Citizen," *Indep. Gaz.*, 3 July 1790; "Observer," ibid., 14 Aug. 1790.
39. *Penn. Packet*, 5 July 1783 offers one example; such comments were, however, quite rare in the war years.
40. Ibid., 20 Aug. 1785; "Honestus," ibid., 3 Sept. 1785.
41. "The Memorial," *Indep. Gaz.*, 12 Nov. 1785, was designed to support the move for reincorporation and so may have painted a particularly bleak picture.
42. Ibid., 17 Nov. 1785; "Petition," *Penn. Packet*, 30 Dec. 1785.
43. *Penn. Statutes*, 12: 280–90 passim; see also 13: 244, 254.
44. *Penn. Eve. Her.*, 18 Sept. 1787; *Penn. Journal*, 4 Apr. and 23 May 1787; *Indep. Gaz.*, 31 Mar. 1787; "Dennis K——y," ibid., 10 July 1787; Mease, *Picture*, pp. 160–61.
45. *Universal Magazine of Knowledge and Pleasure* 85 (July 1789):

17. Numerous essays claimed that criminality was increasing, and it appears from the number of criminals in the city jail for 1787–96 that 1786 and 1787 were years of higher criminality than the period following 1791. See Samuel Harard, ed., *Register of Pennsylvania* . . . , 16 vols. (Philadelphia, 1828–36), 1: 206.
46. "Vice," *Penn. Eve. Her.*, 26 May 1787; ibid., 27 June 1787; "Oration," *Penn. Gaz.*, 1 Oct. 1788; *Fed. Gaz.*, 24 June 1789 (emphasis added), 20 Mar. 1790.
47. *Indep. Gaz.*, 14 Aug. 1787; "Address," *Fed. Gaz.*, 20 Mar. 1789.
48. 7 July and 18 Sept. 1787.
49. *Fed. Gaz.*, 13 June 1789.
50. 3 Jan. 1797.
51. Because Southwark and the Northern Liberties were not parts of incorporated Philadelphia, any crimes committed in those areas would not have been tried in the mayor's court.
52. See Appendix B for the full listing of the statistics and an analysis of their derivation. Using a list of convictions may somewhat overstate the degree of crime by the poorer element, for it is quite possible that more prosperous inhabitants, if they engaged in crime, may have avoided conviction.
53. See Appendix B; for an earlier example that shows the same pattern, see p. 63 above.
54. Percentage computed from the sources cited in Appendix B. On the individual crimes see PCA, Sentence Docket, 2 Dec. 1794–February 1804, pp. 3, 14 (hereinafter PCA, Sentence Docket); and PCA, Philadelphia County Inspectors of the Jail and Penitentiary House Prisoners for Trial Docket, 1798–1802, p. 40 (hereinafter PCA, Trial Docket, 1798–1802).
55. PCA, Philadelphia County Inspectors of the Jail and Penitentiary House Prisoners for Trial Docket, 1790–97, pp. 21, 258, 260, 276, 285, 315, 349, 392, 430; PCA, Trial Docket, 1798–1802, pp. 5, 38, 66, 103, 269; PCA, Sentence Docket, p. 100.
56. *Penn. Statutes*, 12: 511–28 passim.
57. Ibid., 15: 355–57; see also pp. 174–81.
58. Other major cities had had such organizations before the Revolution. See Bridenbaugh, *Cities in Revolt*, pp. 124, 319.
59. 16 Nov. 1790; "To the orderly," *Aurora*, 24 Aug. 1795, implies that the 1790 association no longer existed.
60. *Penn. Gaz.*, 10 Sept. 1791.
61. *An Address to the citizens of Philadelphia, respecting the better government of youth* (Philadelphia, 1795), passim; see also "Philadelphus," *Penn. Eve. Her.*, 10 Aug. 1785.

62. Cf. pp. 155-57 above.
63. "To the orderly," *Aurora*, 24 Aug. 1795.
64. HSP, petitions "To the Senate and House . . ." dated at Philadelphia in December 1798, filed under Y12 7324 f 24; *Porcupine's Gaz.*, 16 Jan. 1798.
65. *Am. Daily Adv.*, 23 Aug. 1800.

Chapter 5: Public Poor Relief, 1760–1776

1. On the selection of overseers, which varied over time, see *Penn. Statutes*, 2: 251; 8: 75; and n. 24 to Chapter Six. By the late 1760s, and possibly in 1760, there were twelve city overseers.
2. Gary B. Nash ("Poverty," pp. 10–17) suggests that the city had little difficulty in maintaining the poor before the 1760s. Hannah B. Roach ("Philadelphia's Colonial Poor Laws," pp. 159–69) presents a different and more convincing view.
3. According to MMHE: 1769–78, p. 31, in the mid-1750s the city normally maintained between 80 and 120 persons. Since these figures were offered after the fact, without documentation, and since they were offered to prove how difficult it had become in the 1770s to maintain the poor, they are, at best, estimates. In January 1764 the city maintained "about" 220 poor people; this number may have included only those housed in the city almshouse. See *Penn. Archives*, 8th ser., 7: 5506.
4. *Penn. Archives*, 8th ser., 7: 5506. See also ibid., pp. 5535–36, 5538 ff.; and Scharf and Westcott, *History*, 1: 242–43.
5. *Penn. Archives*, 8th ser., 7: 5823–24, 5830–31.
6. Ibid., p. 5831; on the hospital, see Williams, *America's First Hospital*.
7. According to Scharf and Westcott (*History*, 2: 1451), people of "benevolence and means" made this suggestion. Nash ("Poverty," p. 14) has attributed the proposal for the house of employment to "a group of wealthy Quaker merchants." However, the sources he cites (ibid., 15 n) clearly indicate that the suggestion came, as it had before, from the overseers, who are not described in the sources as "wealthy Quaker merchants." But wealthy Quaker merchants did figure prominently in the work of the new organization that emerged. See Stephen J. Brobeck, "Changes in the Composition and Structure of Philadelphia Elite Groups, 1756–1790" (Ph.D. diss., University of Pennsylvania, 1973), p. 205; and subsequent discussion in this chapter.
8. *Penn. Archives*, 8th ser., 7: 5857; *Penn. Statutes*, 7: 9–17 (quotation from p. 9).

9. *Penn. Archives*, 8th ser., 7: 6148–50 passim.
10. *Penn. Statutes*, 7: 9–17.
11. Ibid.; MAHM: 1788–96, p. 2. The terms "almshouse" and "house of employment" were normally used interchangeably. The institution was also referred to as the "bettering house."
12. *Penn. Statutes*, 7: 15–16; see also ibid., p. 78.
13. Ibid., pp. 10, 16.
14. *Penn. Archives*, 8th ser., 7: 5982, 6000, 6037–38, 6042, 6054, 6313–15; *Penn. Statutes*, 7: 75–79; HSP, Report of Managers of House of Employment: Committee on Condition of the House, 9 Feb. 1768, in Edward Wanton Smith Collection.
15. *Penn. Archives*, 8th ser., 7: 6097–99, 6101, 6322–24, 6337, 6343, 6369; 8: 7402, 7421.
16. At times the managers were supported by petitions from the suburban areas. For the managers' case, see ibid., 7: 6099–100, 6101–2, 6148–56 passim; 8: 7423–24.
17. MGOP: 1768–74, 15 June 1769; MMHE: 1769–78, p. 8.
18. MMHE: 1769–78, pp. 32–33; these pages were printed in *Penn. Gaz.*, 25 Jan. 1770.
19. MMHE: 1769–78, p. 8.
20. MGOP: 1768–74, 15 June 1769.
21. MMHE: 1769–78, p. 8.
22. The managers here analyzed are those who directed the contributorship in 1766 and in 1769. I do not have lists of the managers who served between these years. The overseers analyzed are those who served in 1768–69 and 1769–70. Lists of names were obtained from MMHE: 1766; MMHE: 1769–78; and MGOP: 1768–74. On the conduct of the analysis, see Appendix A.
23. On the Quaker elite, see Brobeck, "Changes," pp. 271–72, 279, 286–88, 308–9, 317, and passim. On the status of the mechanic-artisan group, see the sources cited in n. 23 to the Introduction.
24. These rules were apparently not always stringently enforced. See p. 117 above.
25. It is not always clear from the rules as written precisely how punishments were to be authorized. The cited rules, first instituted in May of 1769, are given in MAHM: 1788–96, pp. 2–7.
26. See, e.g., MGOP: 1768–74, pp. 3–4, 84, 87, 126, 130, 135. For an especially full and revealing example see HSP, Sam. Rhoads, Jr., Levi Hollingsworth, and Samuel Fisher to Philadelphia Overseers, 17 Nov. 1771(?), in Gratz Collection, under Overseers of the Poor; cf. MGOP: 1768–74, pp. 44–46.
27. MGOP: 1768–74, p. 14.
28. Outdoor relief of a limited nature was given at least through

Notes to Chapter Six

December 1771, and the managers also continued to provide outdoor employment by giving out materials to be spun. See MMHE: 1769–78, pp. 37, 57, 59, 70, 73, 74, 78, 82, 86, 99, 101, 103, 106, 109, 112.
29. MGOP: 1768–74, pp. 50, 51, 53, 57–58; *Penn. Archives*, 8th ser., 8: 6592, 6594, 6634.
30. *Penn. Statutes*, 8: 75–96, and especially pp. 75, 76–77, 79–80, 95–96.
31. MMHE: 1769–78, p. 120; see also pp. 119, 121, 123, 127, 135, 138, 139, 141, 144, 147, 149.
32. Ibid., pp. 177, 185, 190, 192, 194, 195, 197, 198, 199, 202, 203, 207, 208, 211; MGOP: 1768–74, pp. 150–52; MOPCP: 1774–82, 2 Oct. and 20 Nov. 1775.
33. MMHE: 1769–78, pp. 226–33 passim; cf. Philip Padelford, ed., *Colonial Panorama, 1775: Dr. Robert Honymen's Journal for March and April* (San Marino, Calif., 1939), p. 18.
34. *Penn. Statutes*, 8: 474.
35. *Penn. Gaz.*, 9 Jan. 1772.

Chapter 6: Public Poor Relief, 1776–1800

1. Brobeck, "Changes," p. 205. Note that a comparison of the managers for 1785–89 with lists of politically active people shows that only three of twelve managers were Quakers, and two of those had been disowned. See n. 26 to this chapter and lists in Richard A. Ryerson, *The Revolution Is Now Begun: The Radical Committees of Philadelphia, 1765–1776* (Philadelphia, 1978), pp. 264–83 passim.
2. MMHE: 1769–78, pp. 259–60, 265–66, 285, 288–97 passim, 306; MOPCP: 1774–82, meetings of 28 Oct. 1776–22 July 1778 (see especially 28 Oct. and 11 Nov. 1776 and 22 July 1778, and see also meeting of 26 Nov. 1778); *Penn. Eve. Post*, 12 Feb. 1778.
3. MOPCP: 1774–82, 26 Nov. 1778.
4. MMHE: 1769–78, pp. 306 ff.; MAHM: 1780–88, title page.
5. MOPCP: 1774–82, 22 Oct., 26 Nov., and 10 and 31 Dec. 1778; ibid., 8 Feb., 8, 15, and 22 Apr., 10 and 17 June, 8 July, 2 Nov., and 16 Dec. 1779; ibid., letter of 19 Feb. 1779; *Pennsylvania Colonial Records*, 16 vols. (Harrisburg, Pa., 1838–53), 12: 172.
6. MOPCP: 1774–82, 6 Apr. and 6 July 1780, 5 Apr. 1781.
7. *Penn. Statutes*, 9: 358–59; see also Brunhouse, *Counter-Revolution*, pp. 40–41.
8. *Penn. Statutes*, 10: 403.
9. MOPCP: 1774–82, 7, 14, and 28 Feb. and 7 and 28 Mar. 1782.

10. The law did not prove especially helpful in keeping "disorderly" persons out of the city. See MAHM: 1780–88, p. 18. For the 1782 law see *Penn. Statutes*, 10: 401–6.
11. MOPCP: 1774–82, 28 Mar. and 4 and 11 Apr. 1782; MOPCP: 1782–87, 9 Oct. 1783; MAHM: 1780–88, p. 17.
12. MAHM: 1780–88, p. 23. I cannot determine with precision to whom the managers were referring. These favored poor may merely have been the poor of unimpeachable character. Or they may have been persons who, besides having unimpeachable character, had once enjoyed some social position. Whatever the case, just a few paupers could be housed in this section, since only a part of the lower ward in the west wing was to be partitioned.
13. Ibid., p. 30; cf. MAHM: 1788–96, pp. 2–7.
14. MOPCP: 1782–87, 18 Aug. 1785.
15. MAHM: 1780–88, pp. 51–53; *Penn. Packet*, 12 Mar. 1787; "To the Public," ibid., 24 Mar. 1787.
16. *Penn. Packet*, 12 Mar. 1787; see also MAHM: 1780–88, pp. 27–28, 29, 31–32, 36–37, 41–43, 50, 59–61.
17. "To the Public," *Penn. Packet*, 24 Mar. 1787; see also MOPCP: 1782–87, 18 Aug. and 3 Nov. 1785, 15 Feb. 1787.
18. See n. 18 to Chapter Seven.
19. MAHM: 1780–88, pp. 109, 110; MGBGP: 1788–95, pp. 1, 2.
20. *Penn. Packet*, 11 Dec. 1788.
21. MAHM: 1788–96, pp. 52–54 passim.
22. Ibid., pp. 79–82.
23. See, e.g., Main, *Social Structure*, pp. 72–78.
24. By law, overseers were nominated and appointed by city and suburban officials. Actually, the retiring overseers submitted a list of "suitable" persons who had not previously served, and the new overseers were picked from that list. See, e.g., MGOP: 1768–74, pp. 1–2, 56; MOPCP: 1774–82, 17 Feb. 1780; RMCBOP: 1787–96, 25 Mar. 1790, 15 Aug. 1793.
25. MOPCP: 1782–87, 18 Aug. 1785.
26. The period 1784–89 was selected for analysis because it encompasses both the 1785 statement that the overseers were unable to bear the burden of the office and the 1788 "Revolution." The overseers from Southwark, the Northern Liberties, and Moyamensing, a total of nine men for each year, were excluded from the analysis because I have only very scattered listings for these areas. Lists of managers and overseers were obtained from MAHM: 1780–88; MOPCP: 1782–87; RMCBOP: 1787–96.

Notes to Chapter Six

27. I cannot determine if the William Lewis who served as an overseer in 1785-86 was the same man who served in the legislature. On the general analysis, see Appendix A.
28. Titles compiled from the sources in n. 26 to this chapter; from [John?] Macpherson, *Macpherson's Directory for the city and suburbs of Philadelphia* . . . (Philadelphia, 1785); and from Francis White, *The Philadelphia Directory* . . . (Philadelphia, 1785). For the list see ibid., p. 92.
29. The list of the founders of the Republican Society that is used here and elsewhere is given in *Penn. Gaz.*, 24 Mar. 1779.
30. This analysis covers the sets of men indicated in n. 26 to this chapter. On the conduct of the analysis, see Appendix A.
31. Included in this group of mechanic-artisans were two each of the following: carpenter, tailor, sail/mast maker, and tanner and currier. Also included were one each of the following: coach maker, baker, hatter, butcher.
32. This group included eighteen merchants, four shopkeepers, three grocers, and two ship chandlers.
33. The other overseer who can be identified, William Turner, was described in 1785 as a "Captain." By 1791 he was listed merely as a "gentleman" in Clement Biddle, *The Philadelphia Directory* (Philadelphia, 1791). Of the overseers who could not be positively identified, one was either a shopkeeper or a tallow chandler and another was either a grazier or a shopkeeper. Another overseer was probably an iron merchant.
34. Included in the mercantile ranks were ten merchants, a financier, and a shopkeeper.
35. The managers in the mechanic-artisan group were three house carpenters, a biscuit baker, and a man who was either a biscuit baker or a clockmaker. John Wharton, who could not be positively identified, was either a gentleman merchant or a barber.
36. All tax holdings for both overseers and managers are as of 1791. Overseers who were listed in the tax records only for estate holdings are not included in this analysis. The three overseers in this group held estates worth £485, £540, and £550 respectively. On the general analysis, see Appendix A.
37. Twenty-one of the twenty-eight managers could be traced in the tax records. Dr. Joseph Redman is included in the totals even though I have only an estate rating for him. Since his estate holdings were £6,093, he was probably worth a good deal more than that sum. On the other hand, John Wharton's totals would lower the average manager's holdings. The John Wharton who

was a merchant had a main entry of £62, and the barber had a main entry of £40. In addition, there was a John Wharton estate worth a total of £1,965.
38. This mechanic, Raper Hoskins, held taxable property worth £1,284.
39. MAHM: 1788–96, pp. 52–54, 90–91, 462, 500, 502; MGBGP: 1788–95, 25 Nov. 1793, 3 Feb., 2 Mar., 2 June, 1 and 25 Sept., and 6 Oct. 1794.
40. *Penn. Packet*, 19 Nov. 1788, 13 and 14 Feb. 1789; MAHM: 1788–96, pp. 56, 74, 77, 88–89, 91; MGBGP: 1788–95, p. 27; *Penn. Statutes*, 14: 73–74.
41. MAHM: 1788–96, pp. 1–7, 16, 17, 22–23.
42. Ibid., pp. 23, 65; on the regular diet see pp. 25–26.
43. Ibid., pp. 35, 37–38, 175, 191.
44. Ibid., pp. 37–38; see also pp. 16, 94, 95.
45. It is not clear if the hospital was established. See MGBGP: 1788–95, pp. 25, 32–33.
46. The managers did not quote from the vagrant act of 1767. For the quotations and the text of the act, see *Penn. Statutes*, 7: 84–88. The memorial is in MAHM: 1788–96, pp. 79–87.
47. *Penn. Statutes*, 13: 251–55 passim.
48. A total of twenty-seven men served as guardians at some time between March 1793 and March 1794 (lists of guardians were obtained from MAHM: 1788–96 and RMCBOP: 1787–96). Ten of the men served part or all of the time as managers. Twenty-four of the twenty-seven men could be identified in city directories. Of these, 83.3% were from the mercantile group. Included in this group were twelve merchants, five grocers, and three shopkeepers. The other 16.7% were from the mechanic-artisan group and included a baker, a cabinetmaker, a shipwright, and a carpet manufacturer. Nine of those who served as managers could be identified by occupation: 77.8% were from the mercantile group, and the other 22.2% were from the mechanic-artisan group.
49. RMCBOP: 1787–96, 6 Dec. 1793; some pensions were still given, however, as is indicated in the entries of 5 June 1794 and 23 Apr. 1795.
50. Quotations from MAHM: 1788–96, pp. 393, 421; see also pp. 249, 356, 415, 470.
51. MAHM: 1796–1803, 22 June 1796, 22 July 1799.
52. Ibid., 22 June and 11 July 1796; 6 Nov. 1797; 5 and 19 Mar., 17 Sept., and 20 Nov. 1798; 23 Jan., 25 Mar., 22 July, and 11 Nov.

1799; 24 Mar. and 25 Sept. 1800 (quotations from 5 Mar. 1798).
53. *These Ordinances, Rules and Bye-Laws* . . . , paginated separately, were published with *A Compilation of the Laws of the State of Pennsylvania, relative to the poor* . . . (Philadelphia, 1796). For the quotations see the *Ordinances* section, pp. 5–6.
54. HSP, "Ann Parrish Visitations to the Sick. [Penciled in] 1796," in Parrish Collection, Case 61, Bound Volumes, pp. 20, 24; cf. "Memorial," *Aurora*, 28 July 1796.

Chapter 7: Private Poor Relief

1. *Poverty*, p. 159.
2. *Fed. Gaz.*, 13 June 1789; "Charity," *Am. Daily Adv.*, 7 Oct. 1797.
3. "To do good," *Aurora*, 9 July 1796. See also "Philanthropos," *Penn. Journal*, 22 June 1774; "Benevolence," *Penn. Packet*, 17 Aug. 1787; "Humanity," *Phila. Min.*, 2 Jan. 1796.
4. Scharf and Westcott, *History*, 2: 1469, 1480; *Articles agreed upon by those members of the Unitas Fratrum . . . for the support of their widows* (Philadelphia, 1770).
5. Quotation from *Charleston* (So. Car.) *Columbian Herald*, 18 June 1787; cf. the issue of 24 July 1788. On the societies, see Scharf and Westcott, *History*, 2: 1469; *Penn. Gaz.*, 2 Jan. 1791; *Rules and Orders of the Society of Victuallers* . . . (Philadelphia, 1798); Mease, *Picture*, pp. 283, 284, 285; William Douglas, *Annals of the First African Church* (Philadelphia, 1862), pp. 15–17; and *Constitution of the Scots Thistle Society of Philadelphia* (Philadelphia, 1799).
6. For an insightful comment, see Benjamin Rush to Elias Boudinot(?), 9 July 1788, in Rush, *Letters*, 1: 472–73. Sam Bass Warner, in *Private City*, pp. x, 3–4, and passim, presents a decidedly different view.
7. "Plan," *Penn. Packet*, 12 Oct. 1779; HSP, "Plan for a Society to lend Money to the Poor on Interest," ca. 1790–91, in Miers Fisher Papers; *Phila. Min.*, 7 Mar. 1795; "S. R.," *Penn. Gaz.*, 21 Apr. 1772; "Z," *Fed. Gaz.*, 6 Mar. 1790; "Correspondent," *Gaz. of U.S.*, 7 Apr. 1796.
8. *Fed. Gaz.*, 4 Nov. 1793; "Loaf Bread," ibid., 6 Nov. 1793; "Several Bakers," ibid., 7 Nov. 1793; *The Philadelphiad* 2 (1784): 55–57.
9. *Am. Daily Adv.*, 12, 16, and 18 Dec. 1800 (all quotations from the first essay); "Amicus," ibid., 19 Dec. 1800; "Friend," ibid.,

22 Dec. 1800; "A. B.," ibid., 27 Dec. 1800; Scharf and Westcott, *History*, 2: 1469.
10. "J. J.," *Penn. Mer.*, 20 Mar. 1789; *Fed Gaz.*, 15 and 16 Apr. 1789, 4 Feb. 1792; *Aurora*, 23 Aug. 1793; PCA, "Minutes of Common Council Oct. 31st. 1791 to Mar. 21st 1796," pp. 44, 69–70, 81, 92; PCA, "Minutes of Com. Council Vol. 2 Feb. 14th. 1799 to Jan. 13th. 1803," pp. 61, 64, 69, 84.
11. See Chapter One above on winter subscriptions. I am assuming that such subscriptions were designed to aid the poor on a humanitarian basis, without distinction between the "worthy" and the "unworthy" poor, but it is possible that some of these programs attempted to limit assistance to the industrious. The one subscription effort for which there is general documentation, that of 1761–62, did use a recommendation system, supposedly just "to prevent Impositions of ill designing persons, who may feign a pretence of Indigence, and that a just & equal distribution may be made among those who are real Objects of Charity." HSP, Records of the Committee to Alleviate the Miseries of the Poor, Thomas Wharton Papers in Wharton-Willing Collection (quotation from minutes of 1 Jan. 1761 meeting); ibid., James Pemberton's "Acco[.] of the Distribution"; ibid., Ticket No. 179, signed by James Mease.
12. *Penn. Gaz.*, 18 Apr. 1791; *Aurora*, 13 May 1793, 24 June 1799; *Am. Daily Adv.*, 2 July 1796.
13. Powell, *Bring Out Your Dead*, pp. 91, 281; "City-Hall," *Aurora*, 11 Mar. 1794; Mathew Carey, *A Short Account of the Malignant Fever, Lately Prevalent in Philadelphia . . .* , 4th ed. (Philadelphia, 1794), pp. 17, 21.
14. Harry W. Pfund, *A History of the German Society of Pennsylvania*, 2d rev. ed. (Philadelphia, 1964), pp. 1–5, 30; German Society of Pennsylvania Archives (Philadelphia), "Minute's Der Incorporirten Deutschen Gesellschaft [1770–1802]," 18 Oct. 1774, 18 Dec. 1788, 3 Jan. 1789, and passim.
15. *Penn. Eve. Post*, 3 Feb. 1776.
16. For the list of the thirteen founders of the society, see *Penn. Eve. Post*, 8 Feb. 1776. Seven of the eight whose religious affiliation could be identified were Quakers. Only seven of the men could be identified by occupation. Five were from the mercantile group, and two, a baker and a brewer, were from the mechanic-artisan group. The eleven men who could be traced in the 1774 tax list were from the solid middle rank, but not of the top economic rank. Four owned acreage; five owned livestock; six owned servants. See Appendix A.

Notes to Chapter Seven 213

17. "Americanus," *Penn. Gaz.*, 26 June 1760, 3 July 1760; "Society," ibid., 2 Feb. 1774; Scharf and Westcott, *History*, 2: 1475–76.
18. Williams, *America's First Hospital*, pp. 12–14; "No. VI," *Gaz. of U.S.*, 10 Aug. 1799; "No. VII—to the Managers," ibid., 20 July 1799. As Williams shows (p. 151), the number of sick poor aided by the hospital was quite small, especially by the 1780s.
19. See n. 55 to Chapter One.
20. *Aurora*, 30 Oct. 1794. Cf. *Penn. Journal*, 25 Jan. 1765; and Benjamin Rush to John Redman Coxe, 8 Dec. 1795, in Rush, *Letters*, 2: 765.
21. *Penn. Journal*, 3 Oct. 1765; Watson, *Annals*, 1: 406–7; "Speculator," *Penn. Gaz.*, 16 Mar. 1785; Joseph Scott, *The United States Gazatter* . . . (Philadelphia, 1795), s.v. "Phi."
22. A good general discussion of the society's activities in poor relief is Auguste Jorns, *The Quakers as Pioneers in Social Work*, trans. Thomas K. Brown (1912; reprint ed., New York, 1931), pp. 50–98. On the almshouse, see Watson, *Annals*, 3: 287–90; and on the wide variety of outdoor relief granted, see, as illustration, PFMMA, "Minutes of the Committee appointed by the several Monthly Meetings in Philadelphia for the Care of the Poor . . . [for 1773–95]," pp. 33, 35–36, 40, 41, 44, 56, 125, 129, 138, 140, 146, 148–49, and passim (hereinafter PFMMA, MCMMCP: 1773–95). Permission to cite such records was kindly given by Monthly Meeting of Philadelphia Friends.
23. On occasion, nonmembers of the society were housed in the Friends' almshouse. On the general admission procedure see, PFMMA, MCMMCP: 1773–95, pp. 59, 138, and "respecting E. Reading 5:th Mo. 4th, 1781," in 1783 folder; PFMMA, Women's Minutes "1st mo 1757 to 12 mo 1767," p. 80 and passim; PFMMA, "Minutes of the Committee of Twelve from 2nd. Month 6th. 1795 to the First Month 3d 1817 inclusive," 17 Oct. 1796.
24. PFMMA, MCMMCP: 1773–95, pp. 6, 20, 24, 30, 33, 35, 68, 157, 320; PFMMA, "Minutes of the Committee of Twelve . . . ," 5 Aug. and 6 Sept. 1796; PFMMA, "Monthly Meeting of Friends of Philadelphia," box 4, "Accots Committee . . . for the Yr. 1787—" and "General State of the Committee of Twelve[']s Acco.t for the Year 1788 & Report thereon dated 1 Month 9th 1789."
25. *Penny Post*, 9 Jan. 1769; *Penn. Eve. Post*, 8 Jan. 1778; *Aurora*, 20 Nov. 1790; CCA, "Minutes of Vestry March 1761 to April 1784," pp. 179, 185, 186–87, 302, 341, 415, 433, 434; CCA, "Minute Book of the Corporation of the United Episcopal Churches of Christ Church [and] of St. Peters Church . . . 1784 [to 1813]," pp. 11–12, 24.

26. CCA, "Minutes of Vestry . . . ," pp. 159–60; see also n. 28 to this chapter.
27. CCA, "Minutes of Vestry . . . ," pp. 231–40 passim; Scharf and Westcott, *History*, 2: 1676–77.
28. CCA, "Minute Book . . . ," pp. 24–25; CCA, "Minutes of Vestry . . . ," pp. 303–4, 434 (quotation from p. 304).
29. HSP, Collections of the Genealogical Society of Pennsylvania, vol. 297, "First Baptist Church Philadelphia Vol. II Minutes 1760–1850," pp. 20, 26, 28–29, 33, 45, 50, 51–53, 56–57, 62, 75–76, 119, 123, and passim (quotation from p. 33).
30. St. Mary Roman Catholic Church (Philadelphia), Minutes of the Trustees for 1788–1811, 25 July 1791, and passim. These records are maintained at the rectory.
31. Between 1786 and 1798, four other ethnic societies that aided immigrants sprang up. However, because of missing or scanty records, it is virtually impossible to determine if these groups (two Irish, one French, and one Welsh) limited support to the industrious. See *Penn. Journal*, 22 Mar. 1786; Brunhouse, *Counter-Revolution*, pp. 10, 192, 289; Scharf and Westcott, *History*, 2: 1467–68; HSP, Minute Book of the Welsh Society for 1798–1839; and John H. Campbell, *History of the Friendly Sons of St. Patrick and of the Hibernian Society for the Relief of Emigrants from Ireland* (Philadelphia, 1892), pp. 4, 155; "Constitution," *Nat. Gaz.*, 9 Mar. 1793.
32. HSP, SGSM: 1772–1812, Rules adopted 23 Apr. 1772; APS, "St. Andrews Society 1749 [to 1776]," rule 14, dated 7 Dec. 1749 (hereinafter APS, SASM: 1749–76. There are good short histories of both societies in Scharf and Westcott, *History*, 2: 1464–65, 1467.
33. APS, SASM: 1749–76, 30 May 1760, 12 Jan. and 25 Aug. 1761, 30 Oct. 1768, and passim; HSP, SGSM: 1772–1812, 23 July and 23 Oct. 1772, 23 Jan. 1773, 23 July 1774, and passim.
34. APS, SASM: 1749–76, 25 July 1761, 2 Dec. 1768, 27 Sept. and 2 Dec. 1771, 4 Dec. 1772; APS, Book of Minutes of the St. Andrews Society of Philadelphia, 1786–1813, 28 Feb. 1799, and passim; HSP, SGSM: 1772–1812, 23 Jan. 1773, 24 Jan., 23 July, and 24 Oct. 1774, 23 Jan. 1775, and passim.
35. A list of the first officers of the society, whom I am assuming were the founding members, is given in Scharf and Westcott, *History*, 1: 444. The men were traced as outlined in Appendix A.
36. See Chapter Four above.
37. *Aurora*, 9 Aug. 1797; HSP, "Minutes of the Board of Health beginning 26th July 1796 and ending the 3d of May 1798," pp. 69–71 (hereinafter HSP, MBH: 1796–98).

Notes to Chapter Seven

38. "A Useful Hint," *Mer. Daily Adv.*, 19 Aug. 1797; HSP, MBH: 1796–98, p. 71.
39. Advertisement of Jonathan Penrose, *Aurora*, 6 Sept. 1797; "Board of Health," *Penn. Gaz.*, 21 Sept. 1797.
40. Richard Folwell, *Short History of the Yellow Fever, that broke out in the city of Philadelphia, in July, 1797 . . . .*, 2d ed. (Philadelphia, 1798), pp. 16, 18, 19; *Aurora*, 6 Sept. 1797 (quotation from *Aurora*).
41. *Porcupine's Gaz.*, 20 and 25 Sept. 1798; *True Am.*, 27 Aug. 1798; Condie and Folwell, *History of the Pestilence*, p. 78.
42. *Porcupine's Gaz.*, 15 Oct. 1798; Condie and Folwell, *History of the Pestilence*, p. 86; *Am. Daily Adv.*, 9 Oct. 1798; *True Am.*, 17 Nov. 1798.
43. *Plan for the Philadelphia Dispensary for the Medical Relief of the Poor* (Philadelphia, 1786), p. 1.
44. Ibid., pp. 2–4, 8; the list of the first officers (p. 4) who were also founders of the organization was traced as indicated in Appendix A.
45. APS, microfilm of Records of the Philadelphia Dispensary, no. 219 of Pennsylvania Hospital Records, Annual Reports, 1789–90 ff., and meeting of 13 June 1786; see also *Account of the Design, Origin, and present State of the Philadelphia Dispensary* (Philadelphia, 1805).
46. HCA, Minutes of the Female Society for the Relief of the Distressed for November 1795 to 29 Jan. 1798, pp. 1–4, 12–13 (hereinafter HCA, Minutes of Female Society, 1795–98).
47. Ibid., pp. 4, 25–26, 95, 111–12, 147, and passim.
48. Ibid., pp. 12, 29–30, 43–44, 45, 90, 92, 95, 96–97, 101, 106, 109, 110, 115, 117, 124, 128–29, 138–39, 146, 147, 148, 182, and 11 Dec. 1797.
49. HCA, Minutes of the Female Society for the Relief of the Distressed for January 1798 to March 1813, pp. 4–6, 34, 39–41 (hereinafter HCA, Minutes of Female Society, 1798–1813); *Report of the Female Society of Philadelphia for the Relief and Employment of the Poor* (Philadelphia, 1818), pp. 1–5.
50. HCA, Minutes of Female Society, 1795–98, passim; HCA, Minutes of Female Society, 1798–1813, pp. 21–22 and passim.
51. "Advice to a Magdalen," filed under Am 1800 Phila Mag. 6363 f at Library Company of Philadelphia (quotation from this source); *The Constitution of the Magdalen Society* (Philadelphia, 1800). The statement on the occupations of the founders is offered gingerly. The first list of officers located is for 1802, when the organization was incorporated (see Scharf and West-

cott, *History*, 1: 1454–55). I am assuming that this list is a list of founders. Only six of the nine officers could be located in the city directories for 1801 or 1802. Half of the officers came from the normal occupational groups for founders of such organizations; two were merchants and one was a minister. The other half were mechanics or artisans and included a mast maker, a chair maker, and a grazier. Perhaps the higher-than-average number of people from the mechanic-artisan group can be accounted for by the consideration that the women most in need of the help of this society were likely to come from the lower occupational ranks. See Rush, *Autobiography*, p. 247.

52. On the later developments see, e.g., Scharf and Westcott, *History*, 2: 1454, 1470–71, 1484, 1485–86, 1489.
53. The earliest listing of officers I have found is for 1796. See Thomas Stephens, *Stephens's Philadelphia Directory, for 1796* ... (Philadelphia, 1796), pp. 18–19. I am assuming that these were the founders of the organization or that they come from the same background as the founders. Twelve of the fifteen men could be positively identified in the city directories. Seven of the twelve were engaged in mercantile pursuits; two were physicians; two were lawyers; only one, a silk dyer, was from the mechanic-artisan group. The suggestion that these may often have been newly arrived immigrants is based on the fact that, while twelve of the fifteen were listed in either the 1796 or 1797 city directory, only two of the fifteen could be located in the city directories for 1791 or 1792. This finding certainly suggests that the 1796 officers were new arrivals, although they may have come to the city from other parts of America.
54. "To the Public," *Phila. Gaz.*, 6 Oct. 1794.
55. I can find a list of officers for 1800, but not for a period after that. See Cornelius W. Stafford, *The Philadelphia Directory, for 1800* (Philadelphia, 1800), pp. 73–74 of the supplement section; and cf. Scharf and Westcott, *History*, 2: 1468. On the activities of the group, see *Gale's Indep. Gaz.*, 17 Feb. 1797; *Aurora*, 5 Sept. 1797; "Member," *Phila. Gaz.*, 9 Mar. 1799.
56. *Penn. Statutes*, 10: 67–73; HSP, "Plan for improving the condition of the Free Negroes," filed under AB [1789]–9; "A Plan," *Penn. Packet*, 19 Nov. 1789. The committee began operations in 1790.
57. Quotations from HSP, Penn. Abolition Soc.: 1790–1803, pp. 154, 163; see also, e.g., ibid., pp. 13–15, 26, 139, 181.
58. Ibid., pp. 139, 154, 155, 158, 159, 160, 161, 169, 170, 171, 173, 179 (quotations from pp. 154, 155).

Notes to Chapter Eight 217

59. On supervising see also ibid., pp. 209, 216–17; and "To the Free Africans," *Am. Daily Adv.*, 16 Jan. 1796.
60. HSP, Penn. Abolition Soc.: 1790–1803, pp. 23, 25, 36, 38, 39–40, 48, 67, 68–69, 73, 84, 87, 88, 99–100, 101–2, 105, 107, 115, 119, 120–23, 145, 153, 162, 181, 209–10, 226. On education see Chapter Eight below.
61. HSP, Penn. Abolition Soc., 1790–1803, 18 Sept. 1791; cf. 4 Jan. 1791, 22 May 1793, and passim.
62. *The Constitution of the Female Association of Philadelphia for the Relief of Women and Children, in Reduced Circumstances* (Philadelphia, 1803), pp. 12–16 (quotations from pp. 13, 14).
63. *Aurora*, 1 June 1791.

Chapter 8: Educating the Poor

1. Quimby, "Apprenticeship," p. 112.
2. Edward P. Cheyney, *History of the University of Pennsylvania, 1740–1940* (Philadelphia, 1940), pp. 17–27, 34–38, 58 (quotation from p. 23).
3. Labaree and Willcox, *Papers of Benjamin Franklin*, 3: 397–429 (quotation from p. 427).
4. *Penn. Gaz.*, 4 and 8 Apr. 1765; *Penn. Journal*, 18 and 25 Oct. 1764; *Aurora*, 28 Oct. 1790; *Penn. Packet*, 28 Oct. 1790.
5. *Penn. Journal*, 17 Nov. 1773.
6. Some religious groups provided education for the children of their congregations. The extent to which such provision aided the poor cannot be determined, and this examination is accordingly limited to the groups and schools specifically designed to educate the poor. On general education by religious groups, see, e.g., CCA, "Minutes of Vestry . . . ," pp. 45–46, 142, 145, 151, 152; *Am. Daily Adv.*, 6 Feb. 1796; Lawrence A. Cremin, *American Education: The Colonial Experience, 1607–1783* (New York, 1970), p. 537.
7. HSP, "Friends Free School . . . 1750–1778," in Gratz Collection; Mease, *Picture*, pp. 262–63; Scharf and Westcott, *History*, 2: 1465; 3: 1922; *Eine Acte, zur Incorporiung der zur Unterstützung Nothleidender Deutschen beysteurenden Deutschen Gesellschaft in Pennsylvanien* (Philadelphia, 1793), pp. 4–5; Samuel E. Weber, *The Charity School Movement in Colonial Pennsylvania, 1754–1763* (Philadelphia, 1905), passim, but especially pp. 58–64; *Penn. Gaz.*, 13 Aug. 1788.
8. Cremin similarly does not report extensive plans or efforts to educate the poor in Philadelphia. The one exception is the char-

ity school attached to the college; but, as noted, and as Cremin observes, that institution served a very limited number of poor people. See his *American Education*, pp. 378, 401–3, 537.
9. *Penn. Gaz.*, 28 July 1773; *Penn. Packet*, 27 Jan. 1780.
10. This standard argument is presented in, e.g., Jameson, *American Revolution*, p. 128; and Curti, *Growth*, p. 125.
11. *Penn. Packet*, 9 Nov. 1786.
12. *Penn. Mer.*, 26 Oct. 1787. I have found no record of this group establishing any other schools.
13. Ibid., 8 and 22 Nov. 1788.
14. *Penn. Packet*, 12 Aug. 1785, 26 Dec. 1787; *Fed. Gaz.*, 25 July and 9 Dec. 1788; *Aurora*, 16 Dec. 1790.
15. "Sunday Schools," *Penn. Journal*, 30 Mar. 1791; *Phila. Gaz.*, 22 Jan. 1795; Mease, *Picture*, p. 251.
16. HSP, Penn. Abolition Soc.: 1790–1803, p. 53; see also *The Mail*, 22 Sept. 1791.
17. HSP, Penn. Abolition Soc.: 1790–1803, pp. 90, 113, 131.
18. Ibid., pp. 137, 146, 148, 152, 155, 159, 163–64.
19. Ibid., pp. 71, 103, 137, 163, 192, 200–3, 210–11 (quotations from pp. 200, 203).
20. Ibid., pp. 203, 226–27, 233 ff.
21. *Aurora*, 17 May 1796, is the only record of this school discovered.
22. Mease, *Picture*, pp. 252, 254–56; *Constitution of the Female Association*, p. 11; "A. B.," *Gaz. of U.S.*, 12 Dec. 1798; PCA, "Minutes of the Board of Inspectors [of the Philadelphia Jail] from May 1794 to August 1801," 27 July 1798.
23. "To the Citizens," *Indep. Gaz.*, 28 Mar. 1787.
24. Benjamin Rush, "To the Ministers," in Rush, *Letters*, 1: 464–65. Cf. "A Lady," *Indep. Gaz.*, 14 Apr. 1787; and *Penn. Eve. Her.*, 18 July 1787.
25. "H," *Fed. Gaz.*, 4 June 1789; "K," ibid., 16 June 1789; "Friend," ibid., 19 June 1789.
26. "Sketches," *Phila. Gaz.*, 24 Jan. 1795.
27. On Quakers see *Am. Daily Adv.*, 6 Feb. 1796; on Germans, who were also said to oppose a general system of education, see "E," *Gaz. of U.S.*, 2 Aug. 1796.
28. *Aurora*, 5 Feb. 1796.
29. *Am. Daily Adv.*, 9 Feb. 1796; cf. series of essays by "E," *Gaz. of U.S.*, 19 and 29 July and 11 and 27 Aug. 1796.
30. Quotation from *Aurora*, 3 Apr. 1799. See also "Notification," *Am. Daily Adv.*, 18 June 1796; and "The Poor Man's Lot," *U.S. Recorder*, 17 Feb. 1798.
31. As one example of the increased concern, an examination of

Notes to Chapter Eight

Philadelphia newspapers for the period 1760–84 yielded only about a dozen essays concerning education of the poor; over a hundred such items appeared in the period 1785–1800.

32. *Gaz. of U.S.*, 2 Nov. 1790; *Penn. Packet*, 30 Dec. 1790.
33. "To the Citizens," *Indep. Gaz.*, 28 Mar. 1787; "E," *Gaz. of U.S.*, 11 Aug. 1796.
34. Cremin, *American Education*, pp. 568–70; Curti, *Growth*, pp. 98–99, 111–12, 115–16, 123, 130, 138, 147–49.
35. *Gaz. of U.S.*, 14 Dec. 1791; "E," ibid., 29 Aug. 1796.
36. "Extract," *Am. Daily Adv.*, 16 May 1791; *Aurora*, 10 Nov. 1791; "Public Schools," *Gaz. of U.S.*, 2 and 23 June 1792.
37. *Gaz. of U.S.*, 22 June 1791.
38. On the *Aurora*, see pp. 38, 41 above.
39. Compare the society's pronouncements in "Sunday Schools," *Penn. Journal*, 30 Mar. 1791, with the general Pessimist position outlined in this chapter.
40. On the general ideal, see Benjamin Rush to Jeremy Belknap, 5 Jan. 1791, in Rush, *Letters*, 1: 573. There were thirteen founding members of the society; included in that group were at least two Anglicans, two Roman Catholics, two free or fighting Quakers, and Benjamin Rush, who had, until the late 1780s, been numbered among the Presbyterians. The founding meeting of the society was held at St. George's Methodist Church. See *Historic Philadelphia from the Founding until the Early Nineteenth Century* (Philadelphia, 1953), p. 235. The list of first officers is in "Sunday Schools," *Penn. Journal*, 30 Mar. 1791, which was analyzed as indicated in Appendix A.
41. The one possible exception is Mathew Carey. He was a printer who published *The American Museum* and, sometime in 1791, opened a bookselling shop.
42. On the Republican Society and the college, see Brunhouse, *Counter-Revolution*, pp. 152–55.
43. "Sunday Schools," *Penn. Packet*, 12 Aug. 1785; "Lutius," *Indep. Gaz.*, 29 Dec. 1786.
44. *Penn. Mer.*, 8 Nov. 1788; *Fed. Gaz.*, 9 Dec. 1788.
45. "X," *Gaz. of U.S.*, 31 Dec. 1794.
46. "Education," ibid., 19 Dec. 1791; "On the Means," *Penn Journal*, 27 Jan. 1790; *Gale's Indep. Gaz.*, 21 Apr. 1797; *The Mail*, 21 Dec. 1792.
47. "H," *Fed. Gaz.*, 4 June 1789; "On Religious Education," *Penn. Packet*, 20 Nov. 1790.
48. Benjamin Rush, "To the Citizens," *Indep. Gaz.*, 28 Mar. 1787.
49. "A Caladomian," ibid., 3 Sept. 1787.

50. Benjamin Rush, "To the Citizens," ibid., 28 Mar. 1787; *Penn. Eve. Her.*, 18 July 1787.
51. "Education," *Gaz. of U.S.*, 10 Dec. 1791; ibid., 9 Jan. 1793.
52. "H," *Fed. Gaz.*, 4 June 1789; "Z," ibid., 20 Nov. 1789.
53. "Lutius," *Indep. Gaz.*, 29 Dec. 1786; Benjamin Rush, "To the Citizens," ibid., 28 Mar. 1787; *Penn. Packet*, 29 Oct. 1790.
54. Benjamin Rush, "To the Citizens," *Indep. Gaz.*, 28 Mar. 1787. On costs see ibid., 7 Jan. 1787; and *Gaz. of U.S.*, 7 and 10 Dec. 1791.
55. *Penn. Eve. Her.*, 18 July 1787.
56. Ibid.; "Hints," *Penn. Gaz.*, 7 Jan. 1789; *Freeman's Journal*, 7 May 1788.
57. *Gaz. of U.S.*, 14 Dec. 1791; "E," ibid., 2 Aug. 1796; *Fed. Gaz.*, 9 Dec. 1788. These quotations are taken from supporters of education for the poor who claimed to be reporting the views of some of their opponents.
58. *Penn. Packet*, 21 May 1787; *Gaz. of U.S.*, 12 Jan. 1791.
59. "Extract," *Am. Daily Adv.*, 16 May 1791; "To the Citizens," *Indep. Gaz.*, 28 Mar. 1787; cf. "Lutius," ibid., 29 Dec. 1786.

Conclusion

1. *Penn. Statutes*, 10: 67–73 (quotation from p. 67).
2. Gary Nash's examination of the size of Philadelphia's slave population gives an estimate of only 672 in 1775; he shows that the slave population was dwindling. See his "Slaves and Slaveowners," pp. 237, 255. On attitudes toward blacks, see HSP, Penn. Abolition Soc.: 1790–1803, p. 210 and passim.
3. "Address to the Committee," *Phila. Gaz.*, 22 May 1800.
4. Benjamin Rush to Charles Nisbet, 27 Aug. 1784, in Rush, *Letters*, 1: 337.
5. *Phila. Gaz.*, 9 Apr. 1799; cf. "Public Executions," *Nat. Gaz.*, 11 June 1792; and ibid., 19 Dec. 1792.
6. The classic statement is Carl L. Becker, *The History of Political Parties in the Province of New York, 1760–1776* (Madison, Wis., 1909), especially p. 22. The same argument had been developed for Pennsylvania by Charles H. Lincoln in *The Revolutionary Movement in Pennsylvania, 1760–1776* (Philadelphia, 1901), and especially pp. 95–96.
7. The classic statement is Robert E. Brown, *Middle-Class Democracy and the Revolution in Massachusetts, 1691–1780* (Ithaca, N.Y., 1955). See also, e.g., Edmund S. Morgan, *The Birth of the*

Republic, *1763–89*, rev. ed. (Chicago, 1977), p. 7, which repeats the position stated in the 1956 edition (p. 7).
8. Warner, *Private City*, p. 8.
9. Ibid., pp. 5–8; Main, *Social Structure*, pp. 194–95 and passim.
10. Warner, *Private City*, 10–21; Michael Zuckerman, "The Irrelevant Revolution," *American Quarterly* 30 (Summer 1978), pp. 226–37; Maier, "Popular Uprisings," pp. 3–35.
11. Olton, *Artisans*, pp. 34, 39–40; James H. Hutson, "An Investigation of the Inarticulate: Philadelphia's White Oaks," *WMQ* 28 (January 1971): 3–25.
12. David Hawke, *In the Midst of a Revolution* (Philadelphia, 1961), p. 187; Wood, *Creation*, pp. 89–90 and passim. Cf. Olton, *Artisans*, p. 54; and Foner, *Tom Paine*, pp. 52–53.
13. Wood, *Creation*, pp. 42–45 and passim; Maier, "Popular Uprisings," pp. 33–34.
14. Bernard Bailyn, *The Ideological Origins of the American Revolution* (Cambridge, Mass., 1967), pp. 160–319, and especially p. 302.
15. Important examples that focus on cities or towns include Henretta, "Economic Development," pp. 75–92; Allan Kulikoff, "The Progress of Inequality in Revolutionary Boston," *WMQ* 28 (July 1971): 375–412; Miller, *Philadelphia*, pp. 3–19 and passim; Nash, "Urban Wealth" and "Poverty"; Mohl, *Poverty*, especially pp. 14–34; Robert A. Gross, *The Minutemen and Their World* (New York, 1976), especially pp. 208–9, 212, 218, 231, 234; Edward C. Papenfuse, *In Pursuit of Profit: The Annapolis Merchants in the Era of the American Revolution, 1763–1805* (Baltimore, 1975), pp. 138–53, 257–68; Stephanie G. Wolf, *Urban Village: Population, Community, and Family Structure in Germantown, Pennsylvania, 1683–1800* (Princeton, N.J., 1976), especially pp. 120–24. Highly influential statements of the new view are in Jesse Lemisch's "Jack Tar" and "American Revolution."
16. Main, *Social Structure*, p. 194 n; cf. Lemisch, "American Revolution," p. 33 n.
17. Compare Main, *Social Structure*, pp. 281–87, with "A Pennsylvania Farmer," *Penn. Packet*, 15 Feb. 1790; and Benjamin Rush to Thomas Percival, 26 Oct. 1786, and Rush's "To American Farmers About to Settle in the New Parts of the United States," in Rush, *Letters*, 1: 400–6, 503–5.
18. Foner, *Tom Paine*, pp. 47–52.
19. "The Moral Economy of the English Crowd in the Eighteenth Century," *Past & Present* 50 (February 1971): 76–136. On the

influence of this essay, see, e.g., Young, *American Revolution*, pp. 13, 41, 212, 455. Strong support for this general view is given in Dirk Hoerder, *Crowd Action in Revolutionary Massachusetts, 1765–1780* (New York, 1977).

20. Williamson, *American Suffrage*, pp. 92–116; Fletcher M. Green, *Constitutional Development in the South Atlantic States, 1776–1860: A Study in the Evolution of Democracy* (Chapel Hill, N.C., 1930), pp. 47–98; Allan Nevins, *The American States during and after the Revolution, 1775–1789* (New York, 1924), pp. 117–70.
21. Elisha P. Douglass, *Rebels and Democrats: The Struggle for Equal Political Rights and Majority Rule during the American Revolution* (Chapel Hill, N.C., 1955), pp. 162–213; Hoerder, *Crowd Action*, pp. 368–89; Robert J. Taylor, ed., *Massachusetts, Colony to Commonwealth: Documents on the Formation of Its Constitution, 1775–1780* (Chapel Hill, N.C., 1961).
22. Olton, *Artisans*, pp. 10–11, 114–20; Foner, *Tom Paine*, 205–9.
23. Francis Jennings, "The Indian's Revolution," and Joan H. Wilson, "The Illusion of Change: Women and the American Revolution," in Young, *American Revolution*, pp. 321–48, 385–445. A different view of the effect of the Revolution on the position of women is given in Carol R. Berkin and Mary B. Norton, eds., *Women of America: A History* (Boston, 1979), pp. 45–46.
24. McManus, *Black Bondage*, pp. 160–79; Arthur Zilversmit, *The First Emancipation: The Abolition of Slavery in the North* (Chicago, 1967), pp. 109 ff.
25. "The Revolution in Black Life," in Young, *American Revolution*, pp. 351–82.
26. For a valuable and suggestive study of a later period, see Leon F. Litwack, "The Emancipation of the Negro Abolitionist," in *The Antislavery Vanguard: New Essays on the Abolitionists*, ed. Martin Duberman (Princeton, N.J., 1965), pp. 137–55.
27. For a flagrant example of the use of modern standards for judgment, see Wilson, "Illusion" and compare the balanced approach in Berkin and Norton, *Women*, pp. 7–10. On the pronouncements of the revolutionary era, see, in addition to the examples given in the text, Arthur M. Schlesinger, "The Lost Meaning of 'The Pursuit of Happiness,'" *WMQ* 21 (July 1964): 325–27.
28. Rothman, *Discovery*, pp. xii–28 passim.
29. *Poverty*, pp. 159–70, 262.
30. Rothman, *Discovery*, pp. xii–28 passim.
31. The phrasing is from Becker, *History*, p. 22.

Bibliographic Note

This note is not intended to provide an exhaustive listing and analysis of all of the items cited in this study. It is designed to offer a guide to the sources that I found most useful for the study of poverty in Philadelphia during the revolutionary era.

Primary

As the footnotes indicate, the newspapers listed on pp. 183–84 are crucial for an examination of poverty in eighteenth-century Philadelphia. No other sources provide such a wide range of information concerning the responses to poverty and the social history of the city. The records housed at the Philadelphia City Archives are essential for evaluating the role of various governmental agencies. In addition to containing the public poor relief records listed on pp. 184–85, this repository has numerous tax records, records of the reincorporated city, and criminal and jail records from the 1790s. An extensive guide to the City Archives is provided by John Daly, ed., *Descriptive Inventory of the Archives of the City and County of Philadelphia* (Philadelphia, 1970). The Historical Society of Pennsylvania houses many important sources that yield valuable information on the responses to poverty. The most useful in this regard were records of the Philadelphia Society for Alleviating the Miseries of Public Prisons, records of the Pennsylvania Abolition Society concerning the Committee for Improving the Condition of Free Blacks, Miers Fisher Papers, Wharton–Willing Collection, Dreer Collection, Parrish Collection, and St. George's Society Minutes for

1772–1812. The *Guide to the Manuscript Collections of The Historical Society of Pennsylvania*, rev. ed. (Philadelphia, 1949) is a still useful, although not complete, guide. The American Philosophical Society has the records of the St. Andrew's Society of Philadelphia as well as those of the Philadelphia Dispensary. The accounts of the Female Society of Philadelphia are housed at the Haverford College Archives. The German Society of Pennsylvania Archives has the minutes of the German Society. The archives of the Monthly Meeting of Philadelphia Friends contains voluminous records of the various Quaker groups and organizations that dealt with the poor. The minute books of Christ Church and St. Peter's Church for 1761–1813 are available at the Christ Church Archives. The minutes of the trustees of St. Mary's for 1788–1811 are maintained at the rectory of St. Mary Roman Catholic Church of Philadelphia.

Although the Library Company of Philadelphia and the Historical Society of Pennsylvania have extensive holdings of works published in eighteenth-century Philadelphia, the American Antiquarian Society microcard reprints of the items in Charles Evans's *American Bibliography* were invaluable. A short-title Evans and a listing of the items discovered since Evans completed his research is Clifford K. Shipton and James F. Mooney, eds., *National Index of American Imprints through 1800: The Short-Title Evans*, 2 vols. (Worcester, Mass., 1969).

The city directories compiled in 1785 and then for each year after 1790 proved crucial for tracing individuals. My work in the directories was facilitated by using the microfilm of the directories published through 1802 which is available at nominal cost from The Free Library of Philadelphia.

Many important government sources are available in printed editions. The well-indexed James T. Mitchell and Henry Flanders, comps., *The Statutes at Large of Pennsylvania for 1682 to 1801*, 15 vols. (Harrisburg, 1896–1911) is to be preferred to any other editions of the laws of the period. Harry H. Eddy, *Guide to the Published Archives of Pennsylvania* (Harrisburg, Pa., 1949) provides an introduction and general guide to the wide variety of records contained in *Pennsylvania Colonial Records*, 16 vols. (Harrisburg, Pa., 1838–56) and in the nine series of the *Pennsylvania Archives*.

The letters, reminiscences, and other writings of Philadelphians who lived in the period 1760–1800 were, of course, vital. The most useful of such printed works were: L. H. Butterfield, ed., *Letters of Benjamin Rush*, 2 vols. (Princeton, N.J., 1951); George W. Corner, ed., *The Autobiography of Benjamin Rush: His "Travels Through Life" together with his* Commonplace Book *for 1789–1813* (Princeton, N.J., 1948), which is vol. 25 of Memoirs of the American Philosophical Society; Tench Coxe, *A View of the United States of America, in a series of papers written at various times between the years 1787 and 1794* . . . (Philadelphia, 1794); Alexander Graydon, *Memoirs of A Life, Chiefly Passed in Pennsylvania, within the Last Sixty Years, with Occasional Remarks upon the General Occurrences, Character and Spirit of that Eventful Period* (Harrisburg, Pa., 1811); James Mease, *The Picture of Philadelphia, giving an account of its origin, increase and improvement in arts, sciences, manufactures, commerce and revenue* (Philadelphia, 1811); Leonard W. Labaree and William B. Willcox, eds., *The Papers of Benjamin Franklin*, 23 vols. to date (New Haven, Conn., 1959–). John F. Watson, *Annals of Philadelphia, and Pennsylvania, in the Olden Time; being a collection of Memoirs, Anecdotes, and Incidents of the City and Its Inhabitants* . . . , enlarged by Willis P. Hazard, 3 vols. (Philadelphia, 1884) is, as the title suggests, both a history and a primary source, for it contains the observations of persons who lived in the eighteenth-century city.

Traveler accounts are especially useful, primarily for two reasons. The visitors often compared the situation in Philadelphia to that in other areas and they were likely to note things that Philadelphians passed over with little or no comment. Of the various traveler accounts, the following proved most beneficial: Johann D. Schoepf, *Travels in the Confederation*, trans. and ed. Alfred J. Morrison, 2 vols. (Philadelphia, 1911); Duke De La Rochefoucault Liancourt, *Travels through the United States of North America, of the Country of the Iroquois, and Upper Canada, in the Years 1795, 1796, and 1797; with an Authentic Account of Lower Canada*, trans. H. Heuman, 2 vols. (London, 1799); Isaac Weld, *Travels Through the States of North America, and the Province of Upper and Lower Canada, During the Years 1795, 1796, and 1797* (London, 1799).

Secondary

Any examination of eighteenth-century Philadelphia should begin with a close reading of J. Thomas Scharf and Thompson Westcott, *History of Philadelphia, 1609-1884*, 3 vols. (Philadelphia, 1884). This magnificent and encyclopedic monument to scholarship provides information that I found nowhere else. Hannah B. Roach provides the best short history of public poor relief in the colonial city in her "Philadelphia's Colonial Poor Laws," *Pennsylvania Genealogical Magazine*, 22, no. 3 (1962): 159-85. John H. Powell's sprightly *Bring Out Your Dead: The Great Plague of Yellow Fever* in *Philadelphia in 1793* (Philadelphia, 1949) contains a wealth of information. J. Paul Selsam, *The Pennsylvania Constitution of 1776: A Study in Revolutionary Democracy* (Philadelphia, 1936) and Theodore Thayer, *Pennsylvania Politics and the Growth of Democracy, 1740–1776* (Harrisburg, 1953) are still valuable political studies. Robert L. Brunhouse, *The Counter-Revolution in Pennsylvania, 1776–1790* (Harrisburg, 1942) remains the best treatment of politics in the revolutionary era. Important modern studies of aspects of Philadelphia life that I found especially important include: Sam Bass Warner, Jr., *The Private City: Philadelphia in Three Periods of Its Growth* (Philadelphia, 1968); Charles S. Olton, *Artisans for Independence: Philadelphia Mechanics and the American Revolution* (Syracuse, N.Y., 1975); Eric Foner, *Tom Paine and Revolutionary America* (New York, 1976); Richard G. Miller, *Philadelphia— The Federalist City: A Study of Urban Politics, 1789–1801* (Port Washington, N.Y., 1976); William H. Williams, *America's First Hospital: The Pennsylvania Hospital, 1751–1841* (Wayne, Pa., 1976); and Richard A. Ryerson, *The Revolution Is Now Begun: The Radical Committees of Philadelphia, 1765–1776* (Philadelphia, 1978). As the citations of his work indicate, Gary B. Nash has produced several important essays that examine Philadelphia and other major cities of colonial America. He has incorporated those works into his *The Urban Crucible: Social Change, Political Consciousness, and the Origins of the American Revolution* (Cambridge, Mass., 1979) which was not yet available as this study was in press. Billy G. Smith, " 'The Best Poor Man's Country': Living Standards of the 'Lower Sort' in Late Eighteenth-Century Philadelphia," *Working Papers* 2, no. 4 (1979): 1–70 offers an important analysis that covers the 1760–1800 period. The *Pennsylvania Magazine of History and Biography* contains many important essays—and primary sources— that deal with the Philadelphia of 1760–1800.

Of the unpublished work on Philadelphia, I found the following of most help: Ian M. G. Quimby, "Apprenticeship in Colonial Philadelphia" (M. A. thesis, University of Delaware, 1962); Stephen J. Brobeck, "Changes in the Composition and Structure of Philadelphia Elite Groups, 1765–1790" (Ph.D. diss., University of Pennsylvania, 1973); Sharon V. Salinger, "Colonial Labor in Transition: The Decline of Indentured Servitude in Late Eighteenth-Century Philadelphia" which was presented at the 1978 meeting of the Organization of American Historians. Billy G. Smith kindly allowed me to examine sections of his forthcoming dissertation, tentatively titled, "The Working Classes of Philadelphia during the Revolutionary Era" (University of California, Los Angeles) which presents a close analysis of the economic position of the city's working classes.

A useful historiographic essay that includes citations of most of the important recent work that deals with Philadelphia in the colonial era is Douglas Greenberg, "The Middle Colonies in Recent American Historiography," *William and Mary Quarterly*, 3d ser., 36 (July 1979): 396–427.

Of the works that do not focus solely or primarily on Philadelphia, Carl Bridenbaugh, *Cities in Revolt: Urban Life in America, 1743–1776*, rev. ed. (New York, 1971) presents the standard comparative study of the major colonial cities. J. Franklin Jameson, *The American Revolution Considered as a Social Movement* (Princeton, N.J., 1926) offers the classic statement of the view that the Revolution had a democratizing impact upon American society. Merle Curti, *The Growth of American Thought*, 3d ed. (New York, 1964) is a useful general study. Richard B. Morris, *Government and Labor in Early America* (New York, 1946) provides a wealth of information. Jackson T. Main, *The Social Structure of Revolutionary America* (Princeton, N.J., 1965) is an indispensable work. Raymond A. Mohl, *Poverty in New York, 1783–1825* (New York, 1971) is especially valuable since it allows some comparison to be made between two major cities of the period. David J. Rothman, *The Discovery of the Asylum: Social Order and Disorder in the Republic* (Boston, 1971) presents a very different view of poor relief in the eighteenth century.

The continuing debate on the nature of society in late colonial and revolutionary America can be followed by examining the essays that appear in the Third Series of the *William and Mary Quarterly*. Jesse Lemisch, "The American Revolution Seen from the Bottom Up," in *Towards A New Past: Dissenting Essays in American History*, ed. Barton J. Bernstein (New York, 1968), pp. 3–45 provides an important commentary on the issues of the debate as does Gordon S. Wood, "Rhetoric and Reality in the American Revolution," *William and Mary Quarterly*, 3d ser., 23 (January 1966): 3–32. The different interpretations can be seen by comparing Alfred F. Young, ed., *The American Revolution: Explorations in the History of American Radicalism* (DeKalb, Ill., 1976), and especially pp. ix–xv, 449–62 with Pauline Maier, "Popular Uprisings and Civil Authority in Eighteenth-Century America," *William and Mary Quarterly*, 3d ser., 27 (January 1970): 3–35. An example of the development of the debate as it relates to eighteenth-century Philadelphia can be seen by comparing James H. Hutson, "An Investigation of the Inarticulate:

Philadelphia's White Oaks," *William and Mary Quarterly*, 3d ser., 28 (January 1971): 3–25 with Jesse Lemisch and John K. Alexander, "The White Oaks, Jack Tar, and the Concept of the 'Inarticulate,'" *William and Mary Quarterly*, 3d ser., 29 (January 1972): 109–34 with Hutson's "Rebuttal" on pp. 136–42.

Index

African Methodist Episcopal Church, 148
Aged, 8, 97–98, 116
Almshouses, 87–88, 128–129, 205 n. 3. *See also* House of Employment
American character, depicted, 5
American Daily Advertiser, 83
American Revolution: nature of, 174; and public poor relief, 101–6, 120–21; and social change, 1, 4–7, 23–25, 27–28, 47–49, 66, 71, 83–84, 144–45, 160–69 *passim*
Apprentices, 18, 24, 27, 30, 82, 137–38, 143, 146, 148
Artisans. *See* Mechanics and artisans
Association in Southwark for Suppressing Vice and Immorality, 81
Association of the district of Southwark, for suppression of vice and immorality, 82, 83
Aurora, 38, 41, 53, 150–51, 154

Barry, James, 80
Baston, John, 79
Beemery(?), William, 80
Berlin, Ira, 173
Biddle, Charles, 27
Blacks: attitudes toward, 20–21, 137–39, 144, 146–48, 162–63; as criminals, 78–79, 180–81; and education, 144–48; housing patterns and, 20–21; status, 8, 128, 137, 139. *See also* Slavery
Board of Health, 22, 130–31
Bray, Rev. Thomas, 144
Bridenbaugh, Carl, 62
Bryen, Tiberius, 147
Butler, Richard, 80

Carey, Mathew, 154
Carlisle, Alexander, 71
Christ Church, 128–29
Clarkson, Matthew, 81–82
Clothing, styles of, 17–18, 24–25, 160–61, 166
Cobbett, William, 39–41, 82–83
College of Philadelphia, 143–44
Committee for Improving the Condition of the Free Blacks, 137–39, 146–48
Committee to Alleviate the

Miseries of the Poor, 9, 212 n. 11
Community, sense of, 6–7, 171–74
Constitution of 1776: as agent for social change, 32, 66, 71, 74–75, 84, 161–63, 172; opposition to, 30–32, 42–43; provisions of, 31–32
Constitution of 1790, 150, 153, 195–96 n. 23
Constitution of the United States, 172
Continental Congress, 37
Contributors to the Relief and Employment of the Poor within the City of Philadelphia, 89–90, 110–11. *See also* House of Employment; Overseers of the Poor
Coxe, Tench, 27
Crime and disorder: causes, analyzed, 52–53, 76, 82, 137, 155, 157; interest in analysis of, 20–21, 62–63, 73, 76, 85; penal codes and, 17, 63–66, 68, 74–76, 80–81, 84, 106–7; poor and, 5, 63, 73, 77–80; rise in, 76–78, 85, 204 n. 45; trading justices and, 71–73
Crowd action, 30–31, 35–37, 40–41, 73, 83

Debt, imprisonment for, 64–71 *passim*, 84, 162
Deference: absence of, 25, 30, 33, 36, 42, 45, 47, 49, 172; desired for the poor, 5–6, 23, 25, 48–49, 60, 142, 152, 158–59, 161, 164–69 *passim*; moral crusade to support, 49, 53–60 *passim*; poor need to embrace, 22–24, 29. *See also* Education; Poor, the; Poverty
Delaware River, 15
Disease, 21–22, 26, 37–38, 125, 127, 130–31

Disorder, social. *See* Crime and disorder
Divine, Thomas, 80
Donnovan, Elizabeth, 68

Education: of apprentices, 143, 146, 152; background of supporters of, 154–55; interest in, for the poor, 81–82, 99, 137–38, 142–45, 152–58, 218–19 n. 31; lack of a public system, 148–51; medical, and the poor, 127–28; opposition to, for the poor, 158; "Optimist" and "Pessimist" views, contrasted, 142, 152–58 *passim*; lack of, for the poor, 5, 82, 151–52
Edwards, Dr. Enoch, 77–78
Elections: nominations for, 29; of 1789, 44–45; of 1797 and 1798, 37–42
Employment: and debilitation, 12; manufacturing and, for the poor, 13–15; a necessity for the poor, 8, 12–15, 17, 77–78; seasonal nature, 14–16, 77–78, 125
Enlightenment, American, 4, 61, 85, 152–53, 161, 168
Ethnic organizations, 123–25, 129–30, 136–37, 144, 214 n. 31
Eve, Sarah, 50

Faulkner, Ephraim, 35
Federal Gazette, 15, 81
Female Association of Philadelphia, 139, 148
Female Society for Assisting the Distressed, 133–35
First Baptist Church, 129
First Company of Philadelphia Militia Artillery, 34–35
Fisher, James, 79
Fort Wilson: background, 34–35; incident and aftermath, 35–36

Index

Franklin, Benjamin, 126–27, 143, 194 n. 4
Freeman's Journal, 5
French Revolution, and political attitudes, 37, 39–40
Freneau, Philip, 33

Gale, Joseph, 78–79
Gazette of the United States, 151–52
German Society, 125, 144
Grand Juries, 14, 43–44, 73–74, 88
Graydon, Alexander, 5, 164
Grayson, Colonel ———, 35
Green, Esther, 80
Guardians of the Poor of the City of Philadelphia: attitudes of, 116–21 *passim*; authorized, 105–6; background, 118; begin functioning, 111. *See also* House of Employment; Overseers of the Poor

Hamilton, James, 63
Harris, Eleanor, 147
Historians: and analysis of Philadelphia, 6–7; and interpretation of early America, 1, 169–74; and study of poverty, 1, 4
House of Employment: attitudes of managers, 15–16, 91–93, 95, 98–100, 107–21 *passim*; attitudes of poor, 91–92, 95–96, 108–9, 120; background of managers, 92–93, 101, 103, 111–15, 121, 207 n. 1; creation, 87–89, 205 n. 7; failure, 86, 97–101, 111, 115; finances, 90–92, 94, 98–101, 104–5, 108–10, 115–16; inmates of, depicted, 91, 97–98, 108–9, 116–19; rules and regulations, 94–96, 98, 107–8, 116, 119–20

Housing patterns in Philadelphia, 19–22, 161, 191 n. 34
Howe, General William, 104

Immigrants: attitudes toward, 13, 16, 26–27, 137, 194 n. 4; and crime, 17, 78–79, 180–81; economic problems of, 8, 16–17, 125, 136–37; in politics, 27. *See also* Ethnic organizations
Incorporation of Philadelphia (1789), 42–46, 72–73, 198 n. 62, 203 n. 34
Indentured servants, 27–28, 30, 82, 125
Independent Gazetteer, 16–17, 77
Institution of Charity-Schools, 145
Irish Town, 20, 38
Israel, Israel, 37–42 *passim*, 166

Jameson, J. Franklin, 1
Jones, Absalom, 147
Joseph (a black), 80

Labor, system of, 27–28, 47, 164–65
Laborers, day, 8, 15, 19–20, 63, 79
Laurens, Henry, 35–36
Leslie, William, 68
Logan, George, 151

McDowell, Hugh, 79
McNeil, John, 80
Magdalen Society, 135
Main, Jackson Turner, 171
Manufacturing, 13–14, 28, 51, 77–78, 139
Martin, Joe, 79
Massachusetts, 172
Mayor's Court, 62, 79–80
Mechanics and artisans: economic status, 8, 14, 28–29, 33, 93, 125, 188 n. 23; political

views, 29–30, 45, 170; and private poor relief, 123–24, 135, 141; and public poor relief, 86, 92–93, 101, 113–15
Medicine. See Diseases; Education; Poor, the
Mercantile community, members of: denounced, 34–36; and education, 154–55, 158–59; and fear of the poor, 9–10; and politics, 35–36, 43–45; power, 6; and private poor relief, 127, 130, 132, 135–36, 141; and public poor relief, 86, 92–93, 101, 113–15
Militia, the, 30, 34–37, 46, 165
Miller, Richard C., 12, 20
Mobility: attitudes toward socioeconomic, 50–51, 54–56, 58, 60; geographic, 73–74, 81, 88–89, 106–7, 171; socioeconomic, 13, 17, 160–61, 170–71. *See also* Education
"Mobs." *See* Crowd action
Mohl, Raymond, 122, 173
Morgan, Benjamin R., 38–42 *passim*
Morris, Robert, 113–14
Moyamensing, 89, 101, 115–16
Mull, Elizabeth, 120
Mutiny of 1783, 36–37
Mutual aid societies, 123–24, 139–40

Nash, Gary B., 9
Negro Charity School, 145
Newton, Ann, 120
New York City, 74, 173
Northern Liberties, 20–21, 38, 89–90, 101, 115–16, 204 n. 51

O'Hara, Oliver, 79
Outdoor relief, 87–88, 90–92, 94, 96–97, 100–1, 105–10, 115, 118–19, 121
Overseers of the Poor: attitudes of, 23, 94, 101, 103–4, 107–10, 114–20 *passim*; background, 91–93, 101, 103, 112–15, 118, 121; duties, 86–87, 89–90, 106, 111, 117; selection, 86, 106, 208 n. 4

Parker, John, 15
Passyunk, 89–90, 101, 106, 115–16
Patterson, Samuel, 36
Peale, Charles, 18
Pennsylvania Abolition Society, 137, 146–47
Pennsylvania Assembly: committees of, 62, 71, 87; pay of, 29; and penal codes, 62, 64–66, 68–69, 74–76, 80–81, 161–62; and poor relief, 17, 88–90, 96, 100–1, 105–7, 115–16, 118; powers, 31–32; and price regulation, 34, 36; and slavery, 137, 162–63; and yellow fever, 131
Pennsylvania Evening Herald, 16–17, 27, 54, 78
Pennsylvania Hospital, 88, 127
Pennsylvania Journal, 27
Pennsylvania Legislature of 1790–1800, 46, 69–70, 150–51
Pennsylvania Line, 36–37
Pennsylvania Packet, 73
Pennsylvania Senate, 39
Philadelphia: British occupation, 42, 66, 104; as crime center, 74; governmental structure, 29, 42, 44, 46; ordinances, 45–46; police, 62, 66, 76, 83; population, 26, 43; promotional literature on, 13, 15, 26–27, 171. *See also* Suburbs of Philadelphia
Philadelphia Corporation, 29, 42, 44
Philadelphia Dispensary for the Medical Relief of the Poor, 23, 132–33, 141
Philadelphia Gazette, 70

Philadelphia Minerva, 23
Philadelphia Society for Alleviating the Miseries of Public Prisons, 67–71, 130
Philadelphia Society for Assisting Distressed Prisoners, 65–66, 68, 126, 130
Philadelphia Society for the Information and Assistance of Persons Emigrating from Foreign Countries, 16, 136–37
Poor, the: definitions of, 7–8, 33; fear among, 6, 33, 44–45, 73; and frugality, 15–16, 52, 93; limited choices of, 11–12, 17, 22–24; homes of, 22; language of, 5, 23, 32–33, 156; and medical treatment, 22–23, 67, 88, 97, 99, 117, 120, 127, 129, 132–34; number of, 8–9, 14, 16, 48, 87; segments of, differentiated, 26–27, 49–53, 85, 89, 95–96, 107, 116–20 *passim*, 128–30, 132, 140–41; typical occupations, 8, 12, 15, 19; voting patterns, 38–41. *See also* Poverty
Poor law: of 1766, 89–90; of 1771, 96–97; of 1776, 100; of 1782, 105–7; of 1789, 118
Porcupine's Gazette, 39
Poverty: as cause of crime, 16–17, 52, 77–82; ease of falling into, 123–25; "industrious" defined, 8; "industrious" and "idle" contrasted, 49–60 *passim*, 166–67; perceptions of, refined, 48–49, 51, 60; and wealth contrasted, 49–51, 53–60
Powell, Samuel, 45, 154
Price, Dr. ———, 127
Prices, regulation of, 34–36, 172
Private poor relief: dual nature of, 6, 23, 122, 128–41 *passim*, 167–68; reclamation societies, 133–35, 168; simple humanitarianism and, 122, 124–27, 132, 140, 212 n. 11; subscriptions, 9, 16, 37, 62, 73, 104, 124–25, 140; uplift societies, 133, 135–39, 168. *See also* Mutual aid societies; Ethnic organizations; names of individual organizations
Prostitution, 20, 74, 82–83, 135
Public poor relief. *See* Contributors to the Relief and Employment of the Poor within the City of Philadelphia; Guardians of the Poor of the City of Philadelphia; House of Employment; Overseers of the Poor; Poor law

Quakers: and education, 144, 150–51; in politics, 40–41, 45, 103, 105, 126; and private poor relief, 126–28, 130, 132–35, 137, 141; and public poor relief, 86, 92–93, 103, 105, 207 n. 7

Recommendation system, 22–24, 127, 129–33, 193 n. 51
Republicanism, ideals of, 6–7, 31–32, 46, 153, 170, 172
Republican Society, 43–44, 154
Rhetoric, changing style of political, 30, 32–34, 42, 46–47
Roberdeau, Daniel, 34
Rothman, David, 174
Rush, Dr. Benjamin: mentioned, 127; quoted, 6, 8, 21–22, 32, 36–37, 148–49, 152, 157, 159, 164

St. Andrews Society, 129–30
St. Mary's Catholic Church, 129
St. Peter's Church, 128–29
Sanitation, 19, 21–22
Seamen, 8, 15, 20, 34, 79
Shaw, Major Samuel, 35
Shippen, Dr. William, 128

Slavery, 27, 137, 162–63, 172–73
Smith, Billy G., 17
Society for Inoculating the Poor, 127
Society for the Institution of First-Day or Sunday Schools in the City of Philadelphia, and the Districts of Southwark and the Northern-Liberties, 145–46, 152, 154–55, 158
Society for the Suppression of Vice and Immorality, 82–83
Society of Friends. *See* Quakers
Society of the Sons of St. George, 15, 129–30
Southwark, 19–21, 38, 83, 89–90, 101, 116, 204 n. 51
Suburbs of Philadelphia: crime, 74; described, 20–21, 62; police, 62; and public poor relief, 86–87, 89–90, 96–97, 101, 106, 109, 115–16; as residence of the poor, 16, 20, 38–39; voting, 38–40. *See also* names of individual areas
Suffrage: denial, 32; requirements, 28–31, 42, 44–47, 163, 195–96 n. 23
Supreme Executive Council, 34, 36–37, 76

Taverns, 20, 23, 39, 41, 62, 66, 72, 74, 77, 166
Thomas, John, 79
Thompson, E. P., 172
Tolles, Frederick B., 1

Trading justices, 6, 71–73

United States Abolition Societies, 25
Universal Magazine, 76

Wages, 13, 17, 27–28, 34, 45, 117
Watson, John, 18, 21
Wealth, distribution of, 11–12, 160–61, 177
Weiss, Susannah, 134
Weld, Isaac, 25
White, Amous, 147
Whitefield, Rev. George, 143
Williams, Ann, 147
Williams, John, 80, 129
Wilson, James, 35
Women: clothing of, 18, 24; as criminals, 80, 180; in education, 145, 147–48; and House of Employment, 94–95, 97–99, 117, 119–20; and private poor relief, 70, 127, 129, 133–35, 139
Wyatt, Joseph, 79

Yellow fever, 26, 37–38, 125, 130–31
Youths: attitudes and actions of, 50, 74, 81–82, 144, 156; and crime, 73, 75–76, 81–82, 84; education of, 99, 138–39, 143–50; and House of Employment, 94–95, 97, 99, 117; and private poor relief, 129, 134–35